The Psalms,
Prayers of Many Moods

The Psalms,
Prayers of Many Moods

Ronald Quillo

PAULIST PRESS
New York/Mahwah, N.J.

Imprimatur:
Most Reverend Patrick F. Flores, D.D.
Archbishop of San Antonio

Date:
July 13, 1998

The Imprimatur is an official declaration that a book or pamphlet is free of doctrinal or moral error. No implication is contained therein that those who have granted the Imprimatur agree with the contents, opinions or statements expressed.

The text of the psalms is from the New Revised Standard Version of the Bible, copyright © 1989 by the Division of Christian Education of the National Council of the Churches of Christ in the U.S.A. All rights reserved. Used by permission.

The Sequence of Psalms for the Liturgy of the Hours is based on "The Four-Week Psalter" of *The Liturgy of the Hours according to the Roman Rite*, copyright © 1976 by Catholic Book Publishing Company, New York. The quotation from Saint Ambrose on page viii is from the same work, Volume III, p. 347.

Cover design by Nick Markell

Book design by Theresa M. Sparacio and Lynn Else

Library of Congress Cataloging-in-Publication Data

Quillo, Ronald.
    The Psalms, prayers of many moods / Ronald Quillo.
    p. cm.
Includes index.
ISBN 0-8091-3843-3 (alk. paper)
1. Bible. O.T. Psalms—Devotional literature. I. Title.
BS1430.4 .Q55   1999
223´.20520434—dc21   98-47843
                                                      CIP

Published by Paulist Press
997 Macarthur Boulevard
Mahwah, New Jersey 07430

www.paulistpress.com

Printed and bound in the
United States of America

Contents

For My Parents
Ann and Henry Quillo
Who Created a Home
Where I Learned
How to Pray

The LORD is my strength and my shield;
  in him my heart trusts;
so I am helped, and my heart exults,
  and with my song I give thanks to him.

Psalms 28:7

[A] psalm is a blessing on the lips of the people, a hymn in praise of God, the assembly's homage, a general acclamation, a word that speaks for all, the voice of the church, a confession of faith in song. It is the voice of complete assent, the joy of freedom, a cry of happiness, the echo of gladness. It soothes the temper, distracts from care, lightens the burden of sorrow. It is a source of security at night, a lesson of wisdom by day. It is a shield when we are afraid, a celebration of holiness, a vision of serenity, a promise of peace and harmony.

Saint Ambrose
Explanations of the Psalms

Introduction:
Prayers for Many Moods

RICHES OF THE PSALMS

There are many paths to spiritual enrichment, many ways of profiting from the divinely granted joys of life, many methods of surmounting obstacles, many means of enduring sorrow, many avenues to serenity. An inexhaustible resource for such gain is at hand in the inspired message of the Bible's psalms. Pathways through these ancient hymns and prayers can be opened for every generation in a fresh and timely way. Such is my aim in this book. While attentive to contemporary perspectives on personal and communal development, I attempt to help the reader discover or retrieve the wealth of insights that accord with themes of classical spirituality, especially reflection, renewal, discernment, darkness, love, and contemplation.

IF YOU LIKE, BEGIN RIGHT NOW

You may bypass the rest of this introduction. If you are adventuresome or enjoy spontaneity, you may choose to leap right in, to begin on any page with any psalm. You might begin at Psalm 1 and progress numerically; you might have favorite psalms on which to concentrate; or the psalms' titles might guide you to themes or issues that you find intriguing or compelling. How you interact with a given psalm would be highly individualized. The text of the psalm itself, the parallel text, and the accompanying thoughts and images would serve you according to patterns of prayer, meditation, spiritual exercise, study, or reflection that suit you at the moment.

On the other hand, introductory observations and suggestions may heighten your attention to the many valuable features of the Book of Psalms. Initial explanatory comments may guide you toward the vibrant spirituality, the deepening of faith, the improvement in disposition, the attainment of worthy goals, which *The Psalms, Prayers of Many Moods* is designed to facilitate.

THE PLAN OF THIS BOOK

*Psalms with Titles and
Parallel Texts*

The psalms are in numerical order according to the New Revised Standard Version of the Bible. Each psalm, situated in the left column, has a title epitomizing the major theme or idea as I have elaborated it in the parallel text of the right column.

To help you locate a psalm that fits a felt but perhaps still unspecified mood or need, a **categorical list** following this introduction divides the psalms and their titles under four headings: worship, joy, sorrow, and serenity. The headings and titles do not specify every aspect of the psalms but suggest the psalms' wide range of issues, themes, and moods.

The **Psalter,** or Book of Psalms, constitutes the major section of the present book and is immediately preceded by a table displaying numerically the usual **sequence of psalms for the Liturgy of the Hours.** Readers who participate in this prayer of the church may find the table helpful for approaching in a fresh way the psalms of the respective times of day.

Thoughts and Images

Following each psalm are what I designate as an oppressive thought and image and an edifying thought and image associated with the psalm and its title. These thoughts and images are designed, along with the parallel text, to promote personal and creative interaction with the psalm. The concluding prayer recapitulates the psalm's theme, thoughts, and images.

Room for Reactions

The blank spaces in the parallel texts allow you the option of entering your own comments, sketches, or other markings that personalize your approach to particular psalms.

Panorama

The final part of the book contains a panorama or overview of the psalms' approach to spirituality. Summaries of the psalms in numerical order constitute an interpretive presentation of religious development as the psalms in general presume or proclaim that it occurs. The panorama is divided into seventeen titled "panels" or paragraphs so that a kind of sequence can be observed. The psalms are essentially prayers, but a theology of spirituality is at least implicit in them. Surely there are several views of spirituality to be found among the Psalter's many stanzas and verses. I have taken perspectives from each of the psalms and linked them into a unified statement that suggests a course of spiritual progress and desirable personal enrichment.

Some readers interacting with individual psalms may find it valuable to have a sense of the larger picture reflected by the Psalter in its entirety. Some readers may welcome the panorama as a tool for reviewing their challenges and successes or for recalling insights and images that have been helpful. Since each psalm is summarized individually, the panorama may, along with the categorical list, also assist some readers in locating a topic, issue, or theme.

Index

The index at the back of the book tells you what psalms share similar ideas or themes. Also indicated are some psalms' ideas or themes that are not suggested by the titles or not elaborated in the parallel text. You thus have an additional tool for finding the kind of psalm you would like to consider at the moment.

SOME SUGGESTIONS

Individuality

Your way of interacting with the psalms is likely to vary considerably from that of other readers. You will probably modify your method regularly, or at least from time to time. The following observations may facilitate your initial gains or later progress.

The Psalms and Their Parallels

The psalms invite you to enter a spiritual world of vibrant imagery, heightened emotion, and profound insight. Because they were composed in a distant time and culture, their wording may at times seem obscure or alien. On the other hand, many elements of the psalms appear as aspects of common human experience.

There is no substitute for the sacred word of Scripture. To enhance your ability to enter into the psalms' special world, I have added a parallel text that refashions or regenerates what, as I see it, comes to expression in the psalm itself. This regeneration offers the psalm in alternate and interpretive vocabulary, images, and concepts. How you utilize the regenerated parallel text depends on what works best, at least for the moment. You may begin with either the entire psalm or the entire parallel text and then proceed to the other as and if you choose. Or you may prefer skipping back and forth between parts of them. In any case, the dual presentation allows you to become receptive in a new way to the psalms' distinctive spiritual riches.

Manageable Units

The poetic nature of the psalms is reflected in the verse translation. The verses bid you to pause as you read, to savor particular emotions or perspectives, and to allow your own thoughts and feelings to enter. The brief lines of the parallel text similarly invite you to linger and muse. Sometimes in prayer or meditation, a single word or short phrase repeated softly or silently—possibly in pace with slow or deep breathing—will in itself contribute to a desired spiritual effect like healing or serenity. In this manner, you may in a given session choose to dwell exclusively on the title or a specific line of a psalm or its parallel regeneration.

Reconfiguration

You might wish at times to reconfigure a given psalm or verse by changing the speaker. For example, you could imagine that "I am protected" is spoken by someone other than yourself. Conversely, you could imagine that "He is protected" is referring to you rather than to someone else or to someone other than the person who might first come to mind. This technique is particularly valuable when the speaker is evidencing dispositions that are praiseworthy. Thus, "I am protected" could appear to be spoken by you or someone else, such as a friend, a person in need, the Suffering Servant of Isaiah, or Jesus Christ. Precedents for reconfiguration or accommodation of this kind can be found in traditions of spirituality and worship. You may thus associate or compare yourself in new ways with others, especially models of spiritual excellence, and be more thoroughly affected by the corresponding thoughts, feelings, or images that serve your spiritual progress.

Many Moods

The psalms give honest expression to a variety of emotions and thoughts, some regarded as desirable, others regarded as repugnant. The random order and unpredictable shifts accord well with the range and swing of moods we can experience from day to day or even from minute to minute. The Psalter teaches us that practically any disposition of the soul can be an occasion for spiritual enrichment. You may choose to work with a particular psalm even if its mood does not fit yours at the moment. Interacting or praying with a joyful psalm, for example, can help you attain joy even if you are now sad; or selecting a sorrowful psalm when you are happy can reflect your desire to consider the redeeming influence of suffering or to be compassionate with suffering individuals or groups.

The categorical list of psalms under the headings of worship, joy, sorrow, and serenity is based on a general theology of spiritual enrichment. This pattern is reflected in the psalms themselves. We are created by God to find our fulfillment in responding to godly love. The act of **worship** expresses faith in God and the eminent value of acknowledging divine goodness. Conscious and reverent attention to this relationship brings with it the **joy** of loving God more deeply and experiencing in our depths the rewards of rightfully relating to our world and other persons. But spiritual progress inevitably brings **pain,** often because of our faults or the failings of others. Nonetheless, with God's support we can quickly find comfort in the divine plan for us and thus enjoy the **serenity** of new intimacy with God. Our hearts are revived for more fervent worship. So renewed, we learn that the pattern of worship, joy, sorrow, and serenity is circular and ongoing. Experience of this truth opens our eyes and hearts to divine fidelity. We thus grow in our hope-filled conviction that spiritual perfection lies before us.

With this in mind you may choose to move from day to day—or from session to session—from one category to the next so that the focus of the selected psalms considered in turn reflects the circular pattern of spiritual enrichment. You could for example establish a four-day cycle or designate certain days of the week for working with psalms under particular headings. If you simply decide to proceed through the psalms numerically, you will be led through the cycle of spiritual moods according to the psalms' own arrangement.

Venting the Negative

The oppressive thought and image proposed at the end of each psalm allow you to consider, to whatever extent deemed suitable, negative features of your interior world, namely, elements of your mind, heart or imagination that could, if they persist, harm you spiritually or inhibit your spiritual growth. Certain thoughts or fantasies can, at least after a time, poison our outlook or deaden our progress. You may associate a particular feeling with each of them. Facing such elements squarely can be very advantageous. Naming them, looking at them, dwelling on them for an appropriate length of time, or expounding them can bring them more fully to the surface of your spiritual life and, with divine help, let you become free from the dangers of these elements' working in a hidden or unconscious way. The psalmists seem to have had a refined sense of such dangers.

Accenting the Positive

On the other hand the psalms are frequently rhapsodic in expressing religious sentiments and other positive attitudes. The edifying thought and image suggested as alternatives to the oppressive ones offer you occasions to let your spiritual life be nurtured by positive dispositions of your mind, heart, or imagination. Introducing or observing such elements, associating particular feelings with each of them, enjoying their refreshing qualities, or embellishing them can enhance your interior life and, with God's grace, allow your spirituality to become considerably enriched. The psalms are essentially prayers and are clearly dedicated to such enrichment.

After formally interacting with a psalm, you may wish at later times—for a day, a week, or perhaps longer—to repeat occasionally or even frequently the edifying thought or image, especially if oppressive thoughts, images, or feelings unduly persist. Repetition of what is edifying can help reorient you for grace-supported spiritual progress.

For the most part the thoughts and images are derived from suggestions or examples in the respective psalms. As they work with certain psalms and parallel texts, some readers may prefer discovering or inventing their own thoughts and images.

Creative Space

The blank spaces throughout the book need not be filled with your own words or pictures but can be left to be. Emptiness may mark a holy ineffability in drawing close to God.

PARTICULAR ISSUES

Pain, Sorrow, and Death

Some of the psalms speak routinely of pain and torment as natural consequences—self-inflicted or divinely inflicted punishments—of indiscretions or sins committed by individuals, groups, or societies. Rightful punishment is presumed to serve a good purpose. Such perspective constitutes a theology that is consonant with healthy psychology as well as repeated teachings of other books in both Hebrew and Christian Scripture. The text that parallels psalms of this kind generally mirrors such a view.

There are other psalms however, especially those influenced by Israel's wisdom tradition, that in other circumstances regard human sorrow and even death as sadly inexplicable or mysterious afflictions of the innocent. Here one's faith is tested and fortified by a call to acknowledge divine wisdom and to display heightened trust. The figures of Job in Hebrew Scripture and Jesus in Christian Scripture give profound witness to obedience and trust in face of overwhelming and undeserved tribulation. The verses that parallel psalms dealing with apparently inexplicable suffering likewise imitate their spiritual perspectives.

A great number of psalms devote the majority of their verses to matters of sorrow. The stories of enslavement, exile, persecution, war, disease, passion, crucifixion, and death demonstrate the Bible's attunement to the ravages of humanity and reveal God's compassion for the sons and daughters of divine creation. The psalms participate in such sensitivity to the human condition and the innumerable challenges to authentic spiritual growth. Yet, in each era of scriptural witness, the ultimate word is of God's efficacious designs to console, protect, forgive, redeem, liberate, empower, and glorify. This is no less true of the Psalter. Even psalms of sorrow contain—mostly in quite bold terms but at least implicitly—proclamations of faith, sentiments of confidence in a God who loves steadfastly.

Anger

The psalms frequently vent anger over enemies, the wicked who endanger and wound an individual or the nation. The hostility in these verses is aimed at the body as well as the mind and soul. Clearly rage can be an upright expression of outrage over injustice and other evils. Rage can work for the protection of oneself or others, but it never should become an instrument for abuse of any kind. Nor should it linger to poison the soul. The Psalter, like the rest of the Bible in both its Jewish and Christian renditions, declares that even God gets angry—though temporarily, if not reluctantly—not only toward evil opponents of religion but also toward the good of heart who frequently do wrong despite their faith. From differing perspectives then, the Bible presents anger as sometimes acceptable and sometimes reproachable.

Evil that we humans see around or upon us—whether in nature or others—can frequently reflect negativity that we unconsciously bear within ourselves. Psychologically speaking, such seeing "out there" what is really within is called projection. The text that parallels the psalms' rancor in face of iniquity often approaches such outrage as projection. Here the question regards elements of ourselves that are inimical to our faith and spiritual advancement. In these instances, interpretation of the psalms—as in other sections of *The Psalms, Prayers of Many Moods*—is a response formulated more in light of current needs than in view of the biblical author's perceived intent in its discernible historical context. My interpretations thus respect the background of the psalms while giving precedence to their application in the life of faith today.

The Reign of God

Certain references to Israel's king or God's Anointed One (Messiah) in the Psalter and the rest of Hebrew Scripture are interpreted differently by Jews and Christians. The latter may regard such designations as allusions to Jesus Christ. They may similarly interpret *Lord* or the mention of God's Word. The regenerated parallel text allows alternate perspectives. Both Jews and Christians may use this book and appreciate the Psalter as part of their common heritage of faith.

Categorical List

The Psalms are distributed according to title and number.

PSALMS OF WORSHIP

God's Power, Majesty, Tenderness, and Beneficence

Alleluia!, 47, 150
Blessings, 111, 134
Courage, 118
Creation's Glory, 148
Divine Authority, 99
Divine Mercy, 103
Empowerment, 21
Fairness, 75
Forcefulness of God, The, 97
Grace, 115
Happiness, 146
Heroism, 45
Justice, 82
Life in God, 139
Love, God's, 136
Loving God, 145

Majesty of God, The, 95
Messiah, The, 110
Optimism, 93
Power of God, The, 29, 68
Power of Prayer, The, 20
Praise, 117
Providence, 65, 104, 113, 135
Receptivity, 24
Renewal, 96
Self-Knowledge, 36
Sincerity, 50
Success, 149
Togetherness, 147
Trust, 33
Victory, 76

PSALMS OF JOY

Sentiments of Spiritual Exhilaration and Ecstasy

Authority, 112
Clarity, 19
Confidence, 16, 89
Contentment, 63

Dwelling Place of God, The, 48, 84
Detachment, 40
Empowerment, 8
Expectation, 132

PSALMS OF SORROW

Pain and Deprivation, Especially in the Life of Faith

PSALMS OF SERENITY

Resting Close to God in Contentment and Peace

The Sequence of Psalms for the Liturgy of the Hours

Numbers in each section refer to the psalms—and in some instances their respective verses—of the liturgy's Four-Week Psalter.

INVITATORY PSALM FOR ALL DAYS OF ALL WEEKS
95 (alternate 100, 67, or 24)

PSALMS BY WEEKS

Week I		Week II		Week III		Week IV

SUNDAY
Evening Prayer I

| 141:1-9 | | 119:105-112 | | 113 | | 122 |
| 142 | | 16 | | 116:10-19 | | 130 |

Night Prayer

| 4 | | 4 | | 4 | | 4 |
| 134 | | 134 | | 134 | | 134 |

Office of Readings

1		104		145		24
2						66
3						

Morning Prayer

| 63:2-9 | | 118 | | 93 | | 118 |
| 149 | | 150 | | 148 | | 150 |

Daytime Prayer

| 118 | | 23 | | 118 | | 23 |
| | | 76 | | | | 76 |

Week I		Week II		Week III		Week IV

Evening Prayer II

Week I		Week II		Week III		Week IV
110:1-5,7		110:1-5,7		110:1-5,7		110:1-5,7
114		115		111		112

Night Prayer

Week I		Week II		Week III		Week IV
91		91		91		91

MONDAY
Office of Readings

Week I		Week II		Week III		Week IV
6		31:1-17,20-25		50		73
9						

Morning Prayer

Week I		Week II		Week III		Week IV
5:2-10,12-13		42		84		90
29		19:1-6		96		135:1-12

Daytime Prayer

Week I		Week II		Week III		Week IV
19:7-14		119:41-48		119:89-96		119:129-136
7		40:2-14,17-18		71		82
						120

Evening Prayer

Week I		Week II		Week III		Week IV
11		45		123		136
15				124		

Night Prayer

Week I		Week II		Week III		Week IV
86		86		86		86

TUESDAY
Office of Readings

Week I		Week II		Week III		Week IV
10		37		68		102
12						

Morning Prayer

Week I		Week II		Week III		Week IV
24		43		85		101
33		65		67		144:1-10

Week I		Week II		Week III		Week IV

Daytime Prayer

Week I		Week II		Week III		Week IV
119:1-8		119:49-56		119:97-104		119:137-144
13		53		74		88
14		54:1-6,8-9				

Evening Prayer

Week I		Week II		Week III		Week IV
20		49		125		137:1-6
21:2-8,14				131		138

Night Prayer

Week I		Week II		Week III		Week IV
143:1-11		143:1-11		143:1-11		143:1-11

WEDNESDAY
Office of Readings

Week I		Week II		Week III		Week IV
18:2-30		39		89:2-38		103
		52				

Morning Prayer

Week I		Week II		Week III		Week IV
36		77		86		108
47		97		98		146

Daytime Prayer

Week I		Week II		Week III		Week IV
119:9-16		119:57-64		119:105-112		119:145-152
17		55:2-15,17-24		70		94
				75		

Evening Prayer

Week I		Week II		Week III		Week IV
27		62		126		139:1-18,23-24
67				127		

Night Prayer

Week I		Week II		Week III		Week IV
31:1-6		31:1-6		31:1-6		31:1-6
130		130		130		130

Week I		Week II		Week III		Week IV

THURSDAY
Office of Readings

18:31-51		44		89:39-53 90		44

Morning Prayer

57 48		80 81		87 99		143:1-11 147:1-11

Daytime Prayer

119:17-24 25		119:65-72 56:2-7b,9-14 57		119:113-120 79:1-5,8-11,13 80		119:153-160 128 129

Evening Prayer

30 32		72		132		144

Night Prayer

16		16		16		16

FRIDAY
Office of Readings

35:1-2,3c,9-19,22-23, 27-28		38		69:2-22,30-37		78:1-39

Morning Prayer

51 100		51 147:12-20		51 100		51 147:12-20

Daytime Prayer

119:25-32 26 28:1-3,6-9		119:73-80 59:2-5,10-11, 17-18 60		22		119:161-168 133 140:1-9,13-14

Week I		Week II		Week III		Week IV
		Evening Prayer				
41		116:1–9		135		145
46		121				
		Night Prayer				
88		88		88		88

SATURDAY

Office of Readings

Week I		Week II		Week III		Week IV
105		106		107		78:40–72

Morning Prayer

Week I		Week II		Week III		Week IV
119:145–152		92		119:145–152		92
117		8		117		8

Daytime Prayer

Week I		Week II		Week III		Week IV
119:33–40		119:81–88		119:121–128		119:169–176
34		61		34		45
		64				

COMPLEMENTARY PSALMS FOR ALL DAYS OF ALL WEEKS

Midmorning		Midday		Midafternoon
120		123		126
121		124		127
122		125		128

THE PSALTER

The Psalms in Numerical Order

PSALM 1

Centering

1 Happy are those
    who do not follow the advice of the wicked,
  or take the path that sinners tread,
    or sit in the seat of scoffers;
2 but their delight is in the law of the Lord,
    and on his law they meditate day and night.
3 They are like trees
    planted by streams of water,
which yield their fruit in its season,
    and their leaves do not wither.
In all that they do, they prosper.
	Centered on God, focused foremost on no one else or nothing else, one must inevitably flourish. The mind and heart are turned to the very source of life.

4 The wicked are not so,
    but are like chaff that the wind drives away.
5 Therefore the wicked will not stand in the
    judgment,
nor sinners in the congregation of the
    righteous;
	To muse on or be moved by what isolates oneself from this is to flirt with ruin.

6 for the Lord watches over the way of the righteous, but the way of the wicked will perish.	*No venture brings greater happiness than the project of knowing the ways of God.*

Oppressive Thought: I must always do what
    others do.

Edifying Thought: I can be happy
    in my unique way.

Oppressive Image: A barren tree

Edifying Image: A fruit-bearing tree

As a tree draws sustenance from the moisture and nutrients of the soil, let me, O God, rely essentially on you. Then my gifts will come more to light and serve the needs of others, especially those close to me.

PSALM 2

Anger

1 Why do the nations conspire,
   and the peoples plot in vain?
2 The kings of the earth set themselves,
   and the rulers take counsel together,
   against the Lord and his anointed, saying,
3 "Let us burst their bonds asunder,
   and cast their cords from us."

Many forces plague us. Personal and social ills attempt to weaken and even crush us.

4 He who sits in the heavens laughs;
   the Lord has them in derision.

All of this however is folly in face of God's plan.

5 Then he will speak to them in his wrath,
   and terrify them in his fury, saying,
6 "I have set my king on Zion, my holy hill."
7 I will tell of the decree of the Lord:
   He said to me, "You are my son;
   today I have begotten you.

Divine wrath, which is rooted in wisdom and love, is ultimately transforming. We are taken as children and molded into the divine image.

8 Ask of me, and I will make the nations your
   heritage,
   and the ends of the earth your possession.
9 You shall break them with a rod of iron,
   and dash them in pieces like a potter's vessel."
10 Now therefore, O kings, be wise;
    be warned, O rulers of the earth.

Our anger, welling up against evil, may become excessive if we are not prepared to leave punishment ultimately in God's hands. Giving anger up to God, we are secure in knowing we will not escalate evil

11 Serve the Lord with fear,
    with trembling (¹²) kiss his feet,
    or he will be angry, and you will perish in the
    way;
    for his wrath is quickly kindled.
    Happy are all who take refuge in him.

Oppressive Thought: I should never show or
   feel anger.

Edifying Thought: Some things provoke
   rightful and temporary anger.

Oppressive Image: A shattered vessel

Edifying Image: Confident laughter

*M*ay my anger, Lord, be moderate, my aversion be to what harms me or wrongs others. May the breath of your Spirit extinguish fires of hate, temper flames of passion, and intensify the heat of love.

PSALM 3

Protection

1 O Lord, how many are my foes!
   Many are rising against me
2 many are saying to me,
   "There is no help for you in God."
3 But you, O Lord, are a shield around me,
   my glory, and the one who lifts up my head.
4 I cry aloud to the Lord,
   and he answers me from his holy hill.
5 I lie down and sleep;
   I wake again, for the Lord sustains me.
6 I am not afraid of ten thousands of people
   who have set themselves against me all
     around.
7 Rise up, O Lord!
   Deliver me, O my God!
  For you strike all my enemies on the cheek;
   you break the teeth of the wicked.
8 Deliverance belongs to the Lord;
   may your blessing be on your people!

By your power, O God, you provide protection against many ravages.

Your energies can obstruct physical harm, deflect emotional upheaval, and neutralize spiritual onslaught.

Confidence in you, Lord, brings such sustenance, and even transport beyond death.

Oppressive Thought: I will be defeated.

Edifying Thought: In God I have power.

Oppressive Image: A fallen warrior

Edifying Image: An impenetrable shield

*S*trengthened by you, Lord, I rely on power that is not merely my own; I ignore my feeble state and look first to you, my trusted guardian.

PSALM 4

Confidence

1 Answer me when I call, O God of my right!
   You gave me room when I was in distress.
   Be gracious to me, and hear my prayer.

2 How long, you people, shall my honor suffer
     shame?
   How long will you love vain words, and seek
     after lies?

I can burden myself by longing for better times or circumstances.

3 But know that the Lord has set apart the
     faithful for himself;
   the Lord hears when I call to him.

4 When you are disturbed, do not sin;
   ponder it on your beds, and be silent.

5 Offer right sacrifices,
   and put your trust in the Lord.

A key to serenity in less than perfect times (and what time is perfect?) is joy in experiencing whatever is good now.

6 There are many who say, "O that we might see
     some good!
   Let the light of your face shine on us, O
     Lord!"

7 You have put gladness in my heart
   more than when their grain and wine
     abound.

The Lord's grace is boundless, and divine blessings flow into all circumstances, even ones construed to be undesirable.

8 I will both lie down and sleep in peace;
   for you alone, O Lord, make me lie down in
     safety.

I however must see beyond the perceived and calmly rest in the silent folds of God's generosity.

Oppressive Thought: Everything is
   in disarray.

Edifying Thought: Here there is unseen
   good.

Oppressive Image: Tossing and turning

Edifying Image: Sleeping like a baby

O*pen my eyes, O God, to the goodness around me. Heal me of this blindness that prevents me from seeing blessings and hope amid trials and sorrows. May my breadth of vision be a sign of your encompassing wisdom.*

PSALM 5

Anger

1	Give ear to my words, O Lord; give heed to my sighing.	*Your loving attention, O God,* *permits my urgent expression of* *anger toward those who provoke or* *harm me.*

2	Listen to the sound of my cry,
	  my King and my God,
	  for to you I pray.	

3	O Lord, in the morning you hear my voice;
	  in the morning I plead my case to you, and
	    watch.	

4	For you are not a God who delights in
	    wickedness;
	  evil will not sojourn with you.
		My sentiments move toward you,
		dear God, and reveal my desire for
		recompense.

5	The boastful will not stand before your eyes; you hate all evildoers.	

6	You destroy those who speak lies;
	  the Lord abhors the bloodthirsty and
	    deceitful.	

7	But I, through the abundance of your
	    steadfast love,
	  will enter your house,
	  I will bow down toward your holy temple
	  in awe of you.
		Such feelings are safe with you and
		leave the matter to your divine
		judgment.

8	Lead me, O Lord, in your righteousness
	  because of my enemies;
	  make your way straight before me.	

9	For there is no truth in their mouths;
	  their hearts are destruction;
	  their throats are open graves;
	  they flatter with their tongues.
		Let me not be caught in a web of
		self-deceit, a snare in which my
		shameful desires for vengeance
		poison my soul.

10	Make them bear their guilt, O God;
	  let them fall by their own counsels;
	  because of their many transgressions cast them
	    out,
	  for they have rebelled against you.	

11 But let all who take refuge in you rejoice;
　　let them ever sing for joy.
　　Spread your protection over them,
　　　　so that those who love your name may exult
　　　　in you.
12 For you bless the righteous, O Lord;
　　you cover them with favor as with a shield.

In bringing forth my plea, I want to disclose the hurt and to petition for your kind protection from all maliciousness.

Oppressive Thought: I must seek punishment for harm done to me.

Edifying Thought: God is my refuge.

Oppressive Image: An enemy speaking treacheries

Edifying Image: Praying in the temple

Bless all my undertakings this day, O Lord. Grant that every stumbling block or affliction I face may become less formidable to me because of my confidence in your abiding love. May you grant me this day moments of peace, thanksgiving, and healthy respite. Help me to correct wrongs where I can and to let your grace sustain me in my successes.

PSALM 6

Fear

1 O Lord, do not rebuke me in your anger,
　　or discipline me in your wrath.
2 Be gracious to me, O Lord, for I am languishing;
　　O Lord, heal me, for my bones are shaking
　　　　with terror.
3 My soul also is struck with terror,
　　while you, O Lord—how long?
4 Turn, O Lord, save my life;
　　deliver me for the sake of your steadfast love.
5 For in death there is no remembrance of you;
　　in Sheol who can give you praise?
6 I am weary with my moaning;
　　every night I flood my bed with tears;
　　I drench my couch with my weeping.
7 My eyes waste away because of grief;
　　they grow weak because of all my foes.

Fear can leave me feeling isolated and hopeless, sometimes to the point of wondering how near, O God, your supportive hand really is.

Sunken in sorrow, I may weep, not knowing what the outcome may be.

8   Depart from me, all you workers of evil,
      for the Lord has heard the sound of my
         weeping.

9   The Lord has heard my supplication;
      the Lord accepts my prayer.

10 All my enemies shall be ashamed and struck
        with terror;
      they shall turn back, and in a moment be put
        to shame.

When distress drags me to the very bottom, I find the only sure direction is toward you, my God.

Here terror yields to trust in your steadfast love, to confidence in a power that is immeasurably mighty and humbles my own.

Oppressive Thought: There is nothing ahead but sorrow.
Oppressive Image: Floods of tears

Edifying Thought: God is near.

Edifying Image: The Lord wiping tears away

My fears, dear God, are often rooted in a sense of my own limitations. Help me to stop focusing just on my weaker self and find where my greater strengths lie in you.

PSALM 7

Hurt Feelings

1   O Lord my God, in you I take refuge;
      save me from all my pursuers, and deliver
        me,

2   or like a lion they will tear me apart;
      they will drag me away, with no one to
        rescue.

3   O Lord my God, if I have done this,
      if there is wrong in my hands,

4   if I have repaid my ally with harm
      or plundered my foe without cause,

5   then let the enemy pursue and overtake me,
      trample my life to the ground,
      and lay my soul in the dust.

6   Rise up, O Lord, in your anger;
      lift yourself up against the fury of my
        enemies;

Wounded by those I have touched with kindness, I feel overwhelmed by hurt, torn open, and abused.

Under such attack I need your powerful, protective hand, O Lord.

Your divine energy overtakes the destructive forces in and around me.

awake, O my God; you have appointed a
judgment.

7 Let the assembly of the peoples be gathered
around you,
and over it take your seat on high.

For the peace I desire, I must eventually entreat you, O God, to save me.

8 The Lord judges the peoples;
judge me, O Lord, according to my
righteousness
and according to the integrity that is in me.

Give me proper vision to assess the situation rightly.

9 O let the evil of the wicked come to an end,
but establish the righteous,
you who test the minds and hearts,
O righteous God.

Arm me with dispositions that will lessen my vulnerability to ravages of both my soul and body.

10 God is my shield,
who saves the upright in heart.

11 God is a righteous judge,
and a God who has indignation every day.

12 If one does not repent, God will whet his
sword;
he has bent and strung his bow;

Let me not succumb to self-destructive animosity.

13 he has prepared his deadly weapons,
making his arrows fiery shafts.

14 See how they conceive evil,
and are pregnant with mischief,
and bring forth lies.

15 They make a pit, digging it out,
and fall into the hole that they have made.

16 Their mischief returns upon their own heads,
and on their own heads their violence
descends.

17 I will give to the Lord the thanks due to his
righteousness,
and sing praise to the name of the Lord, the
Most High.

My prayer shows firmness and conviction. Counting my blessings, I count first on God's justice.

Oppressive Thought: I will never get over
this.

Edifying Thought: God is just.

Oppressive Image: Torn flesh

Edifying Image: A warm heart

Help me, Lord, not to mistake others' ill moods for attacks on me or those dear to me. When the attacks are real and truly hurtful, let my courage and endurance prevail over my vindictiveness. Let trust in your redeeming power sustain me until all is calm and I can truly do your will.

PSALM 8

Empowerment

1   O Lord, our Sovereign,
     how majestic is your name in all the earth!
  You have set your glory above the heavens.

2   Out of the mouths of babes and infants
    you have founded a bulwark because of your
        foes,
     to silence the enemy and the avenger.

3   When I look at your heavens, the work of your
        fingers,
    the moon and the stars that you have
        established;

4 what are human beings that you are mindful of
        them,
    mortals that you care for them?

5   Yet you have made them a little lower than God,
    and crowned them with glory and honor.

6   You have given them dominion over the works
        of your hands;
    you have put all things under their feet,

7   all sheep and oxen,
    and also the beasts of the field,

8   the birds of the air, and the fish of the sea,
    whatever passes along the paths of the seas.

9   O Lord, our Sovereign,
    how majestic is your name in all the earth!

Before the majesty of God, joy and wonder embellish the thought that so much is in our hands. It may be easier to regard ourselves as victims of malicious opponents or wily nature.

Yet your own Word, O God, allows us to proclaim ourselves governors of our destiny.

For we share your life; by your decree you have endowed us with the very godly power by which circumstances facilitate the good. Our praise of you, O God, our Creator, attunes us to your own life and ways.

Oppressive Thought: I am completely out of control.

Oppressive Image: A critical voice

Edifying Thought: Praising God, I am in charge.

Edifying Image: A soaring bird

When I have risen above my weaknesses, when I feel in control, let my due pride, my just regard for the ascendancy that I have attained, reflect, dear God, my faith in your creative energy. Let me be thankful for what you have given me the power to be. Let me rejoice in the power by which you reign over me and my world.

PSALM 9

Victory

1 I will give thanks to the Lord with my whole
heart;
I will tell of all your wonderful deeds.

Nations who war or those who oppress in any way need to remember that God is just.

2 I will be glad and exult in you;
I will sing praise to your name, O Most High.
3 When my enemies turned back,
they stumbled and perished before you.
4 For you have maintained my just cause;
you have sat on the throne giving righteous
judgment.
5 You have rebuked the nations, you have
destroyed the wicked;
you have blotted out their name forever and
ever.

Short-term gain may be far outweighed by repercussions of God's long-term justice.

6 The enemies have vanished in everlasting ruins;
their cities you have rooted out;
the very memory of them has perished.
7 But the Lord sits enthroned forever,
he has established his throne for judgment.

A nation that is victorious or anyone who feels superior can have cause to give thanks for the blessings that accrue to virtue.

8 He judges the world with righteousness;
he judges the peoples with equity.
9 The Lord is a stronghold for the oppressed,
a stronghold in times of trouble.
10 And those who know your name put their trust
in you,

In any case, humility is in order.

for you, O Lord, have not forsaken those who
seek you.
11 Sing praises to the Lord, who dwells in Zion.
Declare his deeds among the peoples.
12 For he who avenges blood is mindful of them;
he does not forget the cry of the afflicted.

13 Be gracious to me, O Lord.
    See what I suffer from those who hate me;
    you are the one who lifts me up from the
        gates of death,
14 so that I may recount all your praises,
    and, in the gates of daughter Zion,
    rejoice in your deliverance.
15 The nations have sunk in the pit that they
      made;
    in the net that they hid has their own foot
     been caught.

In human relations there are always shades of gray, imperfections on every side.

16 The Lord has made himself known, he has
     executed judgment;
    the wicked are snared in the work of their
     own hands.
17 The wicked shall depart to Sheol,
    all the nations that forget God.

As either black or white can lead to gray, defeats can be misleading, and victories false.

18 For the needy shall not always be forgotten,
    nor the hope of the poor perish forever.
19 Rise up, O Lord! Do not let mortals prevail;
    let the nations be judged before you.
20 Put them in fear, O Lord;
    let the nations know that they are only
     human.

Oppressive Thought: Humans are doomed
   to mutual exploitation.

Edifying Thought: Cooperation and com-
   promise promote harmony.

Oppressive Image: War

Edifying Image: Universal peace

May the God of might bring sobering wisdom to individuals and nations who look first to violence and power as avenues to justice. May the fortitude of a just defense or disciplinary measure be marked by a refined sense of proportion and be sustained by the divine grace that is filled with compassion and mercy.

PSALM 10

Injustice

1 Why, O Lord, do you stand far off?
 Why do you hide yourself in times of trouble?
2 In arrogance the wicked persecute the poor—
  let them be caught in the schemes they have
   devised.
3 For the wicked boast of the desires of their
   heart,
  those greedy for gain curse and renounce the
   Lord.
4 In the pride of their countenance the wicked
   say, "God will not seek it out";
  all their thoughts are, "There is no God."
5 Their ways prosper at all times;
  your judgments are on high, out of their
   sight;
  as for their foes, they scoff at them.
6 They think in their heart, "We shall not be
   moved;
  throughout all generations we shall not meet
   adversity."
7 Their mouths are filled with cursing and deceit
   and oppression;
  under their tongues are mischief and
   iniquity.
8 They sit in ambush in the villages;
  in hiding places they murder the innocent.
 Their eyes stealthily watch for the helpless;
9 they lurk in secret like a lion in its covert;
 they lurk that they may seize the poor;
  they seize the poor and drag them off in
   their net.
10 They stoop, they crouch,
  and the helpless fall by their might.
11 They think in their heart, "God has forgotten,
  he has hidden his face, he will never see it."
12 Rise up, O Lord; O God, lift up your hand;
  do not forget the oppressed.

Blatant or widespread wickedness often appears as a permanent blight.

*God seems not to care.
There seems to be no justice.
Crime seems to pay.*

Evils seem to multiply by their own malicious energy, to breed contempt for virtue, to seduce an ever larger population.

Yet our prayer may rise before you, O God, with the hope that our

13 Why do the wicked renounce God,
        and say in their hearts, "You will not call us
            to account"?
14 But you do see! Indeed you note trouble and
            grief,
        that you may take it into your hands;
    the helpless commit themselves to you;
        you have been the helper of the orphan.
15 Break the arm of the wicked and evildoers;
        seek out their wickedness until you find
            none.
16 The Lord is king forever and ever;
        the nations shall perish from his land.
17 O Lord, you will hear the desire of the meek;
        you will strengthen their heart, you will
            incline your ear
18 to do justice for the orphan and the oppressed,
        so that those from earth may strike terror no
            more.

plea will gain a hearing.

We need to experience anew that amid the mysteries of life we can walk with faith and that your justice will prevail.

Oppressive Thought: There is no justice.

Edifying Thought: God does not forget.

Oppressive Image: A sniper

Edifying Image: A just ruler

*L*ord, *when you seem far away, when you seem not to notice blasphemy and injustice, when criminals seem to profit by their evils, strengthen my faith in your goodness. Help me to hold to the belief that you are the guardian of all the helpless. Help me to marvel at your power.*

PSALM 11

Courage

1 In the Lord I take refuge; how can you say to
        me,
        "Flee like a bird to the mountains;
2 for look, the wicked bend the bow,
        they have fitted their arrow to the string,
            to shoot in the dark at the upright in heart.

Enduring pain, sorrow, or oppression can be like a journey in the dark or a walk over fiery coals. One wants to have finished or to take flight.

3 If the foundations are destroyed,
what can the righteous do?"

4 The Lord is in his holy temple;
the Lord's throne is in heaven.
His eyes behold, his gaze examines
humankind.

By divine grace however one assumes the mantle of courage and takes on the enemy directly.

5 The Lord tests the righteous and the wicked,
and his soul hates the lover of violence.

6 On the wicked he will rain coals of fire and
sulfur;
a scorching wind shall be the portion of their
cup.

7 For the Lord is righteous;
he loves righteous deeds;
the upright shall behold his face.

God, as a comrade in arms, becomes ever more a friend in need.

Oppressive Thought: I am going through
this alone.

Edifying Thought: Facing the enemy can
enhance my courage.

Oppressive Image: A frightened flock of
birds

Edifying Image: A righteous warrior

With God always at my side, what do I need to fear? Only that I may waver in the faith by which I rely on divine defenses. They constantly sustain me. God of power and might, I believe in you.

PSALM 12

Slander

1 Help, O Lord, for there is no longer anyone who
is godly;
the faithful have disappeared from
humankind.

To be really hurt by lies is to wonder whether honesty can anymore prevail.

2 They utter lies to each other;
with flattering lips and a double heart they
speak.

3 May the Lord cut off all flattering lips,

But you, O God, are the source of

the tongue that makes great boasts,

4 those who say, "With our tongues we will
    prevail;
    our lips are our own—who is our master?"

5 "Because the poor are despoiled, because the
    needy groan,
    I will now rise up," says the Lord;
    "I will place them in the safety for which
    they long."

6 The promises of the Lord are promises that are
    pure,
    silver refined in a furnace on the ground,
    purified seven times.

7 You, O Lord, will protect us;
    you will guard us from this generation
    forever.

8 On every side the wicked prowl,
    as vileness is exalted among humankind.

*hope. In turning to your higher
ways, dear Lord, persons who use
words to hide from themselves and
others can learn to speak aright.*

*In openness and truth they can
become refined.*

*Their words become those of the
truly noble.*

Oppressive Thought: I must always be wary
    of deceit.

Oppressive Image: Whispers behind my
    back

Edifying Thought: God is the guardian of
    truth.

Edifying Image: A heart-to-heart talk

*Hold me in your truth, O Lord, that my words may never tarnish me or anyone I mention. May
my utterances, in your grace, only be refining.*

PSALM 13

Desolation

1 How long, O Lord? Will you forget me
    forever?
    How long will you hide your face from
    me?

2 How long must I bear pain in my soul,
    and have sorrow in my heart all day

*The loss of something or someone
precious induces grief that for a
time seems interminable.*

*All consolation, including yours, O
God, appears to be gone, maybe
for good.*

long?
>How long shall my enemy be exalted over me?

3 Consider and answer me, O Lord my God!
>Give light to my eyes, or I will sleep the sleep of death,

4 and my enemy will say, "I have prevailed";
>my foes will rejoice because I am shaken.

5 But I trusted in your steadfast love;
>my heart shall rejoice in your salvation.

6 I will sing to the Lord,
>because he has dealt bountifully with me.

I can feel defeated by evil forces beyond any control, even yours, Lord. Though not feeling touched by you, I can still expect with hope to know your kindness anew.

Such expectancy prepares me for fuller consolation.

Oppressive Thought: What I do not feel must not exist.

Oppressive Image: A heavily veiled face

Edifying Thought: I have pulled through desolation before.

Edifying Image: The gleaming face of the Lord

Feeling alone and empty, I can fall into despair, trusting such sentiments, my God, more than relying on you. Spare me such error. Help me remember my faith of earlier times.

PSALM 14

Pessimism

1 Fools say in their hearts, "There is no God."
>They are corrupt, they do abominable deeds;
>there is no one who does good.

2 The Lord looks down from heaven on humankind
>to see if there are any who are wise,
>who seek after God.

3 They have all gone astray, they are all alike perverse;
>there is no one who does good,
>no, not one.

Sometimes we are foolish enough to deny that God is with us.

From such a perspective everything and everyone else look bleak and godless.

We can then become caught in a downward spiral, feeling victimized or overrun by those we see as malicious. It is honest to admit such feelings.

4 Have they no knowledge, all the evildoers
    who eat up my people as they eat bread,
    and do not call upon the Lord?
5 There they shall be in great terror,
    for God is with the company of the righteous.
6 You would confound the plans of the poor,
    but the Lord is their refuge.
7 O that deliverance for Israel would come from
    Zion!
    When the Lord restores the fortunes of his
    people,
    Jacob will rejoice; Israel will be glad.

Our salvation, or way out of the predicament, however is to remember that God is a refuge to all in need. From the bleak, God can bring forth light and renewal.

Oppressive Thought: Everyone is godless.

Edifying Thought: My outlook affects what happens to me.

Oppressive Image: Overrun by the guilty

Edifying Image: Restored fortune

Help me, Lord, to pray with hope, even in times of greatest struggles. Let me not lose my way; let me not lose my salvation. Let me not lose you.

PSALM 15

Steadfastness

1 O Lord, who may abide in your tent?
    Who may dwell on your holy hill?
2 Those who walk blamelessly, and do what is
    right,
    and speak the truth from their heart;
3 who do not slander with their tongue,
    and do no evil to their friends,
    nor take up a reproach against their
    neighbors;
4 in whose eyes the wicked are despised,
    but who honor those who fear the Lord;
    who stand by their oath even to their hurt;
5 who do not lend money at interest,
    and do not take a bribe against the innocent.

If I refrain from any abusive behavior or speech and remain steadfast in thoughts that are edifying, I will be in a wonderful position to know serenity and to enjoy the presence of God.

Those who do these things shall never be
    moved.

Oppressive Thought: I can do or say what I
    please, whenever I please.

Edifying Thought: God is alive in my good
    words and deeds.

Oppressive Image: Stalled at the bottom of a
    mountain

Edifying Image: Fresh air on a mountaintop

*H*elp me control my thoughts, dear God. Guide me in holding on to ideas, feelings, and images *that are positive, that are holy, that contribute to my psychological, moral, and spiritual health.*

PSALM 16

Confidence

1   Protect me, O God, for in you I take refuge.
2   I say to the Lord, "You are my Lord;
     I have no good apart from you."
3   As for the holy ones in the land, they are the
      noble,
     in whom is all my delight.
4   Those who choose another god multiply their
      sorrows;
     their drink offerings of blood I will not pour
     out
     or take their names upon my lips.
5   The Lord is my chosen portion and my cup;
     you hold my lot.
6   The boundary lines have fallen for me in
      pleasant places;
     I have a goodly heritage.
7   I bless the Lord who gives me counsel;
     in the night also my heart instructs me.
8   I keep the Lord always before me;
     because he is at my right hand, I shall not be
     moved.

The rewards of fidelity to God are endless.

They bring blessings to body, mind, and spirit.

The counsels of God keep one on a path of joy and preserve one from a host of life's ravages.

In this light it is eminently sensible to associate all personal goodness with God and to pray for an increase in the divine presence.

9   Therefore my heart is glad, and my soul
        rejoices;
      my body also rests secure.
10 For you do not give me up to Sheol,
        or let your faithful one see the Pit.
11 You show me the path of life.
        In your presence there is fullness of joy;
        in your right hand are pleasures forevermore.

Hopeful and confident expectation of God's blessings brings fullness of life and even boundless bliss.

Oppressive Thought: I alone must make
    things good.

Edifying Thought: God's power makes
    things good.

Oppressive Image: Turning one's back on
    God

Edifying Image: Hands raised to God

My self-confidence, my hope in myself, is best when it reflects my hope in you, O God. Here, my attitude, far from haughty, is humble assurance of what your influence can do.

PSALM 17

Wanting Protection

1   Hear a just cause, O Lord; attend to my cry;
        give ear to my prayer from lips free of deceit.
2   From you let my vindication come;
        let your eyes see the right.
3   If you try my heart, if you visit me by night,
        if you test me, you will find no wickedness in
            me;
        my mouth does not transgress.
4   As for what others do, by the word of your lips
        I have avoided the ways of the violent.
5   My steps have held fast to your paths;
        my feet have not slipped.
6   I call upon you, for you will answer me, O God;
        incline your ear to me, hear my words.
7   Wondrously show your steadfast love,
        O savior of those who seek refuge

I may pray with a sincere heart.

But when others attack me or seem to undermine the good that I do, I may feel harmed in my innocence, a victim of injustice.

from their adversaries at your right hand.
8   Guard me as the apple of the eye;
      hide me in the shadow of your wings,
9   from the wicked who despoil me,
      my deadly enemies who surround me.
10 They close their hearts to pity;
      with their mouths they speak arrogantly.
11 They track me down; now they surround me;
      they set their eyes to cast me to the ground.
12 They are like a lion eager to tear,
      like a young lion lurking in ambush.
13 Rise up, O Lord, confront them, overthrow
        them!
      By your sword deliver my life from the
        wicked,
14 from mortals—by your hand, O Lord —
      from mortals whose portion in life is in this
        world.
      May their bellies be filled with what you have
        stored up for them;
      may their children have more than enough;
      may they leave something over to their little
        ones.
15 As for me, I shall behold your face in
        righteousness;
      when I awake I shall be satisfied, beholding
        your likeness.

Whatever justice may be, I can rest content in profiting by it because of your power, O God, which confronts all evil.

Whatever your judgment, Lord, I can seek shelter in your goodness and know with firmness of faith that all enemies, whether within or around me, will be vanquished.

Oppressive Thought: I will be outdone.

Edifying Thought: God will vindicate.

Oppressive Image: A lurking lion

Edifying Image: The apple of God's eye

*D*o not let me hastily presume, dear God, that I am the rightful defender of justice. Help me to test whether you have called me to be your agent of right or to leave the matter in your hands.

PSALM 18

Victory

1	I love you, O Lord, my strength.
2	The Lord is my rock, my fortress, and my deliverer,
	my God, my rock in whom I take refuge,
	my shield, and the horn of my salvation, my stronghold.
3	I call upon the Lord, who is worthy to be praised,
	so I shall be saved from my enemies.
4	The cords of death encompassed me;
	the torrents of perdition assailed me;
5	the cords of Sheol entangled me;
	the snares of death confronted me.
6	In my distress I called upon the Lord;
	to my God I cried for help.
	From his temple he heard my voice,
	and my cry to him reached his ears.
7	Then the earth reeled and rocked;
	the foundations also of the mountains trembled
	and quaked, because he was angry.
8	Smoke went up from his nostrils,
	and devouring fire from his mouth;
	glowing coals flamed forth from him.
9	He bowed the heavens, and came down;
	thick darkness was under his feet.
10	He rode on a cherub, and flew;
	he came swiftly upon the wings of the wind.
11	He made darkness his covering around him,
	his canopy thick clouds dark with water.
12	Out of the brightness before him
	there broke through his clouds
	hailstones and coals of fire.
13	The Lord also thundered in the heavens,
	and the Most High uttered his voice.
14	And he sent out his arrows, and scattered them;

Coming through one of life's storms, even the most severe or threatening, constrains me to pause in gratitude for your firm hand, O God, who led me to triumph.

You appeared from heaven in a torrent of power and glory.

Threatened by the floods of death or the waves of perniciousness, I was approached by the Lord of love and mercy.

he flashed forth lightnings, and routed them.

15　Then the channels of the sea were seen,
　　　and the foundations of the world were laid
　　　　bare
　　at your rebuke, O Lord,
　　　at the blast of the breath of your nostrils.

16　He reached down from on high, he took me;
　　　he drew me out of mighty waters.

17　He delivered me from my strong enemy,
　　　and from those who hated me;
　　　for they were too mighty for me.

18　They confronted me in the day of my calamity;
　　　but the Lord was my support.

19　He brought me out into a broad place;
　　　he delivered me, because he delighted in
　　　　me.

20　The Lord rewarded me according to my
　　　righteousness;
　　　according to the cleanness of my hands he
　　　　recompensed me.

21　For I have kept the ways of the Lord,
　　　and have not wickedly departed from my
　　　　God.

22　For all his ordinances were before me,
　　　and his statutes I did not put away from me.

23　I was blameless before him,
　　　and I kept myself from guilt.

24　Therefore the Lord has recompensed me
　　　according to my righteousness,
　　　according to the cleanness of my hands in
　　　　his sight.

25　With the loyal you show yourself loyal;
　　　with the blameless you show yourself
　　　　blameless;

26　with the pure you show yourself pure;
　　　and with the crooked you show yourself
　　　　perverse.

27　For you deliver a humble people,
　　　but the haughty eyes you bring down.

28　It is you who light my lamp;
　　　the Lord, my God, lights up my darkness.

29　By you I can crush a troop,

God showed me fidelity and sincerity as in a mirror, as infinitely greater examples of virtues I had exhibited in my humanness.

For your sons and daughters find in you, rightly or wrongly, qualities they have within themselves.

The way of light was thus opened to me, and I found new strength and courage.

and by my God I can leap over a wall.

30 This God—his way is perfect;
 the promise of the Lord proves true;
 he is a shield for all who take refuge in him.

31 For who is God except the Lord?
 And who is a rock besides our God?—

I was now a channel of God's power, vanquishing the evil forces that came against me.

32 the God who girded me with strength,
 and made my way safe.

33 He made my feet like the feet of a deer,
 and set me secure on the heights.

34 He trains my hands for war,
 so that my arms can bend a bow of bronze.

35 You have given me the shield of your salvation,
 and your right hand has supported me;
 your help has made me great.

36 You gave me a wide place for my steps under me,
 and my feet did not slip.

37 I pursued my enemies and overtook them;
 and did not turn back until they were consumed.

Their power became insignificant.

38 I struck them down, so that they were not able to rise;
 they fell under my feet.

39 For you girded me with strength for the battle;
 you made my assailants sink under me.

And I enjoyed my new strength.

40 You made my enemies turn their backs to me,
 and those who hated me I destroyed.

41 They cried for help, but there was no one to save them;
 they cried to the Lord, but he did not answer them.

42 I beat them fine, like dust before the wind;
 I cast them out like the mire of the streets.

43 You delivered me from strife with the peoples;
 you made me head of the nations;
 people whom I had not known served me.

44 As soon as they heard of me they obeyed me;
 foreigners came cringing to me.

45 Foreigners lost heart,
 and came trembling out of their strongholds.

46 The Lord lives! Blessed be my rock,

Before such a Lord I sing blessings

and exalted be the God of my salvation,
47   the God who gave me vengeance
      and subdued peoples under me;
48   who delivered me from my enemies;
      indeed, you exalted me above my
         adversaries;
      you delivered me from the violent.
49   For this I will extol you, O Lord, among the
         nations,
      and sing praises to your name.
50   Great triumphs he gives to his king,
      and shows steadfast love to his anointed,
      to David and his descendants forever.

and praise.

To you, my God, I proclaim my love.

Oppressive Thought: I am alone in my battle.

Edifying Thought: God strengthens me.

Oppressive Image: Drowning

Edifying Image: God as my rock

Let me never forget, O Lord, that by your designs, creation should become your kingdom, a domain of goodness and success. As part of your plan, I can succeed, can overcome all obstacles to fulfilling whatever your dream may be for me. Let me always remember how much help you have already provided so that in times of struggle, I can still praise you for your goodness and still hope for victory through you.

PSALM 19

Clarity

1   The heavens are telling the glory of God;
      and the firmament proclaims his handiwork.
2   Day to day pours forth speech,
      and night to night declares knowledge.
3   There is no speech, nor are there words;
      their voice is not heard;
4   yet their voice goes out through all the earth,
      and their words to the end of the world.
      In the heavens he has set a tent for the sun,

In moments of wonderful insight it can become refreshingly clear how much of this world and the universe is ordered for the good.

God's love pours out over all like

5 which comes out like a bridegroom from his
      wedding canopy,
      and like a strong man runs its course with
      joy.
6 Its rising is from the end of the heavens,
      and its circuit to the end of them;
      and nothing is hid from its heat.
7 The law of the Lord is perfect,
      reviving the soul;
   the decrees of the Lord are sure,
      making wise the simple;
8 the precepts of the Lord are right,
      rejoicing the heart;
   the commandment of the Lord is clear,
      enlightening the eyes;
9 the fear of the Lord is pure,
      enduring forever;
   the ordinances of the Lord are true
      and righteous altogether.
10 More to be desired are they than gold,
      even much fine gold;
   sweeter also than honey,
      and drippings of the honeycomb.
11 Moreover by them is your servant warned;
      in keeping them there is great reward.
12 But who can detect their errors?
      Clear me from hidden faults.
13 Keep back your servant also from the insolent;
      do not let them have dominion over me.
   Then I shall be blameless,
      and innocent of great transgression.
14 Let the words of my mouth and the meditation
      of my heart
      be acceptable to you,
      O Lord, my rock and my redeemer.

*intense sunlight bringing both
luminosity and warmth.*

*How exhilarating it is, day or
night, to look to heaven, delight in
its message, and learn of God's
ways.*

*Walking in these ways, true to
divine energies suffusing nature
and the universe, is to taste ultimate sweetness.*

*To be in tune with the divine plan
is to desire repentance from any
hesitance, let alone recalcitrance,
in connection with directions
designed by the Lord.*

Oppressive Thought: God's ways remain hid-
    den to me.

Oppressive Image: An eclipse of the sun

Edifying Thought: What the Lord wants of
    me is clear.

Edifying Image: Sunrise

*L*ord *my God, when your Word to me is not clear, help me to be patient. When your Word to me is clear, help me to be receptive. Heal the weakness whereby I let your clarity be obscured by my stubbornness. Open my mind and heart to the divine wisdom you so generously share with us.*

PSALM 20

The Power of Prayer

1 The Lord answer you in the day of trouble!
　　The name of the God of Jacob protect you!
2 May he send you help from the sanctuary,
　　and give you support from Zion.
3 May he remember all your offerings,
　　and regard with favor your burnt sacrifices.
4 May he grant you your heart's desire,
　　and fulfill all your plans.
5 May we shout for joy over your victory,
　　and in the name of our God set up our
　　　banners.
　　May the Lord fulfill all your petitions.
6 Now I know that the Lord will help his
　　anointed;
　　he will answer him from his holy heaven
　　with mighty victories by his right hand.
7 Some take pride in chariots, and some in horses,
　　but our pride is in the name of the Lord our
　　　God.
8 They will collapse and fall,
　　but we shall rise and stand upright.
9 Give victory to the king, O Lord;
　　answer us when we call.

It is a loving deed to pray for those in need.

Confidence in the Lord's generosity and protectiveness helps not only those we pray for, but flows back to us as renewed faith and courage.

*Anyone chosen to stand in our lead or in the lead of those we pray for is like the Lord's anointed, the Messiah elected as the agent of God's wonderful designs.
Through the leader, model, guide, or friend, those in need can be blessed with their hearts' desires.*

We pray with new conviction for all of them.

Oppressive Thought: Prayer cannot help in
　　this case.

Oppressive Image: A broken staff

Edifying Thought: We are strong in the
　　Lord.

Edifying Image: Standards raised in victory

*M*ay my confidence in my prayers, dear God, mean my confidence in your power. Help me to remain confident of your abiding love, of your eternal desire to redeem and glorify us all.

PSALM 21

Empowerment

1 In your strength the king rejoices, O Lord,
       and in your help how greatly he exults!
2 You have given him his heart's desire,
       and have not withheld the request of his lips.
3 For you meet him with rich blessings;
       you set a crown of fine gold on his head.
4 He asked you for life; you gave it to him—
       length of days forever and ever.
5 His glory is great through your help;
       splendor and majesty you bestow on him.
6 You bestow on him blessings forever;
       you make him glad with the joy of your
          presence.

7 For the king trusts in the Lord,
       and through the steadfast love of the Most
          High he shall not be moved.
8 Your hand will find out all your enemies;
       your right hand will find out those who hate
          you.
9 You will make them like a fiery furnace
       when you appear.
   The Lord will swallow them up in his wrath,
       and fire will consume them.
10 You will destroy their offspring from the earth,
       and their children from among humankind.
11 If they plan evil against you,
       if they devise mischief, they will not
          succeed.
12 For you will put them to flight;
       you will aim at their faces with your bows.
13 Be exalted, O Lord, in your strength!
       We will sing and praise your power.

The king who will stand in our midst is your Anointed One, O Lord, the Messiah. By your power this agent of your majesty stands uncommonly strong, but not alone.

The one royally crowned stands also for us, representing your victory, O God, in our own lives. Our hearts can be filled with thanksgiving as we reflect on what you, our God, accomplish in us.
By you, and through the presence of your Anointed One, our present and future are safeguarded.
We remain unvanquished.

Indeed we suffer from weakness and poor choices.

But these are steadily purged as we rely on and recognize your mighty presence, our Lord and God.

45

Oppressive Thought: I am alone in my plight.

Edifying Thought: I praise God's might.

Oppressive Image: Being devoured

Edifying Image: A crown of gold

Lord, my God, I am weak and helpless indeed, but only when I am so weak as not to believe in you. I struggle, I fall, I hurt; yet in you I have power to prevail. By your power I can maximize my strengths and draw fully on the joys available to me in this life.

PSALM 22

Endurance

1 My God, my God, why have you forsaken me?
     Why are you so far from helping me, from the
       words of my groaning?
2 O my God, I cry by day, but you do not answer;
     and by night, but find no rest.
3 Yet you are holy,
     enthroned on the praises of Israel.
4 In you our ancestors trusted;
     they trusted, and you delivered them.
5 To you they cried, and were saved;
     in you they trusted, and were not put to
       shame.
6 But I am a worm, and not human;
     scorned by others, and despised by the
       people.
7 All who see me mock at me;
     they make mouths at me, they shake their
       heads;
8 "Commit your cause to the Lord; let him
       deliver—
     let him rescue the one in whom he delights!"
9 Yet it was you who took me from the womb;
     you kept me safe on my mother's breast.
10 On you I was cast from my birth,
     and since my mother bore me you have been

The one who is the ultimate source of my strength, the God who sustains me in every trial or sorrow, at times seems so distant or removed. Then I can hardly imagine how I might go on.

Nothing seems to be helping, which makes no sense because the Lord has been so reliable in the past.

46

my God.

11 Do not be far from me,
    for trouble is near
    and there is no one to help.

12 Many bulls encircle me,
    strong bulls of Bashan surround me;

13 they open wide their mouths at me,
    like a ravening and roaring lion.

14 I am poured out like water,
    and all my bones are out of joint;
    my heart is like wax;
    it is melted within my breast;

15 my mouth is dried up like a potsherd,
    and my tongue sticks to my jaws;
    you lay me in the dust of death.

16 For dogs are all around me;
    a company of evildoers encircles me.
My hands and feet have shriveled;

17 I can count all my bones.
They stare and gloat over me;

18 they divide my clothes among themselves,
    and for my clothing they cast lots.

19 But you, O Lord, do not be far away!
    O my help, come quickly to my aid!

20 Deliver my soul from the sword,
    my life from the power of the dog!

21 Save me from the mouth of the lion!
    From the horns of the wild oxen you have
    rescued me.

22 I will tell of your name to my brothers and
    sisters;
    in the midst of the congregation I will praise
    you:

23 You who fear the Lord, praise him!
    All you offspring of Jacob, glorify him;
    stand in awe of him, all you offspring of
    Israel!

24 For he did not despise or abhor
    the affliction of the afflicted;
he did not hide his face from me,
    but heard when I cried to him.

Though I feel crushed, and even plagued with self-hate, something deep within me holds on.

Security in my earliest knowledge of God, however vague, sustains my prayer for help. I am tired of feeling attacked by wild emotions, tired of feeling drained by powerful addictions, so tired that I sometimes wonder if life is any more a prospect for me. Torn by assaults of every kind, I turn again to God for refuge. Feeling sustained by only a thread of hope, I can expect that somehow I will endure.

God hears all entreaties.

25 From you comes my praise in the great
      congregation;
      my vows I will pay before those who fear
      him.
26 The poor shall eat and be satisfied;
      those who seek him shall praise the Lord.
      May your hearts live forever!
27 All the ends of the earth shall remember
      and turn to the Lord;
      and all the families of the nations
      shall worship before him.
28 For dominion belongs to the Lord,
      and he rules over the nations.
29 To him, indeed, shall all who sleep in the earth
      bow down;
      before him shall bow all who go down to the
      dust,
      and I shall live for him.
30 Posterity will serve him;
      future generations will be told about the
      Lord,
31 and proclaim his deliverance to a people yet
      unborn,
      saying that he has done it.

The day will come when I will remind myself and others of the Lord's compassion and goodness. I will be visibly thankful and renewed. In such hope I can even shape a vision I want to pass down, a vision of life in a wonderful world where God is recognized anew as powerfully just, as mighty forever.

Oppressive Thought: God has abandoned
    me.

Edifying Thought: God is faithful and just.

Oppressive Image: Attacked by a lion

Edifying Image: A merry heart

When I turn from you, O God, when I lose touch with what I should cherish most, when I struggle against whatever situations would tear me from you, help me to stand firm in what I know from my earlier days. Help me to live by the beliefs I have proclaimed in moments of innocent and wonderful trust. Help me to remember that you will always be found anew, by me and by a world that likewise longs for you.

PSALM 23

Serenity

1 The Lord is my shepherd, I shall
    not want.
2 He makes me lie down in
    green pastures;
  he leads me beside still waters;
3 he restores my soul.
    He leads me in right paths
    for his name's sake.
4 Even though I walk through the
    darkest valley,
  I fear no evil;
for you are with me;
  your rod and your staff —
  they comfort me.
5 You prepare a table before me
    in the presence of my
    enemies;
you anoint my head with oil;
  my cup overflows.
6 Surely goodness and mercy
    shall follow me
  all the days of my life,
and I shall dwell in the house of
    the Lord
  my whole life long.

An act of faith or an image of serenity can scarcely be matched for the power it brings to surmount every obstacle, endure any pain, and find every moment on life's paths a treasure. The power is not only from one's personal resources, but eminently from God, who cares deeply for all who stand within the circle of divine protection. So protected and so led, one can rest confident that now, for this moment, everything for needed contentment, joy, and thanks is granted. And so it will always be for anyone who can stay mindful that, above all, the Creator is perpetually kind and loving, enduringly a strength and comfort. Any fear that appears to belie God's providential care is but transitory. In face of transition, in defiance of threats to one's image of a loving God, prayer becomes an act of courage supported by experience of godly reliability.

Oppressive Thought: If things were different,
  I would be at peace.

Edifying Thought: For now I have everything I need.

Oppressive Image: A dark valley

Edifying Image: Restful waters

How foolish I am, Lord, when I trust other guides more than you. I am prey to my weaker, anxious, or rapacious desires when I look for situations or persons who are not in your plan for me. How peaceful I am when I remember that you have me on a path, that you are providing for me, that you are bringing me to something great beyond measure.

PSALM 24

Receptivity

1 The earth is the Lord's and all that is in it,
    the world, and those who live in it;
2 for he has founded it on the seas,
    and established it on the rivers.
3 Who shall ascend the hill of the Lord?
    And who shall stand in his holy place?
4 Those who have clean hands and pure
        hearts,
        who do not lift up their souls to what
            is false,
        and do not swear deceitfully.
5 They will receive blessing from the Lord,
    and vindication from the God of their
        salvation.
6 Such is the company of those who seek
        him,
    who seek the face of the God of Jacob.
7 Lift up your heads, O gates!
    and be lifted up, O ancient doors!
    that the King of glory may come in.
8 Who is the King of glory?
    The Lord, strong and mighty,
    the Lord, mighty in battle.
9 Lift up your heads, O gates!
    and be lifted up, O ancient doors!
    that the King of glory may come in.
10 Who is this King of glory?
    The Lord of hosts,
        he is the King of glory.

With God filling everything, with the divine hand supporting my whole world, with everything about me, about us, flowing from the Creator's abundance, I am fully disposed for joy and plenty.

I can drive away such splendor by hateful, unkind words when perhaps my self-disdain recoils, when inner judgments are hurled at others, guilty or innocent. My utterances then become a darkness, my bleak creation, which God does not lift, except by my invitation, except by my readiness to be filled beyond the present measure of God's power in me, in us, in our world. Shall we not then become bigger?

Let it be to our greater glory, and the greater glory of God, that we say, "Enter, Lord! We are your temple."

Oppressive Thought: God's presence is limited.

Edifying Thought: God's all-surpassing love fills our world.

Oppressive Image: Dirty hands

Edifying Image: A clean heart

*W*hy *am I so frequently closed, O Lord, cut off from your abundant heavenly presence? Help me, my God, to open my heart, perhaps to a capacity it has never known. Let me be filled and transformed by you. Let me see my world swelling with your blessings and love.*

PSALM 25

Needing Guidance

1   To you, O Lord, I lift up my soul.
2   O my God, in you I trust;
    do not let me be put to shame;
    do not let my enemies exult over me.
3   Do not let those who wait for you be put to shame;
    let them be ashamed who are wantonly treacherous.
4   Make me to know your ways, O Lord;
    teach me your paths.
5   Lead me in your truth, and teach me,
    for you are the God of my salvation;
    for you I wait all day long.
6   Be mindful of your mercy, O Lord, and of your steadfast love,
    for they have been from of old.
7   Do not remember the sins of my youth or my transgressions;
    according to your steadfast love remember me,
    for your goodness' sake, O Lord!
8   Good and upright is the Lord;
    therefore he instructs sinners in the way.
9   He leads the humble in what is right,
    and teaches the humble his way.

Errors of my past can weigh heavily, continuing to burden my spirit, afflicting my mind and heart, revealed in sufferings of my body. Persons can malign me, like persistent and cruel reflections of a shame I feel for myself.

My wrongful ways thus have their vengeance, over and over. Yet my soul aspires to other ways, awaits relieving vindication.

Such ways you, O God, reveal; such paths become the rules by which your divine compassion can guide me rightly, bring me peace,

10   All the paths of the Lord are steadfast love and
        faithfulness,
        for those who keep his covenant and his
        decrees.

11   For your name's sake, O Lord,
        pardon my guilt, for it is great.

12   Who are they that fear the Lord?
        He will teach them the way that they should
        choose.

13   They will abide in prosperity,
        and their children shall possess the land.

14   The friendship of the Lord is for those who fear
        him,
        and he makes his covenant known to them.

15   My eyes are ever toward the Lord,
        for he will pluck my feet out of the net.

16   Turn to me and be gracious to me,
        for I am lonely and afflicted.

17   Relieve the troubles of my heart,
        and bring me out of my distress.

18   Consider my affliction and my trouble,
        and forgive all my sins.

19   Consider how many are my foes,
        and with what violent hatred they hate me.

20   O guard my life, and deliver me;
        do not let me be put to shame, for I take
        refuge in you.

21   May integrity and uprightness preserve me,
        for I wait for you.

22   Redeem Israel, O God,
        out of all its troubles.

and make me whole.

To fail by such new measures could be to meet another vengeance, to hurt again in my new shame.

I must thus accept fresh rules, your saving guidance, O God, with fear, with wise respect for your firmness.

In this I find a warm, loving friend, a strong companion on a way of refuge.

Oppressive Thought: There is no way out.

Edifying Thought: God shows me the way.

Oppressive Image: An embarrassed youth

Edifying Image: A kind mentor

How it hurts to be caught, Lord, constrained by habits that grip me as vices. How I long to be enveloped in virtues, the strengths by which I am free, rapt in love of you and others. You free me, Lord; you strengthen me by your power and grace.

PSALM 26

Wanting Vindication

1 Vindicate me, O Lord,
   for I have walked in my integrity,
   and I have trusted in the Lord without
      wavering.
2 Prove me, O Lord, and try me;
   test my heart and mind.
3 For your steadfast love is before my eyes,
   and I walk in faithfulness to you.
4 I do not sit with the worthless,
   nor do I consort with hypocrites;
5 I hate the company of evildoers,
   and will not sit with the wicked.
6 I wash my hands in innocence,
   and go around your altar, O Lord,
7 singing aloud a song of thanksgiving,
   and telling all your wondrous deeds.
8 O Lord, I love the house in which you dwell,
   and the place where your glory abides.
9 Do not sweep me away with sinners,
   nor my life with the bloodthirsty,
10 those in whose hands are evil devices,
   and whose right hands are full of bribes.
11 But as for me, I walk in my integrity;
   redeem me, and be gracious to me.
12 My foot stands on level ground;
   in the great congregation I will bless the
      Lord.

Byways and brambles, blockages and hurdles slow my course to the Holy Place.

There and not yet there, knowing you, my God, and finding you, I often tread circuits instead of thoroughfares. On this journey even the innocent may endure that due the guilty, the recompense of fouling deeds, of stinging wrongs.

But by your ways, O God, I can find that supposed wrongs work rightly.

Your holy justice prevails.

On that I can stake my life.

Oppressive Thought: God is unfair.

Edifying Thought: God does wonders for me.

Oppressive Image: A band of criminals

Edifying Image: Washed hands

Do not leave me a victim, Lord, of my own weaknesses. Help me to move forward into closer union with you. Help me to find myself free of fault, free of wounds, and ready to sing your praises.

PSALM 27

Protection

1   The Lord is my light and my salvation;
      whom shall I fear?
 The Lord is the stronghold of my life;
      of whom shall I be afraid?
	To dwell close to God, to seek solace in God daily is to be immune from ravages of many kinds.

2   When evildoers assail me
      to devour my flesh—
 my adversaries and foes—
      they shall stumble and fall.	

3   Though an army encamp against me,
      my heart shall not fear;
 though war rise up against me,
      yet I will be confident.
	Sheltered in the godly, there is nothing to fear.

4   One thing I asked of the Lord,
      that will I seek after:
 to live in the house of the Lord
      all the days of my life,
 to behold the beauty of the Lord,
      and to inquire in his temple.
	Whatever horror, whatever doubt, whatever hesitance we may have learned growing up, taken in as scarcely doubted realities, accepted in the household of our youth, is forever harmless in the light and love of God's protecting presence.

5   For he will hide me in his shelter
      in the day of trouble;
 he will conceal me under the cover of his tent;
      he will set me high on a rock.	

6   Now my head is lifted up
      above my enemies all around me,
 and I will offer in his tent
      sacrifices with shouts of joy;
 I will sing and make melody to the Lord.	

7 Hear, O Lord, when I cry aloud, be gracious to me and answer me!	
8 "Come," my heart says, "seek his face!" Your face, Lord, do I seek.	

9   Do not hide your face from me.
 Do not turn your servant away in anger,
      you who have been my help.
 Do not cast me off, do not forsake me,
      O God of my salvation!
	Attacks on the body or the feelings, assaults on the mind and its wishes, or skirmishes against the heart and its dreams are all diffused in the lovely warmth, the comfort and

10 If my father and mother forsake me,	

the Lord will take me up.

11 Teach me your way, O Lord,
    and lead me on a level path
    because of my enemies.

12 Do not give me up to the will of my adversaries,
    for false witnesses have risen against me,
    and they are breathing out violence.

13 I believe that I shall see the goodness of the
        Lord
    in the land of the living.

14 Wait for the Lord;
    be strong, and let your heart take courage;
    wait for the Lord!

glow of a love that shelters, of a divine, caressing goodness.

Oppressive Thought: I am forever a
    victim of my upbringing.

Edifying Thought: I am protected and
    spared.

Oppressive Image: Beaten down

Edifying Image: A head held high

*D*ear God, my creator, however disposed to fall or fail, I may rely on your will that I remain safe
and sound. Under your protection from worldly forces, I may put more trust in you than in
my limited perspectives or false persuasions. You are my loving master.

PSALM 28

Security

1 To you, O Lord, I call;
    my rock, do not refuse to hear me,
  for if you are silent to me,
    I shall be like those who go down to the Pit.

2 Hear the voice of my supplication,
    as I cry to you for help,
  as I lift up my hands
    toward your most holy sanctuary.

3 Do not drag me away with the wicked,
    with those who are workers of evil,
  who speak peace with their neighbors,

O Lord, my God, hear me.
Save me in my distress.

Do not let the vicious influences of enemies have their way with me. You are my help, my constant

while mischief is in their hearts.

4 Repay them according to their work,
   and according to the evil of their deeds;
repay them according to the work of their
      hands;
   render them their due reward.

5 Because they do not regard the works of the
      Lord,
   or the work of his hands,
he will break them down and build them up no
      more.

6 Blessed be the Lord,
   for he has heard the sound of my pleadings.

7 The Lord is my strength and my shield;
   in him my heart trusts;
so I am helped, and my heart exults,
   and with my song I give thanks to him.

8 The Lord is the strength of his people;
   he is the saving refuge of his anointed.

9 O save your people, and bless your heritage;
   be their shepherd, and carry them forever.

refuge and safeguard.

*May all forces against me answer
to you and desist.*

*Then will I be strong and full of
thanks.*

Oppressive Thought: I will surely go down
   like all the others.

Edifying Thought: I am strong in my trust.

Oppressive Image: A pit

Edifying Image: A sanctuary

Sometimes, O Lord, I feel assailed from all sides. Whether my greater enemies are from within or without, you are my refuge against them all. I call upon you; I put my trust in you. I remember that I am safe.

PSALM 29

The Power of God

1 Ascribe to the Lord, O heavenly beings,
   ascribe to the Lord glory and strength.
2 Ascribe to the Lord the glory of his name;

*In raging, God need not hurt. In
fury, God need not demean. Like a
storm that blasts and rumbles,*

worship the Lord in holy splendor.

3 The voice of the Lord is over the waters;
    the God of glory thunders,
    the Lord, over mighty waters.

4 The voice of the Lord is powerful;
    the voice of the Lord is full of majesty.

5 The voice of the Lord breaks the cedars;
    the Lord breaks the cedars of Lebanon.

6 He makes Lebanon skip like a calf,
    and Sirion like a young wild ox.

7 The voice of the Lord flashes forth flames of
    fire.

8 The voice of the Lord shakes the wilderness
    the Lord shakes the wilderness of Kadesh.

9 The voice of the Lord causes the oaks to whirl,
    and strips the forest bare;
    and in his temple all say, "Glory!"

10 The Lord sits enthroned over the flood;
    the Lord sits enthroned as king forever.

11 May the Lord give strength to his people!
    May the Lord bless his people with peace!

that drenches, quakes, and howls, godly energies can flow mightily, revealing power, dominion, grandeur, and dignity.

To elicit wholesome fear, to command respect, is the prerogative of one who knows that nurturing, instructive love must begin at times with firmness.

Weeding out excesses, tending all growth relentlessly, taking praise as is fitting, God provides a setting of stability.

Oppressive Thought: I cannot hold out
    under the strain.

Oppressive Image: A fallen tree

Edifying Thought: A whirlwind can test and
    strengthen me.

Edifying Image: A thrilling thunderstorm

Your might, O God, is fearsome but not numbing. I am moved, challenged, energized, by your displays of power. Because you are otherwise calm and kind, I accept your forceful ways as elements of refined, relentless love. You are my firm and honored guide.

PSALM 30

Security

1 I will extol you, O Lord, for you have drawn me
    up,
    and did not let my foes rejoice over me.

Lord, you did let me suffer, nearly to a point of total loss, but not to be left there for long.

2 O Lord my God, I cried to you for help,
     and you have healed me.
3 O Lord, you brought up my soul from Sheol,
     restored me to life from among those gone
       down to the Pit.
4 Sing praises to the Lord, O you his faithful ones,
     and give thanks to his holy name.

Rejoicing in a new day, I come away from the stress, a night of torment and dismay. By day I know your constancy, your enduring goodness and compassion. I no longer believe, in presumptuous reckoning, that you will spare me every pain and fright.

5 For his anger is but for a moment;
     his favor is for a lifetime.
   Weeping may linger for the night,
     but joy comes with the morning.
6 As for me, I said in my prosperity,
     "I shall never be moved."
7 By your favor, O Lord,
     you had established me as a strong
       mountain;
   you hid your face;
     I was dismayed.
8 To you, O Lord, I cried,
     and to the Lord I made supplication:
9 "What profit is there in my death,
     if I go down to the Pit?
   Will the dust praise you?
     Will it tell of your faithfulness?
10 Hear, O Lord, and be gracious to me!
     O Lord, be my helper!"

But I hold with surety to your wondrous name, the mark of faithfulness for which my thanks and praise are insufficient match.

11 You have turned my mourning into dancing;
     you have taken off my sackcloth
     and clothed me with joy,
12 so that my soul may praise you
       and not be silent.
     O Lord my God, I will give
       thanks to you forever.

Oppressive Thought: I shall never be disturbed.

Edifying Thought: God wants the best for me.

Oppressive Image: Weeping

Edifying Image: Dancing

When I needlessly burden myself, O Lord, by resenting the presence of pain in my life, help me remember that you know my sorrow, that you are kind, and that you wisely assess all the effects of my trials. I trust you above all else.

PSALM 31

Needing Courage

1 In you, O Lord, I seek refuge;
      do not let me ever be put to shame;
      in your righteousness deliver me.
2 Incline your ear to me;
      rescue me speedily.
   Be a rock of refuge for me,
      a strong fortress to save me.
3 You are indeed my rock and my fortress;
      for your name's sake lead me and guide me,
4 take me out of the net that is hidden for me,
      for you are my refuge.
5 Into your hand I commit my spirit;
      you have redeemed me, O Lord, faithful God.
6 You hate those who pay regard to worthless
         idols,
      but I trust in the Lord.
7 I will exult and rejoice in your steadfast love,
      because you have seen my affliction;
      you have taken heed of my adversities,
8 and have not delivered me into the hand of the
         enemy;
      you have set my feet in a broad place.
9 Be gracious to me, O Lord, for I am in distress;
      my eye wastes away from grief,
      my soul and body also.
10 For my life is spent with sorrow,
      and my years with sighing;
   my strength fails because of my misery,
      and my bones waste away.
11 I am the scorn of all my adversaries,
      a horror to my neighbors,
   an object of dread to my acquaintances;

There is no greater strength, no greater refuge, no greater hope than you, my God.

I may be shamed by those who turn from you or ignore you; I may suffer from physical or mental anguish; I may be incapacitated or seem to be barred from life itself; I may see nothing but dreadful grief; I may be rejected by those who think they know better; to my loved ones I may be lost in oblivion; I and my reputation may be the object of fearful threats; or I may even be held torturously by my adversaries.

those who see me in the street flee from me.

12 I have passed out of mind like one who is dead;
    I have become like a broken vessel.
13 For I hear the whispering of many—
    terror all around!—
as they scheme together against me,
    as they plot to take my life.
14 But I trust in you, O Lord;
    I say, "You are my God."
15 My times are in your hand;
    deliver me from the hand of my enemies and
        persecutors.

But you, God, respond quickly to me; you protect me; you lead me to safer circumstances; you show your kindness, giving me hope in a future you have lovingly designed.

16 Let your face shine upon your servant;
    save me in your steadfast love.
17 Do not let me be put to shame, O Lord,
    for I call on you;
let the wicked be put to shame;
    let them go dumbfounded to Sheol.
18 Let the lying lips be stilled
    that speak insolently against the righteous
    with pride and contempt.
19 O how abundant is your goodness
    that you have laid up for those who fear you,
and accomplished for those who take refuge in
        you,
    in the sight of everyone!
20 In the shelter of your presence you hide them
    from human plots;
you hold them safe under your shelter
    from contentious tongues.

You silence voices within and without me, cries that scorn and disparage me.

21 Blessed be the Lord,
    for he has wondrously shown his steadfast
        love to me
    when I was beset as a city under siege.

Your ways summon my respect.

22 I had said in my alarm,
    "I am driven far from your sight."
But you heard my supplications
    when I cried out to you for help.

And even when I despair, you are wondrously present, ready to help me find new courage and new pride in you.

23 Love the Lord, all you his saints.
    The Lord preserves the faithful,
    but abundantly repays the one who acts
    haughtily.

24   Be strong, and let your heart take courage,
      all you who wait for the Lord.

Oppressive Thought: I am cut off from the sight of God.

Edifying Thought: Into your hands I commend my spirit.

Oppressive Image: Lying lips

Edifying Image: A refuge

In face of threats and attacks, amid all of life's afflictions, I reclaim the courage I have known, sure that you were at my side. I need never relinquish, O God, my confidence in your power. Even in weakness, I can remain strong.

PSALM 32

Confession

1   Happy are those whose transgression is
      forgiven,
        whose sin is covered.
2   Happy are those to whom the Lord imputes no
      iniquity,
        and in whose spirit there is no deceit.
3   While I kept silence, my body wasted away
      through my groaning all day long.
4   For day and night your hand was heavy upon
      me;
      my strength was dried up as by the heat of
      summer.
5   Then I acknowledged my sin to you,
      and I did not hide my iniquity;
   I said, "I will confess my transgressions to the
      Lord,"
      and you forgave the guilt of my sin.
6   Therefore let all who are faithful
      offer prayer to you;
   at a time of distress, the rush of mighty waters
      shall not reach them.
7   You are a hiding place for me;

To hide one's faults and failings, especially from oneself, is to invite inner turmoil. Pressing on as righteous, declining to express what is concealed, suppressing what could be admitted is poisonous to the soul and constricting to the spirit. To speak boldly however, to confess one's sins, to bring inner darkness into the light of God is to know freedom, renewal, creativity, and joy.

In the welcoming, forgiving presence of the Lord, one is protected from dishonesty which, like a flood, engulfs and destroys.

you preserve me from trouble;
    you surround me with glad cries of
        deliverance.
8   I will instruct you and teach you the way you
        should go;
    I will counsel you with my eye upon you.

*And one learns anew to follow
God's kind and caring lead.*

9   Do not be like a horse or a mule, without
        understanding,
    whose temper must be curbed with bit and
        bridle,
    else it will not stay near you.
10 Many are the torments of the wicked,
    but steadfast love surrounds those who trust
        in the Lord.
11 Be glad in the Lord and rejoice, O righteous,
    and shout for joy, all you upright in heart.

Oppressive Thought: No one knows.

Edifying Thought: Confession brings
    release.

Oppressive Image: Taut reins

Edifying Image: A song of joy

Free me, Lord, from the self-deceit whereby I hide my faults, pretending they are of no account. Refresh my soul as I admit how I have failed; let me begin anew to know forgiveness. Accepted by you, I accept myself in an honest way, and thus become more acceptable in the eyes of those I love. You are my way of truth.

PSALM 33

Trust

1   Rejoice in the Lord, O you righteous.
    Praise befits the upright.
2   Praise the Lord with the lyre;
    make melody to him with the harp of ten
        strings.
3   Sing to him a new song;
    play skillfully on the strings, with loud

*My desperate plans and hasty scur-
rying are puny, futile, frenzied
machinations, compared with the
designs of my Creator.*

shouts.

4 For the word of the Lord is upright,
   and all his work is done in faithfulness.
5 He loves righteousness and justice;
   the earth is full of the steadfast love of the
   Lord.
6 By the word of the Lord the heavens were
   made,
   and all their host by the breath of his mouth.
7 He gathered the waters of the sea as in a bottle;
   he put the deeps in storehouses.
8 Let all the earth fear the Lord;
   let all the inhabitants of the world stand in
   awe of him.
9 For he spoke, and it came to be;
   he commanded, and it stood firm.
10 The Lord brings the counsel of the nations to
   nothing;
   he frustrates the plans of the peoples.
11 The counsel of the Lord stands forever,
   the thoughts of his heart to all generations.
12 Happy is the nation whose God is the Lord,
   the people whom he has chosen as his
   heritage.
13 The Lord looks down from heaven;
   he sees all humankind.
14 From where he sits enthroned he watches
   all the inhabitants of the earth—
15 he who fashions the hearts of them all,
   and observes all their deeds.
16 A king is not saved by his great army;
   a warrior is not delivered by his great
   strength.
17 The war horse is a vain hope for victory,
   and by its great might it cannot save.
18 Truly the eye of the Lord is on those who fear
   him,
   on those who hope in his steadfast love,
19 to deliver their soul from death,
   and to keep them alive in famine.
20 Our soul waits for the Lord;
   he is our help and shield.

How ludicrous am I, how frivolous my people, in having our way and ignoring the ways of the one who fashioned the universe and directs its noble courses toward harmony and beauty.

Hardly a speck in the grandiose, I am not lost but become grand myself when I submit to God's all-knowing call, the voice for which I really long.

Trusting in this submission, my people and I can pride ourselves, not first in our own achievements, but more on the godly works of which we gladly sing.

21 Our heart is glad in him,
      because we trust in his holy name.
22 Let your steadfast love, O Lord, be upon us,
      even as we hope in you.

Oppressive Thought: I must do it myself.

Edifying Thought: The plans of the Lord stand firm forever.

Oppressive Image: Starving for guidance

Edifying Image: A starry sky

Save me, Lord, from confusion. Let me appreciate what I and those close to me can accomplish through the insights and talents nurtured in us by you. But let me not think for a moment that our designs or achievements are ours alone. Surrendering my plans to you, I evade surrendering to destructive pride.

PSALM 34

Confidence

1 I will bless the Lord at all times;
      his praise shall continually be in my mouth.
2 My soul makes its boast in the Lord;
      let the humble hear and be glad.
3 O magnify the Lord with me,
      and let us exalt his name together.
4 I sought the Lord, and he answered me,
      and delivered me from all my fears.
5 Look to him, and be radiant;
      so your faces shall never be ashamed.
6 This poor soul cried, and was heard by the Lord,
      and was saved from every trouble.
7 The angel of the Lord encamps
      around those who fear him, and delivers them.
8 O taste and see that the Lord is good;
      happy are those who take refuge in him.
9 O fear the Lord, you his holy ones,

I have learned a hard-won lesson: that there is no substitute for praising God and trusting in divine power to rescue and renew. To let such praise rise from my lips is to energize my very soul, to let it resonate with the healing energy of divine grace.
To know such power is to be illuminated from within, to be suffused with a light that can shine from one's very face.

There was nothing that I needed to dread.

for those who fear him have no want.

10 The young lions suffer want and hunger,
   but those who seek the Lord lack no good
      thing.

11 Come, O children, listen to me;
   I will teach you the fear of the Lord.

12 Which of you desires life,
   and covets many days to enjoy good?

13 Keep your tongue from evil,
   and your lips from speaking deceit.

14 Depart from evil, and do good;
   seek peace, and pursue it.

15 The eyes of the Lord are on the righteous,
   and his ears are open to their cry.

16 The face of the Lord is against evildoers,
   to cut off the remembrance of them from the
      earth.

17 When the righteous cry for help, the Lord
      hears,
   and rescues them from all their troubles.

18 The Lord is near to the brokenhearted,
   and saves the crushed in spirit.

19 Many are the afflictions of the righteous,
   but the Lord rescues them from them all.

20 He keeps all their bones;
   not one of them will be broken.

21 Evil brings death to the wicked,
   and those who hate the righteous will be
      condemned.

22 The Lord redeems the life of his servants;
   none of those who take refuge in him will be
      condemned.

God tends me at every moment through angelic protectors and through a sweet presence that gives me joy when I simply accept it. No more time will I waste in mouthing untruths or behaving impiously.

Peace and comfort in the presence of the Lord are mine simply for the sincere wanting.

I have no one or no thing surer on which to rely.

Oppressive Thought: God is deaf to me.

Edifying Thought: Those who seek the Lord lack now nothing they really need.

Oppressive Image: Broken bones

Edifying Image: Protective angels

I sing of your great power, O Lord. You protect me from harm; you let me perform deeds I would have never expected. My very reliance on you is the source of energy by which I come into my own, am transformed, find my way, do what I am to do. With you I am at peace.

PSALM 35

Vindication

1 Contend, O Lord, with those who contend with
    me;
  fight against those who fight against me!
2 Take hold of shield and buckler,
  and rise up to help me!
3 Draw the spear and javelin
  against my pursuers;
say to my soul,
  "I am your salvation."
4 Let them be put to shame and dishonor
  who seek after my life.
Let them be turned back and confounded
  who devise evil against me.
5 Let them be like chaff before the wind,
  with the angel of the Lord driving them on.
6 Let their way be dark and slippery,
  with the angel of the Lord pursuing them.
7 For without cause they hid their net for me;
  without cause they dug a pit for my life.
8 Let ruin come on them unawares.
And let the net that they hid ensnare them;
  let them fall in it—to their ruin.
9 Then my soul shall rejoice in the Lord,
  exulting in his deliverance.
10 All my bones shall say,
  "O Lord, who is like you?
You deliver the weak
  from those too strong for them,
  the weak and needy from those who despoil
    them."
11 Malicious witnesses rise up;
  they ask me about things I do not know.
12 They repay me evil for good;
  my soul is forlorn.
13 But as for me, when they were sick,
  I wore sackcloth;
  I afflicted myself with fasting.

Be again, O Lord, my champion.

*Let me so love you that any evil,
any distraction from you, any
unholy force within me or around
me, may come to nothing.*

*May my hope in your holy pres-
ence and in your angelic powers
cause all my perniciousness to be
self-defeating.*

*Give me the joy of knowing again
that you are my protector. My
whole being, into my very bones,
will thus rejoice in you.*

*So enlivened, so renewed, I can
clearly see the scantiness of unholy
or sinful powers.*

I prayed with head bowed on my bosom,
14   as though I grieved for a friend or a brother;
I went about as one who laments for a mother,
        bowed down and in mourning.
15 But at my stumbling they gathered in glee,
        they gathered together against me;
ruffians whom I did not know
        tore at me without ceasing;
16 they impiously mocked more and more,
        gnashing at me with their teeth.

I can jest at their weakness, which eventually must submit to your will and judgment.

17 How long, O Lord, will you look on?
        Rescue me from their ravages,
        my life from the lions!
18 Then I will thank you in the great
                congregation;
        in the mighty throng I will praise you.
19 Do not let my treacherous enemies rejoice over
                me,
        or those who hate me without cause wink
                the eye.

Though trying to be kind, though aiming for compassion, I have indeed been tormented by such weakness and abused by such weaklings.

20 For they do not speak peace,
        but they conceive deceitful words
        against those who are quiet in the land.
21 They open wide their mouths against me;
        they say, "Aha, Aha,
        our eyes have seen it."
22 You have seen, O Lord; do not be silent!
        O Lord, do not be far from me!

My cry for justice issues from my pain, is the call of a mourner who seeks deliverance.

23 Wake up! Bestir yourself for my defense,
        for my cause, my God and my Lord!
24 Vindicate me, O Lord, my God,
        according to your righteousness,
        and do not let them rejoice over me.
25 Do not let them say to themselves,
        "Aha, we have our heart's desire."
        Do not let them say, "We have swallowed you
                up."

26 Let all those who rejoice at my calamity
        be put to shame and confusion;
let those who exalt themselves against me
        be clothed with shame and dishonor.

Yet I do not seek a vengeance of my own.

27 Let those who desire my vindication
        shout for joy and be glad,

I turn to your wondrous kindness, and I trust in your power to vindi-

and say evermore,
"Great is the Lord,
who delights in the welfare of his servant."

28 Then my tongue shall tell of your
righteousness
and of your praise all day long.

cate, to set things right in such a way that my heart will be glad in knowing anew your marvels as my God.

Oppressive Thought: I must be my own vindicator.

Edifying Thought: The Lord is more powerful than any enemy.

Oppressive Image: Sunk in a pit

Edifying Image: Praising God publicly

If I am my only defender, O Lord, if I rely solely on myself for strength and purpose, my determination is hollow and frail. My capacities are duly fortified when, by your grace, I let you take up my cause. Whether I am resisting my own weakness, repelling attacks, or fighting for justice, I am at my best when I claim you as my vindicator.

PSALM 36

Self-knowledge

1 Transgression speaks to the wicked
deep in their hearts;
there is no fear of God
before their eyes.

2 For they flatter themselves in their own eyes
that their iniquity cannot be found out and
hated.

3 The words of their mouths are mischief and
deceit;
they have ceased to act wisely and do good.

4 They plot mischief while on their beds;
they are set on a way that is not good;
they do not reject evil.

The wicked or malicious can be so self-righteous that they are blind to their own faults or attempt to cover their tracks while plotting still more evil.

5 Your steadfast love, O Lord, extends to the
heavens,
your faithfulness to the clouds.

6 Your righteousness is like the mighty

When I look, O God, to your love, steadfast and strong as a mountain, I see that you are light itself, that I have to count myself among

mountains,
>   your judgments are like the great deep;
>   you save humans and animals alike, O Lord.
7   How precious is your steadfast love, O God!
>   All people may take refuge in the shadow of
>   your wings.
8   They feast on the abundance of your house,
>   and you give them drink from the river of
>   your delights.
9   For with you is the fountain of life;
>   in your light we see light.
10   O continue your steadfast love to those who
>   know you,
>   and your salvation to the upright of heart!
11   Do not let the foot of the arrogant tread on me,
>   or the hand of the wicked drive me away.
12   There the evildoers lie prostrate;
>   they are thrust down, unable to rise.

those who must turn to you to know their deepest, sometimes regrettable, inner condition.

Your light then becomes a font of life, a renewing force by which all that deals death and negativity is rendered helpless.

Oppressive Thought: I am clearly faultless.

Edifying Thought: God's judgments give me life.

Oppressive Image: A darkened heart

Edifying Image: Emerging into light

Honesty about myself, O Lord, is one of my greatest difficulties. When I draw close to you, when I recognize your at once affirming and challenging presence, I see my faults with far more clarity. My regrets however are not defeating. They constrain me rather to move forward in hope because the very power by which you enlighten me is the force that in due time—and with my cooperation—renders my imperfections negligible.

PSALM 37

Vindication

1   Do not fret because of the wicked;
>   do not be envious of wrongdoers,
2   for they will soon fade like the grass,
>   and wither like the green herb.

Spending time and expending energy bemoaning the success of those who do me wrong can be quite unprofitable and really a waste of

3   Trust in the Lord, and do good;
     so you will live in the land, and enjoy
        security.
4   Take delight in the Lord,
     and he will give you the desires of your
        heart.
5   Commit your way to the Lord;
     trust in him, and he will act.
6   He will make your vindication shine like the
        light,
     and the justice of your cause like the
        noonday.
7   Be still before the Lord, and wait patiently for
        him;
     do not fret over those who prosper in their way,
     over those who carry out evil devices.
8   Refrain from anger, and forsake wrath.
     Do not fret—it leads only to evil.
9   For the wicked shall be cut off,
     but those who wait for the Lord shall inherit
        the land.
10   Yet a little while, and the wicked will be no
        more;
     though you look diligently for their place,
        they will not be there.
11   But the meek shall inherit the land,
     and delight themselves in abundant
        prosperity.
12   The wicked plot against the righteous,
     and gnash their teeth at them;
13   but the Lord laughs at the wicked,
     for he sees that their day is coming.
14   The wicked draw the sword and bend their
        bows
     to bring down the poor and needy,
     to kill those who walk uprightly;
15   their sword shall enter their own heart,
     and their bows shall be broken.
16   Better is a little that the righteous person has
     than the abundance of many wicked.
17   For the arms of the wicked shall be broken,
     but the Lord upholds the righteous.

my best resources. Pining for the correction or punishment of an enemy may be to pine away in bitterness and resentment, which eat at my spirit, drain me bodily, dispose me for ongoing frustration.

If I believe that my creator is wise, if I believe that justice pervades every aspect of the divine plan, then I can trust that revenge need not be up to me.

Then I can rest tranquilly, imbibing the peace which comes with firm reliance on God. I can be unpretentious, modest in my claims, childlike and humble in my demands.

18 The Lord knows the days of the blameless,
    and their heritage will abide forever;
19 they are not put to shame in evil times,
    in the days of famine they have abundance.
20 But the wicked perish,
    and the enemies of the Lord are like the
        glory of the pastures;
    they vanish—like smoke they vanish away.
21 The wicked borrow, and do not pay back,
    but the righteous are generous and keep
        giving;
22 for those blessed by the Lord shall inherit the
        land,
    but those cursed by him shall be cut off.
23 Our steps are made firm by the Lord,
    when he delights in our way;
24 though we stumble, we shall not fall headlong,
    for the Lord holds us by the hand.
25 I have been young, and now am old,
    yet I have not seen the righteous forsaken
    or their children begging bread.
26 They are ever giving liberally and lending,
    and their children become a blessing.
27 Depart from evil, and do good;
    so you shall abide forever.
28 For the Lord loves justice;
    he will not forsake his faithful ones.
    The righteous shall be kept safe forever,
        but the children of the wicked shall be cut
        off.
29 The righteous shall inherit the land,
    and live in it forever.
30 The mouths of the righteous utter wisdom,
    and their tongues speak justice.
31 The law of their God is in their hearts;
    their steps do not slip.
32 The wicked watch for the righteous,
    and seek to kill them.
33 The Lord will not abandon them to their power,
    or let them be condemned when they are
        brought to trial.
34 Wait for the Lord, and keep to his way,

I can make no greater investment than my great and modest act of faith. How can it be otherwise if God is wholly good?

To delight in the goodness and beauty of the divine mystery is to be disposed for the divine bounty.

Because I am made like God, I am made for God.

To delight in what I am essentially made for is to have what is essentially fulfilling, to have happiness as such. But the Creator likewise blesses the creature through other gifts of creation. Happiness with God is thus conjoined with blessings from God's world. Such are the joys of God's kingdom so that the deepest desires of my heart may be granted in many ways. I can thus afford to be as bountiful as God is, to give of myself and my possessions as though I do not care how far I go.

I can leave all nastiness to the wicked, to those whose malicious plotting and scheming come to nothing but self-defeat. In acting like God, I imitate God's limitless love. And precisely because of that

and he will exalt you to inherit the land;
    you will look on the destruction of the
      wicked.

35 I have seen the wicked oppressing,
    and towering like a cedar of Lebanon.
36 Again I passed by, and they were no more;
    though I sought them, they could not be
      found.
37 Mark the blameless, and behold the upright,
    for there is posterity for the peaceable.
38 But transgressors shall be altogether
      destroyed;
    the posterity of the wicked shall be cut off.
39 The salvation of the righteous is from the Lord;
    he is their refuge in the time of trouble.
40 The Lord helps them and rescues them;
    he rescues them from the wicked, and saves
      them,
    because they take refuge in him.

love, a love that issues with God's promise of fidelity, I can trust in being replenished to whatever extent I need.

Centering love and justice in God, I can find ongoing refreshment and peace.

Oppressive Thought: The wicked have the
    advantage.

Edifying Thought: Delight in the Lord, and
    receive the blessing you most desire.

Oppressive Image: A withered plant

Edifying Image: A land of bounty

Help me find peace, my Lord, in caring less about revenge on those who hurt me. Sinful ways are ultimately futile. Fill me with the love that comes from you, a love that is generous, caring deeply for others, expending oneself in ways that lead to true contentment. Let me know the joy that comes as your gift, as life-giving grace itself.

PSALM 38

Affliction

1 O Lord, do not rebuke me in your anger,
    or discipline me in your wrath.
2 For your arrows have sunk into me,
    and your hand has come down on me.

Lord, I admit that I have erred, have done wrong, have followed the treacherous path, the path not designed by you for me, the path

3 There is no soundness in my flesh
    because of your indignation;
there is no health in my bones
    because of my sin.

4 For my iniquities have gone over my head;
    they weigh like a burden too heavy for me.

5 My wounds grow foul and fester
    because of my foolishness;

6 I am utterly bowed down and prostrate;
    all day long I go around mourning.

7 For my loins are filled with burning,
    and there is no soundness in my flesh.

8 I am utterly spent and crushed;
    I groan because of the tumult of my heart.

9 O Lord, all my longing is known to you;
    my sighing is not hidden from you.

10 My heart throbs, my strength fails me;
    as for the light of my eyes—it also has
        gone from me.

11 My friends and companions stand aloof from
        my affliction,
    and my neighbors stand far off.

12 Those who seek my life lay their snares;
    those who seek to hurt me speak of ruin,
    and meditate treachery all day long.

13 But I am like the deaf, I do not hear;
    like the mute, who cannot speak.

14 Truly, I am like one who does not hear,
    and in whose mouth is no retort.

15 But it is for you, O Lord, that I wait;
    it is you, O Lord my God, who will
        answer.

16 For I pray, "Only do not let them rejoice over
        me,
    those who boast against me when my foot
        slips."

17 For I am ready to fall,
    and my pain is ever with me.

18 I confess my iniquity;
    I am sorry for my sin.

19 Those who are my foes without cause are
        mighty,

where my freedom and creativity were not best utilized, were wasted, were abused. I can even see that the affliction I suffer, the torment of spirit that resounds in my body, echoes in my emotions, is the outflow, the partner or correlate, of my sin and foolishness.

For my unhappy spirit mourns and withers, exposing itself in all my being.

Do I rightly see my plight as a loving demonstration of your corrective care? Am I being taught by you some consequences of my wrongs? Or is my affliction a self-inflicted wound, the issue of my own distorted choices, the very upshot of my sad behavior? Are others as much repulsed by me as I in my pain imagine? Do they really fuel my sorrow with their taunts? Or is it more the case that I see in them what I am in fact doing to myself?

Whatever the case, Lord, however much I or you or others are responsible for my torment, I turn to you for comfort and healing. You know me through and through.

I resolve to change, to follow with new diligence the ways of your wisdom.

and many are those who hate me
    wrongfully.
20 Those who render me evil for good
    are my adversaries because I follow after
    good.
21 Do not forsake me, O Lord;
    O my God, do not be far from me;
22 make haste to help me,
    O Lord, my salvation.

*Have mercy, Lord, and give me a
new life.*

Oppressive Thought: I can ignore implica-
    tions; this is desirable and good.

Edifying Thought: This is self-defeating.

Oppressive Image: A festering wound

Edifying Image: The closeness of the Lord

I do not always see, O God, a connection between my suffering and my sins. In this case, though, O merciful Lord, I know in my heart that I have indeed contributed to my own misery. My behavior and attitude have caused me hurt. Why you did not spare me this pain? Whether others see as clearly as I do the connection of my pain with my fault, I am not sure. I am surely convinced of your goodness. And I beg of you help to change my ways and thus renew my life. Be with me, my good God.

PSALM 39

Punishment

1 I said, "I will guard my ways
    that I may not sin with my tongue;
  I will keep a muzzle on my mouth as long
    as the wicked are in my presence."
2 I was silent and still;
    I held my peace to no avail;
  my distress grew worse,
3   my heart became hot within me.
  While I mused, the fire burned;
    then I spoke with my tongue:
4 "Lord, let me know my end,
    and what is the measure of my days;
  let me know how fleeting my life is.

*Sometimes, Lord, I am so con-
sumed with my sorrow or pain
that I feel a compelling need for
assurance that most of my remaining life will not be like this. I did
try to endure it all placidly. But
with the continued torment, I
moaned, trying at least not to
complain in such a way that I
irreverently repudiated your sense
of what I rightly deserved.*

5 You have made my days a few handbreadths,
  and my lifetime is as nothing in your sight.
  Surely everyone stands as a mere breath.

6 Surely everyone goes about like a shadow
  Surely for nothing they are in turmoil;
    they heap up, and do not know who will
    gather.

7 "And now, O Lord, what do I wait for?
    My hope is in you.

8 Deliver me from all my transgressions.
    Do not make me the scorn of the fool.

9 I am silent; I do not open my mouth,
    for it is you who have done it.

10 Remove your stroke from me;
    I am worn down by the blows of your hand.

11 "You chastise mortals
    in punishment for sin,
  consuming like a moth what is dear to them;
    surely everyone is a mere breath.

12 "Hear my prayer, O Lord,
    and give ear to my cry;
    do not hold your peace at my tears.
  For I am your passing guest,
    an alien, like all my forebears.

13 Turn your gaze away from me, that I may smile
    again,
    before I depart and am no more."

In this case, my pain is a just punishment.

But my emotions have by now become explosive. I must blurt it out: How much more of this is there? Let it not go on for long. Let my few and fleeting days upon this earth be a time of essential gladness.

I will never disparage your holy judgment.

But I do not want to despair. You are my hope as well as my judge. I have learned my lesson. Have mercy on me, O Lord.

Oppressive Thought: I should never complain.

Edifying Image: The Lord is merciful.

Oppressive Image: A muzzle on my mouth

Edifying Thought: Deliverance from scorn

When you punish me, Lord, when my suffering is the rightful consequence of my wrongful action, help me to endure the pain with a sense of due remorse. Help me to remember that you love me and guide me. Help me to live in hope, to trust in your mercy. Help me to understand that you will give me strength not to sin again

PSALM 40

Detachment

1 I waited patiently for the Lord;
    he inclined to me and heard my cry.
2 He drew me up from the desolate pit,
    out of the miry bog,
and set my feet upon a rock,
    making my steps secure.
3 He put a new song in my mouth,
    a song of praise to our God.
Many will see and fear,
    and put their trust in the Lord.
4 Happy are those who make
    the Lord their trust,
who do not turn to the proud,
    to those who go astray after false gods.
5 You have multiplied, O Lord my God,
    your wondrous deeds and your thoughts
        toward us;
    none can compare with you.
Were I to proclaim and tell of them,
    they would be more than can be counted.
6 Sacrifice and offering you do not desire,
    but you have given me an open ear.
Burnt offering and sin offering
    you have not required.
7 Then I said, "Here I am;
    in the scroll of the book it is written of me.
8 I delight to do your will, O my God;
    your law is within my heart."
9 I have told the glad news of deliverance
    in the great congregation;
see, I have not restrained my lips,
    as you know, O Lord.
10 I have not hidden your saving help within my
        heart,
    I have spoken of your faithfulness and your
        salvation;
    I have not concealed your steadfast love and

What a joy it is to be unburdened of frustrating desires for such as possessions, pleasures, status, and relationships. To hope patiently for them without insisting that they come at once or come at all, to leave to God whether they enter my life is to know tranquility, is to be able to sing out each day a song of thanks for the many blessings showered on me. For these are real gifts and thus truly pleasing, not imagined ones that I regret not having. To rest in the pleasure of blessings surely given and to abide in hope of God's future generosity is to know security in divine abundance and firmness in divine fidelity.

I need not plan my future by prescriptions that have become routine, by expectations that have become bad habits, by desires that have become destructive addictions. Creatively setting my mind and heart on a possible future, I can surrender my efforts into God's hands and become a new creation of the divine will, a new child of divine love.

your faithfulness
from the great congregation.

11 Do not, O Lord, withhold
your mercy from me;
let your steadfast love and your faithfulness
keep me safe forever.

12 For evils have encompassed me
without number;
my iniquities have overtaken me,
until I cannot see;
they are more than the hairs of my head,
and my heart fails me.

13 Be pleased, O Lord, to deliver me;
O Lord, make haste to help me.

Turn to me soon, O God!

14 Let all those be put to shame and confusion
who seek to snatch away my life;
let those be turned back and brought to
dishonor
who desire my hurt.

15 Let those be appalled because of their shame
who say to me, "Aha, Aha!"

16 But may all who seek you
rejoice and be glad in you;
may those who love your salvation
say continually, "Great is the Lord!"

*Let my will converge with yours in
such a way that I am not a slave
to old desires but, by your loving
favor, by your grace, and by your
greatness, a master of my new destiny.*

17 As for me, I am poor and needy,
but the Lord takes thought for me.
You are my help and my deliverer;
do not delay, O my God.

Oppressive Thought: I must have this at
once.

Edifying Thought: The Lord is gracious and
generous.

Oppressive Image: A dark pit

Edifying Image: A new song

When I want too many goods too soon, O Lord, help me to remember that I have you, who
are all good. Calm my insistent desires. Let me, resting in you, be content with all the good
I now enjoy, believing and trusting that what you have in store for me is really all I need. Help
me to become detached from what distracts me from you and your will. Free me from the greed of
my imagination.

PSALM 41

Self-Esteem

1 Happy are those who consider the poor;
    the Lord delivers them in the day of
      trouble.
2 The Lord protects them and keeps them
    alive
    they are called happy in the land.
    You do not give them up to the will of
      their enemies.
3 The Lord sustains them on their sickbed;
    in their illness you heal all their
      infirmities.
4 As for me, I said, "O Lord, be gracious to
    me;
    heal me, for I have sinned against you."
5 My enemies wonder in malice
    when I will die, and my name perish.
6 And when they come to see me, they
    utter empty words,
    while their hearts gather mischief;
    when they go out, they tell it abroad.
7 All who hate me whisper together about
    me
    they imagine the worst for me.
8 They think that a deadly thing has
    fastened on me,
    that I will not rise again from where I
      lie.
9 Even my bosom friend in whom I trusted,
    who ate of my bread, has lifted the
      heel against me.
10 But you, O Lord, be gracious to me,
    and raise me up, that I may repay
      them.
11 By this I know that you are pleased with
    me
    because my enemy has not triumphed
      over me.

One who gives to those in need, say, by sharing wealth or goods, is dear to the heart of God. The joy, the sense of blessedness that comes with such giving breathes of God's own generosity. That is why this imitation of divine caring is a way of entering into the very care that God provides for oneself. Here God satisfies needs for such as peace, health, and freedom from animosity. The latter is a special kind of release.

For when I feel disdained by someone, I may see in that person the very attitudes that characterize my own thoughts about myself, except that I may be unaware that I hold myself in such low esteem. Their supposed lack of love for me, or even their apparently hurtful or destructive dispositions toward me, may be my very own dispositions toward myself, albeit unconscious ones.

Becoming released from disdain, then, can mean allowing God to turn me around toward sincerity and love, whether the so-called enemies' attitudes toward me are real or the products of my suffering imagination.

12 But you have upheld me because of my integrity,
    and set me in your presence forever.
13 Blessed be the Lord, the God of Israel,
    from everlasting to everlasting. Amen and Amen.
	To be so turned or healed is to find anew the immeasurable domain of divine peace.

Oppressive Thought: Their plots make me unhappy.

Edifying Thought: The Lord provides for me in my need.

Oppressive Image: Broadcasting bad news

Edifying Image: A helping hand

In giving to others or in serving them, O Lord, let me find contentment. Help my soul enjoy being steeped in your kind of generosity, the ceaseless outpouring of your loving self, your providential power, into your whole created order. Let me not be fooled by hidden fears about myself, lurking judgments that are more products of my darkness than of my clearer contented vision.

PSALM 42

Needing Hope

1 As a deer longs for flowing streams,
    so my soul longs for you, O God.
2 My soul thirsts for God,
    for the living God.
  When shall I come and behold the face of
    God?
3 My tears have been my food
    day and night
  while people say to me continually,
    "Where is your God?"
4 These things I remember,
    as I pour out my soul:
  how I went with the throng,
    and led them in procession to the house of
    God,
  with glad shouts and songs of thanksgiving,
    a multitude keeping festival.

I have known ecstasy, the thrill of God's exciting presence. I have felt the rush of God's spirit over me and around me as I swooned from an unnamable delight in divine energy. God's closeness is thus for me more than a memory, more than a longing for an escaped past.

Rather, such intimacy, having once transformed me, remains an abiding sense that God is always nearby no matter how it may seem otherwise.

5 Why are you cast down, O my soul,
       and why are you disquieted within me
   Hope in God; for I shall again praise him,
       my help (6) and my God.
   My soul is cast down within me;
       therefore I remember you
   from the land of Jordan and of Hermon,
       from Mount Mizar.
7 Deep calls to deep
       at the thunder of your cataracts;
   all your waves and your billows
       have gone over me.
8 By day the Lord commands his steadfast love
       and at night his song is with me,
       a prayer to the God of my life.
9 I say to God, my rock,
       "Why have you forgotten me?
   Why must I walk about mournfully
       because the enemy oppresses me?"
10 As with a deadly wound in my body,
       my adversaries taunt me,
   while they say to me continually,
       "Where is your God?"
11 Why are you cast down, O my soul,
       and why are you disquieted within me
   Hope in God; for I shall again praise him,
       my help and my God.

For me to wonder, then, where God is in my life, for me to heed anyone's question regarding God's fidelity to me, is simply to confess that I again am journeying to something fresh and sweet and deep, toward the God who lies ever before me.

The hurt of God's apparent distance is—I hope, contemplating what God has taught me—only a momentary bridge to joys that are old and new, past and future, to a song of praise that rises from a heart restored.

Oppressive Thought: God has forgotten me.

Edifying Thought: I will praise God again.

Oppressive Image: A deadly wound

Edifying Image: Flowing, rushing water

When my soul is downcast, O God, when the mood is darkened by my lonely negativity, renew in me good sense. Help me to remember that what I long for is what I already have, your faithful love. Clinging to what I believe is present rather than to what I think is absent is to abide in the ever-brightening light in which I find new life.

PSALM 43

Vindication

1 Vindicate me, O God, and defend my cause
 against an ungodly people;
 from those who are deceitful and unjust
 deliver me!
2 For you are the God in whom I take refuge;
 why have you cast me off?
 Why must I walk about mournfully
 because of the oppression of the enemy?
3 O send out your light and your truth;
 let them lead me;
 let them bring me to your holy hill
 and to your dwelling.
4 Then I will go to the altar of God,
 to God my exceeding joy;
 and I will praise you with the harp,
 O God, my God.
5 Why are you cast down, O my soul,
 and why are you disquieted within me
 Hope in God; for I shall again praise him,
 my help and my God.

*When I feel persecuted or abused,
Lord, when I am maligned by my
own poor thoughts about myself or
by the seeming barbs of others, I
can rest, assured that you are my
help and vindication.*

*I have no need to attend to my
own justification as long as I am
born in the light of your truth, as
long as trust in you truly teaches
me that such defensiveness serves
no other purpose than to fence me
from your consoling presence, from
your transforming touch.*

Oppressive Thought: I must defend myself.

Edifying Thought: God brings injustice to
 light.

Oppressive Image: Deceitful people

Edifying Image: The altar of God

*May my defense against undue attacks, O Lord, whether they come from myself or others, be
not merely my own maneuvering but first and foremost my firm reliance on your power to
protect me, uphold me, and suitably call the oppressor to task.*

PSALM 44

Suffering

1	We have heard with our ears, O God,
	    our ancestors have told us,
	what deeds you performed in their days,
	    in the days of old:

2	you with your own hand drove out the nations
	    but them you planted;
	you afflicted the peoples,
	    but them you set free;

3	for not by their own sword did they win the
	      land,
	    nor did their own arm give them victory;
	but your right hand, and your arm,
	    and the light of your countenance,
	    for you delighted in them.

I have been blessed, O Lord, with a precious heritage. The faith by which I live was born in a community of people who were part of a long tradition. They knew your power and your love. Over and over, you revealed to them and their faith that they could trust in you for support, care, and protection.

4	You are my King and my God; you command victories for Jacob.

5	Through you we push down our foes;
	    through your name we tread down our
	      assailants.

6	For not in my bow do I trust, nor can my sword save me.

7	But you have saved us from our foes,
	    and have put to confusion those who hate
	      us.

8	In God we have boasted continually,
	    and we will give thanks to your name
	      forever.

It is for such blessings as these that I call on you now. I know that I can do nothing of enduring value without you. I believe that what I accomplish is sustained in its ultimate worth by your kind and mighty hand.

9	Yet you have rejected us and abased us, and have not gone out with our armies.
10	You made us turn back from the foe, and our enemies have gotten spoil.
11	You have made us like sheep for slaughter, and have scattered us among the nations.
12	You have sold your people for a trifle demanding no high price for them.
13	You have made us the taunt of our neighbors the derision and scorn of those around us.

I cannot however help but feel that at this moment, Lord, you have abandoned me. I simply pray from my heart and tell you how I feel, not judging that I know or understand all of your mysterious ways. I simply shed my tears before you. It seems you are walking in another direction, letting evil and malicious forces take their toll on me.

14 You have made us a byword among the
   nations,
      a laughingstock among the peoples.
15 All day long my disgrace is before me,
      and shame has covered my face
16 at the words of the tautness and revilers,
      at the sight of the enemy and the avenger.
17 All this has come upon us,
      yet we have not forgotten you,
      or been false to your covenant.
18 Our heart has not turned back,
      nor have our steps departed from your way,
19 yet you have broken us in the haunt of jackals
      and covered us with deep darkness.
20 If we had forgotten the name of our God,
      or spread out our hands to a strange god,
21 would not God discover this?
      For he knows the secrets of the heart.
22 Because of you we are being killed all day
      long
      and accounted as sheep for the slaughter.
23 Rouse yourself! Why do you sleep, O Lord
      Awake, do not cast us off forever!
24 Why do you hide your face?
      Why do you forget our affliction and
      oppression?
25 For we sink down to the dust;
      our bodies cling to the ground.
26 Rise up, come to our help.
      Redeem us for the sake of your steadfast
      love.

How can you permit this? How can you who have protected us all so much in the past allow this kind of affliction, this kind of persecution and torment, to go on another day?

I believe, Lord, in your constant presence and protection. Yet from my hurt and struggling heart, from the darkness of my grieving soul, I ask you to come to my side. I feel that you are far away, and I beg you to grant me the kind of relief for which my faith and the faith of my people has been born.

Prove us right, dear God. Reveal to me again your love and might. Spare me this suffering, and awaken in me a new faith.

Oppressive Thought: God favors the enemy.

Edifying Thought: My trust in God has never failed me.

Oppressive Image: Sunk in the dust

Edifying Image: God's strong hand

You have taught me, Lord, through those guided by your wisdom, to rely on you for protection and support. Why then, my God, do you now seem so distant? I cling to the thought that my feelings are part of your plan. Nonetheless I beg for mercy. Spare me the long endurance of this suffering. Come to my help so that I can soon thank you again.

PSALM 45

Heroism

1 My heart overflows with a goodly theme;
     I address my verses to the king;
     my tongue is like the pen of a ready scribe.

2 You are the most handsome of men;
     grace is poured upon your lips;
     therefore God has blessed you forever.

3 Gird your sword on your thigh, O mighty one,
     in your glory and majesty.

4 In your majesty ride on victoriously
     for the cause of truth and to defend the right
     let your right hand teach you dread deeds.

5 Your arrows are sharp
     in the heart of the king's enemies;
     the peoples fall under you.

6 Your throne, O God, endures forever and ever
     Your royal scepter is a scepter of equity;

7   you love righteousness and hate wickedness.
  Therefore God, your God, has anointed you
     with the oil of gladness beyond your
      companions;

8   your robes are all fragrant with myrrh and
      aloes and cassia.
  From ivory palaces stringed instruments make
     you glad;

9 daughters of kings are among your ladies of
     honor;
     at your right hand stands the queen in gold
     of Ophir.

10 Hear, O daughter, consider and incline your ear
     forget your people and your father's house,

11   and the king will desire your beauty.
  Since he is your lord, bow to him;

12   the people of Tyre will seek your favor with
      gifts,
     the richest of the people (^{13}) with all kinds of
      wealth.
  The princess is decked in her chamber with

Through the image of the Anointed One, the Messiah, I am blessed with an icon of a friend, and more than a friend, whom I could praise.

God has blessed you with qualities and talents, skills and virtues, which set you over my heart. You appear to me as one so beautified by sacred endowment and goodness, one so elevated in stature and esteem, that you have become a hero.
You are a power by which I find more good than evil in life.

I thank God for all that you are, both to me and many others who revere, love, respect, and hold in awe what you embody. Perhaps some of what I see in you is a reflection of blessings or beautiful features which, bafflingly, are bestowed on me or for which I myself in the plan of God am destined in my own way.

gold-woven robes
14 in many-colored robes she is led to the king
behind her the virgins, her companions,
follow.
15 With joy and gladness they are led along
as they enter the palace of the king.
16 In the place of ancestors you, O king, shall have
sons;
you will make them princes in all the earth.
17 I will cause your name to be celebrated in all
generations;
therefore the peoples will praise you forever
and ever.

*Nonetheless, as long as I see your
ability to inspire and care, as long
as I myself am inspired by your
prolific goodness, kindness, and
generosity, my heart will swell with
pride for you; and my words of
praise will continue humbly to
redound to your grandeur.*

Oppressive Thought: I am envious of you.

Edifying Thought: I find true joy in recognizing your goodness.

Oppressive Image: A hostile competitor

Edifying Image: A great friend

*L*ord my God, in the image of the Messiah you let me see the earthly expression of your power, beauty, and love. May my contemplation of these royal features lead me to greater trust in your redeeming presence. May I likewise contemplate in humbler gratitude the grandeur of your rule and the care by which you nurture power, beauty, and love in me.

PSALM 46

Steadfastness

1 God is our refuge and strength,
a very present help in trouble.
2 Therefore we will not fear, though the earth
should change,
though the mountains shake in the heart of
the sea;
3 though its waters roar and foam,
though the mountains tremble with its
tumult.
4 There is a river whose streams make glad the

*I may be surrounded, engulfed, by
uproar, commotion, or frenzy.
Yet the divine power by which I
live becomes the energy, the constant resource, by which I endure.*

My project is in God's hands.

city of God,
the holy habitation of the Most High.

5 God is in the midst of the city; it shall not be moved;
God will help it when the morning dawns.

6 The nations are in an uproar, the kingdoms totter;
he utters his voice, the earth melts.

7 The Lord of hosts is with us;
the God of Jacob is our refuge.

8 Come, behold the works of the Lord;
see what desolations he has brought on the earth.

9 He makes wars cease to the end of the earth;
he breaks the bow, and shatters the spear
he burns the shields with fire.

10 "Be still, and know that I am God!
I am exalted among the nations,
I am exalted in the earth."

11 The Lord of hosts is with us;
the God of Jacob is our refuge.

Its completion, its success, is a matter of godly support. I need not join the fray— not now. I need not defend myself against unruly and frenzied tactics.

A calm holds me fast, a peace from God keeps me secure. The Lord subdues senseless tumult, makes serenity out of silliness.

I need only heed the voice of heaven, the strong and quiet message of divine fidelity.

Oppressive Thought: I am surrounded by ruinous forces.

Oppressive Image: Trembling mountains

Edifying Thought: The Lord brings me peace.

Edifying Image: Stillness in a city

When it seems, O God, that I cannot go on, that amid all this madness and turmoil progress is impossible, I turn to you, the center of my tranquility. In you I find anew my strength, my hope, my energy. In you I find my best self. In you I endure and succeed.

PSALM 47

Alleluia!

1 Clap your hands, all you peoples;
shout to God with loud songs of joy.

My heart overflows with joy as I contemplate the glory of God. The

2 For the Lord, the Most High, is awesome,
       a great king over all the earth.
3 He subdued peoples under us,
       and nations under our feet.
4 He chose our heritage for us,
       the pride of Jacob whom he loves.
5 God has gone up with a shout,
       the Lord with the sound of a trumpet.
6 Sing praises to God, sing praises;
       sing praises to our King, sing praises.
7 For God is the king of all the earth;
       sing praises with a psalm.
8 God is king over the nations;
       God sits on his holy throne.
9 The princes of the peoples gather
       as the people of the God of Abraham.
   For the shields of the earth belong to God;
       he is highly exalted.

divine majesty is overwhelming, an awesome and mighty power. In praise of God I find my own true strength and know with conviction that weakness means being alone amid much, being in dreadful, godless isolation.

My lot, my grace, however is to be blessed, inspired to sing of God's endless wonders.

Oppressive Thought: The world is dreary.

Oppressive Image: An empty throne

Edifying Thought: God is a mighty ruler.

Edifying Image: Clapping hands

When I raise a song of praise to your grandeur, O Lord, I become greater myself. You allow me to sense more deeply the dignity you see in me. You are my Lord and Creator. You are my pride and my strength. I am what I am because of you. Help me to best use all your gifts and grace.

PSALM 48

The Dwelling Place of God

1 Great is the and Lord greatly to be praised
       in the city of our God.
   His holy mountain, (2) beautiful in
           elevation,
       is the joy of all the earth,
   Mount Zion, in the far north,
       the city of the great King.

To visit a shrine or other holy place, to enter a sacred edifice or city, is to come upon the divine presence in a special way, to meet God as lingering and constant.

3   Within its citadels God
        has shown himself a sure defense.

4   Then the kings assembled,
        they came on together.

5   As soon as they saw it, they were astounded
        they were in panic, they took to flight;

6   trembling took hold of them there,
        pains as of a woman in labor,

7   as when an east wind shatters
        the ships of Tarshish.

8   As we have heard, so have we seen
        in the city of the Lord of hosts,
    in the city of our God,
        which God establishes forever.

9   We ponder your steadfast love,
        O God,
        in the midst of your temple.

10   Your name, O God, like your praise,
        reaches to the ends of the earth.
    Your right hand is filled with victory

11   Let Mount Zion be glad,
        let the towns of Judah rejoice
        because of your judgments.

12   Walk about Zion, go all around it,
        count its towers,

13   consider well its ramparts;
        go through its citadels,
    that you may tell the next generation

14   that this is God,
    our God forever and ever.
        He will be our guide forever.

Knowing God in such a manner may engage an inner awareness, so that the heights to which my spirit may soar in meeting God in this place relate directly to the depths of myself where God is also at home.

To explore corners and walkways of a holy place, to sense the divine in the solidity, warmth, beauty or freshness of this blessed location, may be to somehow come to know better, even to appreciate with greater love, my own interior corners and walkways where God has found a place. In the shrine or holy place then is awesome power, a source of joy for faith, an occasion of fear for any force of evil. The strength and grace of such a place are mighty, the contours of a dwelling where unfailing courage can be found again and again.

Oppressive Thought: God has gone from
    this place.

Edifying Thought: God's dwelling is secure.

Oppressive Image: Ruins

Edifying Image: Sturdy walls and turrets

When I tread on sacred ground, Lord, when I linger in a holy place, let my sense of your presence remind me of your omnipresence. Let me recall with thankfulness and praise that your sometimes gentle, sometimes powerful influence is everywhere. Let me remain confident that your grace works effectively in me and aligns with countless other graces at work in your people and in your world.

PSALM 49

Eternal Life

1 Hear this, all you peoples;
  give ear, all inhabitants of the world,
2 both low and high,
  rich and poor together.
3 My mouth shall speak wisdom;
  the meditation of my heart shall be
    understanding.
4 I will incline my ear to a proverb;
  I will solve my riddle to the music of the
    harp.
5 Why should I fear in times of trouble,
  when the iniquity of my persecutors
    surrounds me,
6 those who trust in their wealth
  and boast of the abundance of their riches?
7 Truly, no ransom avails for one's life,
  there is no price one can give to God for it.
8 For the ransom of life is costly,
  and can never suffice
9 that one should live on forever
  and never see the grave.
10 When we look at the wise, they die;
  fool and dolt perish together
    and leave their wealth to others.
11 Their graves are their homes forever,
  their dwelling places to all generations,
    though they named lands their own.
12 Mortals cannot abide in their pomp;
  they are like the animals that perish.
13 Such is the fate of the foolhardy,
  the end of those who are pleased with their
    lot.
14 Like sheep they are appointed for Sheol;

To be in touch with God, to be attuned to divine ways, is to sing with wisdom, to proclaim God's truth through what may sound to many like enigmas, to express with compelling clarity what touches every person of every background or circumstance.

So disposed, I can profess with confidence that attacks on me— whether by myself or others— emerge from a trivial power, from a surfeit of useless energy and resources. Surely I cannot ultimately be spared from death, but neither can anything or anyone who attacks me. Death is too certain. From that standpoint, the destructive energies directed against me are clearly effective.

Death shall be their shepherd;
straight to the grave they descend,
and their form shall waste away;
Sheol shall be their home.

15 But God will ransom my soul from the power of
Sheol,
for he will receive me.
16 Do not be afraid when some become rich,
when the wealth of their houses increases.
17 For when they die they will carry nothing
away;
their wealth will not go down after them.
18 Though in their lifetime they count themselves
happy
—for you are praised when you do well for
yourself—
19 they will go to the company of their ancestors,
who will never again see the light.
20 Mortals cannot abide in their pomp;
they are like the animals that perish.

Yet—and here is the wonderful antidote to such negativity—my confidence is in the mighty, life-giving power of God. For divinity outdoes all destruction. And it is by that godly energy that I and the best in me live now and will live forever, something that cannot be said of the ephemeral, of everything inflated by vanity and darkness.

Oppressive Thought: Attacks from within or
without have ultimate power over me.

Edifying Thought: This too will pass.

Oppressive Image: Tarnished wealth

Edifying Image: In the arms of God

Help me to live rightly, Lord, to live by your Word and your inspiration. Help me to ignore, or even cast aside, forces that lead me into deception, hurtfulness, or even cruelty. Help me to live by the light, your light, by which the good I do endures. Help me to practice virtue in such a way that the effects of my works live on while I live on in you forever.

PSALM 50

Sincerity

1 The mighty one, God the Lord,
speaks and summons the earth
from the rising of the sun to its setting.

In face of the divine majesty, before the eternal power by which all that is temporal is held to meaningful-

2 Out of Zion, the perfection of beauty,
    God shines forth.

3 Our God comes and does not keep silence,
    before him is a devouring fire,
    and a mighty tempest all around him.

4 He calls to the heavens above
    and to the earth, that he may judge his
        people:

5 "Gather to me my faithful ones,
    who made a covenant with me by sacrifice!"

6 The heavens declare his righteousness,
    for God himself is judge.

7 "Hear, O my people, and I will speak,
    O Israel, I will testify against you.
    I am God, your God.

8 Not for your sacrifices do I rebuke you;
    your burnt offerings are continually before
        me.

9 I will not accept a bull from your house,
    or goats from your folds.

10 For every wild animal of the forest is mine,
    the cattle on a thousand hills.

11 I know all the birds of the air,
    and all that moves in the field is mine.

12 "If I were hungry, I would not tell you,
    for the world and all that is in it is mine.

13 Do I eat the flesh of bulls,
    or drink the blood of goats?

14 Offer to God a sacrifice of thanksgiving,
    and pay your vows to the Most High.

15 Call on me in the day of trouble;
    I will deliver you, and you shall glorify me."

16 But to the wicked God says:
    "What right have you to recite my statutes,
    or take my covenant on your lips?

17 For you hate discipline,
    and you cast my words behind you.

18 You make friends with a thief when you see
        one,
    and you keep company with adulterers.

19 "You give your mouth free rein for evil,
    and your tongue frames deceit.

ness, in the sacred place where God is present specially for me, can I, should I, shudder?

Dare I risk being seared by the warmth and energy of my Savior, of my Partner in the fullest love, in the divine gift of accepting, affirming, and supportive presence by which I am spared of any taint and all destruction?

Such warmth can sear when what I bring to the relationship, what I offer as a sign of my own love, is too bereft of myself, too short of what we are together. Then God rightly proclaims that such an offering—whether from my heart, lips, or hands—bespeaks in irony the opposite of what it says. A proclamation like this, an utterance of divine justice or perhaps even divine hurt, becomes a judgment, a stunning cry that shakes the casual, upsets the assumed, negates the pretended.

20   You sit and speak against your kin;
      you slander your own mother's child.
21   These things you have done and I have been
      silent;
      you thought that I was one just like yourself.
    But now I rebuke you, and lay the charge
      before you.
22   "Mark this, then, you who forget God,
      or I will tear you apart, and there will be no
      one to deliver.
23   Those who bring thanksgiving as their
      sacrifice honor me;
    to those who go the right way
    I will show the salvation of God."

Dare I turn from pretense, however small or great, and find anew, afresh, my way in the daily journey of partnership, of covenant with my God, the Lord of heaven and earth? May my heart and soul ever utter the truth. May every sign of my love perdure in the sincerity and purity of faithfulness and thanksgiving.

Oppressive Thought: I am totally secure in the expressions of my faith.

Edifying Thought: God heals me of insincerity.

Oppressive Image: Selfish flattery

Edifying Image: A praiseworthy offering

Y*our presence before me, my Lord and God, always prompts me to be honest about myself. For you are the light in which I see all truth, even those truths that are so hard to see, truths about myself, my character, my strengths, my weaknesses. Help me, Lord, as I work by your grace and in your loving presence to find myself, to abandon my weaker self, and to be my better self.*

PSALM 51

Repentance

1   Have mercy on me, O God,
      according to your steadfast love;
    according to your abundant mercy
      blot out my transgressions.
2   Wash me thoroughly from my iniquity,
      and cleanse me from my sin.
3   For I know my transgressions,
      and my sin is ever before me.

God of love and justice, I acknowledge in your wonderful presence that I have wandered outside the boundaries of your holy will.

To my own mind and from the weakness, limits, and distortions of

4 Against you, you alone, have I sinned,
   and done what is evil in your sight,
   so that you are justified in your sentence
   and blameless when you pass judgment.
5 Indeed, I was born guilty,
   a sinner when my mother conceived me.
6 You desire truth in the inward being;
   therefore teach me wisdom in my secret
   heart.
7 Purge me with hyssop, and I shall be clean;
   wash me, and I shall be whiter than snow.
8 Let me hear joy and gladness;
   let the bones that you have crushed rejoice.
9 Hide your face from my sins,
   and blot out all my iniquities.
10 Create in me a clean heart, O God,
   and put a new and right spirit within me.
11 Do not cast me away from your presence,
   and do not take your holy spirit from me.
12 Restore to me the joy of your salvation,
   and sustain in me a willing spirit.
13 Then I will teach transgressors your ways,
   and sinners will return to you.
14 Deliver me from bloodshed, O God,
   O God of my salvation,
   and my tongue will sing aloud of your
   deliverance.
15 O Lord, open my lips,
   and my mouth will declare your praise.
16 For you have no delight in sacrifice;
   if I were to give a burnt offering, you would
   not be pleased.
17 The sacrifice acceptable to God is a broken
   spirit;
   a broken and contrite heart, O God, you will
   not despise.
18 Do good to Zion in your good pleasure;
   rebuild the walls of Jerusalem,
19 then you will delight in right sacrifices,
   in burnt offerings and whole burnt offerings;
   then bulls will be offered on your altar.

my own heart, I have desired and chosen what seemed fitting and beneficial.

Yet your ways, through law or example or conscience, tell me of my error. I regret having wasted my time, my energies and your support. How much closer I could have come to you and to my own proper destiny. Yet my choice, my sin, has delayed the beauty and joy of such a journey. My choice has been part of a pattern in my life since my earliest years. Somehow I have never been wise enough or strong enough to be consistent in following your ways, your loving designs for me.

Accept now, dear God, my confession. Heal and renew me in my repentance. Let your loving embrace transform my heart and mind and soul so that I will be totally renewed and readied for fresh advancement on my journey with you.

Oppressive Thought: I always do what is
    right in God's eyes.

Edifying Thought: God teaches me what is
    right.

Oppressive Image: A dirty body

Edifying Image: Fresh, clean snow

I have deviated, dear God, from the path you have designed for me. My error, my fault, my reck-lessness felt so right. But I was listening more to my weaker self, to my darkened selfishness, than to you. I am sorry, O God, for having so strayed. I confess my sin and promise to right my ways. Direct me, O God, on my special course of happiness and peace.

PSALM 52

Humiliation

1 Why do you boast, O mighty one,
    of mischief done against the godly?
    All day long (²) you are plotting
      destruction.
    Your tongue is like a sharp razor,
    you worker of treachery.
3 You love evil more than good,
    and lying more than speaking the truth.
4 You love all words that devour,
    O deceitful tongue.

There is a part of me that is smug, thinking erroneously that it gained the upper hand when ignoring, or even deriding, what is admirable and virtuous in myself or in others.

5 But God will break you down forever;
    he will snatch and tear you from your tent;
    he will uproot you from the land of the living.
6 The righteous will see, and fear,
    and will laugh at the evildoer, saying,
7 "See the one who would not take refuge in
      God,
    but trusted in abundant riches,
    and sought refuge in wealth!"

God however can bring me to my senses. Allowing the kind of experience that shatters false images, deceitful facades, or too-cool self-assurance, divine power wisely and lovingly calls me to my true and better self.

8 But I am like a green olive tree
    in the house of God.
    I trust in the steadfast love of God
    forever and ever.
9 I will thank you forever,

So the better parts of me can stand with a dignity that, neither self-effacing nor self-inflating, bespeaks rightful gratitude for what, by grace, I truly am.

because of what you have done.
In the presence of the faithful
I will proclaim your name, for it is good.

Oppressive Thought: I cannot make much
more progress.

Edifying Thought: God holds a mirror
before me.

Oppressive Image: A boaster

Edifying Image: A sturdy, fruitful olive tree.

Save me from haughtiness, O Lord. Give me the sense to be cautious in assuming too quickly that I am right or acting rightly. For if I trust myself too much, my rightness becomes self-righteousness. Then I need to be corrected, brought back to my senses by your influence, the kind direction that I may find upsetting. Mold me into a person who stands firm through spiritual insight, through wisdom that comes with knowing you.

PSALM 53

Faith Distorted

1   Fools say in their hearts, "There is no
        God."
    They are corrupt, they commit
        abominable acts;
    there is no one who does good.
2   God looks down from heaven on
        humankind
    to see if there are any who are wise,
    who seek after God.
3   They have all fallen away, they are all
        alike perverse;
    there is no one who does good,
    no, not one.
4   Have they no knowledge, those
        evildoers,
    who eat up my people as they eat
        bread,
    and do not call upon God?
5   There they shall be in great terror,

The follies of immorality may lead to a sense of godlessness. But not knowing God, misapprehending the wondrous power of divine presence, may by its own misdirected might lead to abominations. With such a prospect before me, I would do well to ask myself daily whether I recognize enough the power of God, whether I see sufficiently all the circumstances in which divine might is working, is active for my good and that of all those I love.

To miss such presence, to fail to be

95

in terror such as has not been.
For God will scatter the bones of the
ungodly;
they will be put to shame, for God has
rejected them.
6   O that deliverance for Israel would come
from Zion!
When God restores the fortunes of his
people,
Jacob will rejoice; Israel will be glad.

*energized and supported by the
recognition of all that God does for
me, might even become so habitual
and unquestioned as to provoke
God's pity, if not God's wrath. Are
such divine dispositions not to be
feared, not to be acknowledged
with healthy respect? Better to
repent of my folly and rest assured
of God's loving kindness.*

Oppressive Thought: God is nowhere in this
situation.

Edifying Thought: God's loving presence is
everywhere.

Oppressive Image: Scattered bones

Edifying Image: A gladsome people

*I need your help, O God. I need to be spared the folly of not noticing you, of ignoring your prov-
idential presence in all that I do. You have given me talents. You support and guide me on
my ways of personal creativity and independence. But you also caution me to remember you, to
have confidence in you, to learn from you during all my days. Help me, Lord, when my faith is
tentative.*

PSALM 54

Providence

1   Save me, O God, by your name,
and vindicate me by your
might.
2   Hear my prayer, O God;
give ear to the words of m
mouth.
3   For the insolent have risen
against me,
the ruthless seek my life;
they do not set God before
them.
4   But surely, God is my helper;

*Typically, Lord, I am besieged by
desires that leave me frustrated.
Not that having what I want would
necessarily be bad. But not having
what I want feels bad and leaves
me with a mind-set, with a stubborn conviction that I am neglected
or unblessed, that what I have or
am cannot be sufficient to taste
life's true goodness, the sweetness
with which you have endowed your
creation. But you see through all of*

the Lord is the upholder of
my life.
5   He will repay my enemies for
their evil.
In your faithfulness, put an
end to them.
6   With a freewill offering I will
sacrifice to you;
I will give thanks to your
name, O Lord, for it is
good.
7   For he has delivered me from
every trouble,
and my eye has looked in
triumph on my enemies.

*this and give me the power to see
as well, to recognize that in turning
to you before all else, in preferring
you to all else, my enemies are
defeated, my desires are dissolved
in the rush of your love. So I turn
them over to you. I give over my
needless desires to your discretion.
You alone I trust as the arbiter of
my destiny, as the designer of beauty in my life. Trusting you, accepting what I have and am as suitably
disposed for the coming of your
kingdom brings refreshment to my
spirit, is a victory of your grace.*

Oppressive Thought: What I desire I need to
be happy.

Edifying Thought: God has given me
enough to be truly happy.

Oppressive Image: Ruthless attackers

Edifying Image: A wonderful helper

*I torture myself, Lord, when I misdirect my faith, when I believe that everything I want is neces-
sary for my happiness. I forget that not all my desires are sustained by your designs for me. I confuse myself when I suppose that everything I long for will benefit me or my world. Give me, my Lord,
the gift of discretion. Help me to pursue my desires prudently.*

PSALM 55

Betrayal

1   Give ear to my prayer, O God;
do not hide yourself from my supplication.
2   Attend to me, and answer me;
I am troubled in my complaint.
I am distraught (³) by the noise of the enemy,
because of the clamor of the wicked.
For they bring trouble upon me,
and in anger they cherish enmity against me.

*Sometimes I feel so alone, so
deprived of life's sweetness, that I
want to run, to find solace in a
quiet haven of refreshment and
peace.*

4   My heart is in anguish within me,
        the terrors of death have fallen upon me.
5   Fear and trembling come upon me,
        and horror overwhelms me.
6   And I say, "O that I had wings like a dove!
        I would fly away and be at rest;
7   truly, I would flee far away;
        I would lodge in the wilderness;
8   I would hurry to find a shelter for myself
        from the raging wind and tempest."
9   Confuse, O Lord, confound their speech;
        for I see violence and strife in the city.
10 Day and night they go around it on its walls,
    and iniquity and trouble are within it;
11   ruin is in its midst;
    oppression and fraud
        do not depart from its marketplace.
12 It is not enemies who taunt me—
        I could bear that;
    it is not adversaries who deal insolently with
        me—
    I could hide from them.
13 But it is you, my equal,
        my companion, my familiar friend,
14 with whom I kept pleasant company;
        we walked in the house of God with the
            throng.
15 Let death come upon them;
        let them go down alive to Sheol;
        for evil is in their homes and in their hearts.
16 But I call upon God,
        and the Lord will save me.
17 Evening and morning and at noon
        I utter my complaint and moan,
        and he will hear my voice.
18 He will redeem me unharmed
        from the battle that I wage,
        for many are arrayed against me.
19 God, who is enthroned from of old,
        will hear, and will humble them—
    because they do not change,
        and do not fear God.

How wondrous would such comfort be, freedom from the attacks and taunts, the disparagement and neglect, not only of associates and comrades but also of my dearest friends, those for whom I care the most, those with whom I am most intimate. A darkness seems to have possessed us all. Betrayal, hurt, and mistrust have poisoned every-thing.

Yet the part of me that knows of God, the spirit within me that has once tasted divine sweetness, knows that escape solves nothing. The darkness swells in my own heart and eyes. The firm, reliable hand of the Lord is there and always has been. God's assuring, enlivening strength is being offered to me with compassion and kind-ness. I need only to accept this gift with fervent trust.

20 My companion laid hands on a friend
    and violated a covenant with me

21 with speech smoother than butter,
    but with a heart set on war;
with words that were softer than oil,
    but in fact were drawn swords.

22 Cast your burden on the Lord,
    and he will sustain you;
he will never permit
    the righteous to be moved.

23 But you, O God, will cast them down
    into the lowest pit;
the bloodthirsty and treacherous
    shall not live out half their days.
But I will trust in you.

I can surrender my heavy heart to God.

Oppressive Thought: It is all their fault.

Edifying Thought: God is my strength.

Oppressive Image: A ruined marketplace

Edifying Image: A peaceful heart

*O*ur living and working together, Lord, accords with your designs for family, community, and society. In a world oppressed by its own sinfulness, interaction can become trying; life with others can become a burden. I need your reassurance, Lord. When I feel misunderstood, taken for granted, or attacked, help me to remember that you stand faithfully by me. You support and direct me; you correct me and provide healing.

PSALM 56

Oppression

1 Be gracious to me, O God, for people
    trample on me;
all day long foes oppress me;

2 my enemies trample on me all day long,
    for many fight against me.
O Most High, (3) when I am afraid,
    I put my trust in you.

4 In God, whose word I praise,

The hurts of scorn and ridicule are some of life's hardest trials. Not appreciated, ignored, dismissed, or even hated, I crumble and cry. To defend myself, to preserve some sense of dignity, I can react immediately with a plea for vengeance. Even in prayer I can lay before

in God I trust; I am not afraid;
what can flesh do to me?

5 All day long they seek to injure my
cause;
all their thoughts are against me for
evil.

6 They stir up strife, they lurk,
they watch my steps.
As they hoped to have my life,

7 so repay them for their crime;
in wrath cast down the peoples, O
God!

8 You have kept count of my tossings;
put my tears in your bottle.
Are they not in your record?

9 Then my enemies will retreat
in the day when I call.
This I know, that God is for me.

10 In God, whose word I praise,
in the Lord, whose word I praise,

11 in God I trust; I am not afraid.
What can a mere mortal do to me?

12 My vows to you I must perform, O God;
I will render thank offerings to you.

13 For you have delivered my soul from
death,
and my feet from falling,
so that I may walk before God
in the light of life.

*you, dear God, my longing for vin-
dication; I can delight in imagining
their behaviors obliterated. That
however carries me only so far. It
can even work against me.*

*If I dwell in bitterness and hate, I
miss an occasion of remembering
the wellspring of my true delight,
miss another chance to enjoy you,
my God, the font of all compassion
and love. You are balm to my soul.
You are my most reliable source of
energy, the Lord most worthy of my
trust. You are my protector. When
I remember you and your power,
the hurtful and harmful words of
others mean little. You are my light
and my God. What is done in
darkness means nothing, comes to
nothing. May I praise you and love
you with every new day.*

Oppressive Thought: I must forever curse
my enemies.

Oppressive Image: Trampled underfoot

Edifying Thought: God is my protector and
light.

Edifying Image: God being moved by my
tears

When I feel maligned or afflicted by others, Lord, help me to remember that you are my protection and support. Let my initial and perhaps natural desires for vengeance turn with suitable speed into trust in your guidance. Your power works, my God, to right wrongs. Your justice
takes my pain into account.

PSALM 57

Protection

1 Be merciful to me, O God, be merciful to me,
   for in you my soul takes refuge;
 in the shadow of your wings I will take refuge,
   until the destroying storms pass by.
2 I cry to God Most High,
   to God who fulfills his purpose for me.
3 He will send from heaven and save me,
   he will put to shame those who trample on
      me.
 God will send forth his steadfast love and his
   faithfulness.
4 I lie down among lions
   that greedily devour human prey;
 their teeth are spears and arrows,
   their tongues sharp swords.
5 Be exalted, O God, above the heavens.
   Let your glory be over all the earth.
6 They set a net for my steps;
   my soul was bowed down.
 They dug a pit in my path,
   but they have fallen into it themselves.
7 My heart is steadfast, O God,
   my heart is steadfast.
 I will sing and make melody.
8   Awake, my soul!
 Awake, O harp and lyre!
   I will awake the dawn.
9 I will give thanks to you, O Lord, among the
      peoples;
   I will sing praises to you among the nations.
10 For your steadfast love is as high as the
      heavens;
   your faithfulness extends to the clouds.
11 Be exalted, O God, above the heavens.
   Let your glory be over all the earth.

There is no substitute for the protective power of God.

I may suffer as the tongues of the unkind disparage me. Pain and fear may be my lot as vengeful parties poison my sources of security.

Yet malicious words and deeds cannot long defeat me. Godly warmth and friendship, godly might and artifice are for me an enduring shelter. The dark wilds of the earth are fleeting and due no honor. I need not crumble before them. God is my loving protector.

From my soul arises my song of praise.

In melodies of confidence and gratefulness, my heart is joyful and my life is renewed.

101

Oppressive Thought: Their words and deeds
    are too much for me.

Edifying Thought: God's might surrounds
    me.

Oppressive Image: Storms of destruction

Edifying Image: Safety among lions

Unkind, even vicious words, O Lord, hurt me. Help me to remember though that their power is fleeting if I refuse to believe them. My power to believe in what is right and true comes from you, my God. Believing in you, opening my heart to you in love and praise, I believe more in the real truth of myself. Through you I know more who I am and am less fooled.

PSALM 58

Wanting Justice

1 Do you indeed decree what is right, you gods?
    Do you judge people fairly?

2 No, in your hearts you devise wrongs;
    your hands deal out violence on earth.

3 The wicked go astray from the womb;
    they err from their birth, speaking lies.

4 They have venom like the venom of a serpent,
    like the deaf adder that stops its ear,

5 so that it does not hear the voice of charmers
    or of the cunning enchanter.

6 O God, break the teeth in their mouths;
    tear out the fangs of the young lions, O
      Lord!

7 Let them vanish like water that runs away;
    like grass let them be trodden down and
      wither.

8 Let them be like the snail that dissolves into
      slime;
    like the untimely birth that never sees the
      sun.

9 Sooner than your pots can feel the heat of
      thorns,
    whether green or ablaze, may he sweep
      them away!

When I see injustice and cruelty, when I sorrow at the misery inflicted by wicked hands, it seems that some cruel idols, some powers of darkness must be the instigators. If such idols live within me, if part of me has honored judgments by which I am the one who is unkind or cruel, may God help me.

May the almighty who reigns supreme, whom I call on to rule my life, show me my sins and by the divine righteousness that I love drive from me all my idols, crush out what is poisonous and destructive.

10 The righteous will rejoice when they see
        vengeance done;
      they will bathe their feet in the blood of the
        wicked.
11 People will say, "Surely there is a reward for
        the righteous;
      surely there is a God who judges on earth."

May I know afresh the taste of
goodness. May I and all who
honor you delight anew in your
power and justice.

Oppressive Thought: Idols rule the earth.

Edifying Thought: God reigns in justice.

Oppressive Image: Venom

Edifying Image: Meadows in spring

When I see injustice, Lord, help me to look first at myself very carefully. Let me see in your divine light what roots of injustice hide within me. Open my eyes to their insidious presence so that with your help I can overcome their influence and deprive them of their habitation. Prepare me, Lord, to be your more fitting instrument of justice.

PSALM 59

Wanting Vindication

1 Deliver me from my enemies, O my God;
      protect me from those who rise up
        against me.
2 Deliver me from those who work evil;
      from the bloodthirsty save me.
3 Even now they lie in wait for my life;
      the mighty stir up strife against me.
    For no transgression or sin of mine, O
        Lord,
4   for no fault of mine, they run and make
        ready.
    Rouse yourself, come to my help and see!
5   You, Lord God of hosts, are God of
        Israel.
    Awake to punish all the nations;
      spare none of those who treacherously
        plot evil.

Surely there are times, O Lord, when I am not the source, at least not the primary one, of the distresses I bear. Sadly there are those who wrongly accuse me, who disdain me for what I am not, who unduly invade my privacy, who drain my resources like callous thieves, who attack me in abhorrent self-righteousness and even rally others against me.

But you, my God, are powerful. You stand at my side as a faithful companion. You love me dearly and have set a course to protect me ultimately against all evil.

6 Each evening they come back,
   howling like dogs
   and prowling about the city.

7 There they are, bellowing with their
      mouths,
   with sharp words on their lips—
   for "Who," they think, "will hear us?"

8 But you laugh at them, O Lord;
   you hold all the nations in derision.

9 O my strength, I will watch for you;
   for you, O God, are my fortress.

10 My God in his steadfast love will meet
      me;
   my God will let me look in triumph on
      my enemies.

11 Do not kill them, or my people may forget;
   make them totter by your power, and
      bring them down,
   O Lord, our shield.

12 For the sin of their mouths, the words of
      their lips,
   let them be trapped in their pride.
   For the cursing and lies that they utter,

13 consume them in wrath;
   consume them until they are no more.
   Then it will be known to the ends of the
      earth
   that God rules over Jacob.

14 Each evening they come back,
   howling like dogs
   and prowling about the city.

15 They roam about for food,
   and growl if they do not get their fill.

16 But I will sing of your might;
   I will sing aloud of your steadfast love
      in the morning.
   For you have been a fortress for me
   and a refuge in the day of my distress.

17 O my strength, I will sing praises to you,
   for you, O God, are my fortress,
   the God who shows me steadfast love.

May I know your power now! May I feel tenderness in which you hold me and protect me. May I rejoice in your fidelity to me and be renewed by the energies of your love. With your love flowing out of you and me, may I see my oppressors learn their lessons. May they see that negligence, insult, offensiveness, abuse, and even viciousness confront a counterforce, power, and light that rise infinitely above all darkness. May you, and I with you, O Lord, take the affronts and respond to the perpetrators in such a way that they will be embarrassed by their folly, humiliated by their carelessness, stunned by their impudence, horrified by their maliciousness, and brought to repentance. May their regret for their misdeeds transform them. May their attitudes and ways be forcefully changed. May they surprise themselves with their newness and learn to rejoice in the power of love.

On you and your love, my God, I rely like a trusting child. With all my heart I believe that you will always be true to me.

Oppressive Thought: I cannot endure their attacks.

Edifying Thought: God is my vindicator.

Oppressive Image: Prowling dogs

Edifying Image: A fortress

I believe, O God, that you will be true to your Word, that eventually in this life or the next the evils that assail me will be subdued. I believe that if I cooperate with your ways, all my fears and afflictions will vanish. You promise as well, dear Lord, to show us from time to time, even in current stages of our lives, signs of this eternal bliss. If you so will then, God, let me be the one to see wrongs against me righted. Let me, to your praise and glory, see evil turned to good.

PSALM 60

Needing Restoration

1 O God, you have rejected us, broken our
      defenses;
    you have been angry; now restore us!
2 You have caused the land to quake; you
      have torn it open;
    repair the cracks in it, for it is tottering.
3 You have made your people suffer hard
      things;
    you have given us wine to drink that
      made us reel.
4 You have set up a banner for those who fear
      you,
    to rally to it out of bowshot.
5 Give victory with your right hand, and
      answer us,
    so that those whom you love may be
      rescued.
6 God has promised in his sanctuary:
    "With exultation I will divide up Shechem,
    and portion out the Vale of Succoth.
7 Gilead is mine, and Manasseh is mine;
    Ephraim is my helmet;
    Judah is my scepter.

Now that my valiant efforts have failed, now that I have succumbed to the attacks, now that I have collapsed under the weight of it all, now that I am poisoned, I refuse to grant that I am ruined.

If I have done wrong, if this state of mine is the rightful outcome of my ways, I confess them, my God, as an affront to you. By your designs, by the patterns you have established for me, for all of us, in your creation, in your world, I may suffer justly. But it is not your justice that I call to your attention, God. That is clear

8 Moab is my washbasin;
   on Edom I hurl my shoe;
   over Philistia I shout in triumph."
9 Who will bring me to the fortified city?
   Who will lead me to Edom?
10 Have you not rejected us, O God?
   You do not go out, O God, with our
      armies.
11 O grant us help against the foe,
   for human help is worthless.
12 With God we shall do valiantly;
   it is he who will tread down our foes.

enough to you in several ways, touching important parts of my life and duly involving both those dear to me and those more distant.

I know you, O Lord. You have shown me your mercy. This is what I dare, emboldened by faith, to recall to you. Be merciful again and save me!

Oppressive Thought: I am defeated.

Oppressive Image: Earthquakes

Edifying Thought: God will restore me.

Edifying Image: A victory banner

There are surely times, O Lord, when I seem to be suffering the rightful consequences of my folly. I err; I act imprudently; I do what is wrong. I thus do what, by your inspiration or plan, can provoke loss or pain in me. Help me, Lord. Lead me in the right direction. Teach me to do good. Forgive my sin. Relieve me, please, of my affliction.

PSALM 61

Protection

1 Hear my cry, O God;
   listen to my prayer.
2 From the end of the earth I call to you,
   when my heart is faint.
   Lead me to the rock
   that is higher than I;
3 for you are my refuge,
   a strong tower against the enemy.
4 Let me abide in your tent forever,
   find refuge under the shelter of your wings.
5 For you, O God, have heard my vows;
   you have given me the heritage of those who

When I feel lost amid life's tribulations, when I seem a foreigner even to myself, I long for your warmth and strength, O Lord.

For you give me comfort and protection in all my ills. You reward my faith with your abundant kindness, with a love you have shown to all those who have taught me fear your name.

6 Prolong the life of the king;
   may his years endure to all generations!
7 May he be enthroned forever before God;
   appoint steadfast love and faithfulness to
      watch over him!
8 So I will always sing praises to your name,
   as I pay my vows day after day.

how to know you.
Bless and protect the ones I honor
with my allegiance. Let me see in
your kindness to them another sign
of your loyalty to me.

Day by day, then, my glad heart
sings your praises.

Oppressive Thought: I am lost.

Edifying Thought: God watches over all of
   us.

Oppressive Image: A faint heart

Edifying Image: A tower of defense

In so many ways, my God, you reach out to me. You tend to me with kindness. You recognize my needs and take care of me. You see danger approaching and provide protection. I have every reason to trust you, praising you for your kindness and fidelity.

PSALM 62

Security

1 For God alone my soul waits in silence;
   from him comes my salvation.
2 He alone is my rock and my salvation,
   my fortress; I shall never be shaken.
3 How long will you assail a person,
   will you batter your victim, all of you,
   as you would a leaning wall, a tottering
      fence?
4 Their only plan is to bring down a person of
      prominence.
   They take pleasure in falsehood;
   they bless with their mouths,
      but inwardly they curse.
5 For God alone my soul waits in silence,
   for my hope is from him.

No matter where I turn for sustenance, no matter what I look to for support and power, whether to my own cleverness, to my own capacities, to wealth, to influence, to others' prowess, to others' authority, without God's might and wisdom, I am nothing. God alone is my ever faithful, all-providing friend.

6 He alone is my rock and my salvation,
     my fortress; I shall not be shaken.
7 On God rests my deliverance and my honor;
     my mighty rock, my refuge is in God.
8 Trust in him at all times, O people;
     pour out your heart before him;
   God is a refuge for us.
9 Those of low estate are but a breath,
     those of high estate are a delusion;
   in the balances they go up;
     they are together lighter than a breath.
10 Put no confidence in extortion,
     and set no vain hopes on robbery;
     if riches increase, do not set your heart on
      them.
11 Once God has spoken;
     twice have I heard this:
   that power belongs to God,
12   and steadfast love belongs to you, O Lord.
   For you repay to all
     according to their work.

God alone gives substance to fleeting objects of trust. Whatever blessings I enjoy (I must remind my sometimes feeble heart) are gifts from God. I cannot forget that God alone is my greatest treasure.

Ultimately whatever hope I have is in God alone. God alone.

Oppressive Thought: Power and wealth are my greatest needs.

Edifying Thought: My security depends on God.

Oppressive Image: A tottering fence

Edifying Image: A mighty rock

I reach out anxiously; I scurry about frightfully; I look relentlessly for persons or things on which I can truly rely. When I find only disappointment, O God, when I am left insecure and unsatisfied, it is because I have not found you there. Help me to find you as the heart of all that I desire.

PSALM 63

Contentment

1 O God, you are my God, I seek you,
     my soul thirsts for you;
   my flesh faints for you,

What a fool I am when I forget how important God is to me.

as in a dry and weary land where there is
no water.

2 So I have looked upon you in the sanctuary,
   beholding your power and glory.

3 Because your steadfast love is better than
   life,
   my lips will praise you.

4 So I will bless you as long as I live;
   I will lift up my hands and call on your
   name.

5 My soul is satisfied as with a rich feast,
   and my mouth praises you with joyful
   lips

6 when I think of you on my bed,
   and meditate on you in the watches of
   the night;

7 for you have been my help,
   and in the shadow of your wings I sing
   for joy.

8 My soul clings to you;
   your right hand upholds me.

9 But those who seek to destroy my life
   shall go down into the depths of the
   earth;

10 they shall be given over to the power of the
    sword,
    they shall be prey for jackals.

11 But the king shall rejoice in God;
    all who swear by him shall exult,
    for the mouths of liars will be stopped.

In my better moments, in fruitful prayer or rewarding action, I have tasted the divine sweetness. I have felt the glow of godly presence in my special place of quiet. I have experienced the peace of resting tranquilly in the arms of the Lord.

I have known the deep contentment of sensing closeness with the God of my life, the God of all creation. More than I need food or drink to live, I need my God to have true life.

To ignore this is to be an enemy to myself. To accept it, to delight in it, is to assume charge of my life like a kindly ruler. Through praising God and rejoicing in divine goodness, I reject my self-defeating ways, nullify them, and realize my most wonderful dream.

Oppressive Thought: I can do without God.

Edifying Thought: To long for the Lord is to
long for life.

Oppressive Image: Prey

Edifying Image: Sweet dreams

I have been blessed, O Lord, at least on occasion, with cherished spiritual experience. I have known your wonderful presence. I have enjoyed the tranquility of feeling close to your divine heart. Such godly presence is my greatest source of contentment and power. Let such moments multiply. Let me grow spiritually. Let me enjoy you more.

PSALM 64

Self-Defeat

1 Hear my voice, O God, in my complaint
  preserve my life from the dread enemy.
2 Hide me from the secret plots of the wicked
  from the scheming of evildoers,
3 who whet their tongues like swords,
  who aim bitter words like arrows,
4 shooting from ambush at the blameless;
  they shoot suddenly and without fear.
5 They hold fast to their evil purpose;
  they talk of laying snares secretly,
  thinking, "Who can see us?
6   Who can search out our crimes?
  We have thought out a cunningly conceived
    plot."
  For the human heart and mind are deep.
7 But God will shoot his arrow at them;
  they will be wounded suddenly.
8 Because of their tongue he will bring them to
    ruin
  all who see them will shake with horror.
9 Then everyone will fear;
  they will tell what God has brought about
  and ponder what he has done.
10 Let the righteous rejoice in the Lord
  and take refuge in him.
  Let all the upright in heart glory.

When such afflictions as loneliness, depression, or worry tear at my soul, often my own thoughts war against me. Quietly, craftily, they poison my attitude and bring me down. They proclaim that I must have or be this or that.

They insinuate that without this or that I must be miserable. And I, fool that I am, accept such distortions. My own irrational thoughts become my worst enemies.

But God, who reigns in truth, exposes them in their corruption and shatters them.

Holding onto God, I walk in light and in the freedom of my best self.

Oppressive Thought: Without that I am nothing.

Edifying Thought: God is my truth.

Oppressive Image: Secret plots

Edifying Image: An honest heart

Rescue me, O God, when I fool myself about what I need. Help me to see that not everything I want fulfills me or brings me true happiness. Through your inspiration, the breath of salvific divine life that I accept through faith, I can sort things out. Then I recognize how and when I burden myself with senseless thoughts. Grant me wisdom, Lord.

PSALM 65

Providence

1　Praise is due to you,
　　　O God, in Zion;
　　and to you shall vows be performed,
2　　　O you who answer prayer!
　　To you all flesh shall come.
3　When deeds of iniquity overwhelm us,
　　　you forgive our transgressions.
4　Happy are those whom you choose and bring
　　　　near
　　　to live in your courts.
　　We shall be satisfied with the goodness of your
　　　　house,
　　　your holy temple.
5　By awesome deeds you answer us with
　　　　deliverance,
　　　O God of our salvation;
　　you are the hope of all the ends of the earth
　　　and of the farthest seas.
6　By your strength you established the
　　　　mountains;
　　　you are girded with might.
7　You silence the roaring of the seas,
　　　the roaring of their waves,
　　　the tumult of the peoples.
8　Those who live at earth's farthest bounds are
　　　　awed by your signs;
　　　you make the gateways of the morning and the
　　　　evening shout for joy.
9　You visit the earth and water it,
　　　you greatly enrich it;
　　the river of God is full of water;
　　　you provide the people with grain,
　　　for so you have prepared it.
10　You water its furrows abundantly,
　　　settling its ridges,
　　softening it with showers,
　　　and blessing its growth.

When you, O God, communicate to my spirit that I am acceptable to you as I am, when I sorrow for my sins and realize that you no longer hold anything against me, my eyes are opened afresh to your boundless goodness and providence. I am newly one with you. I am content in my spiritual home. My surroundings then overflow with your blessings.

Though life has its fiercer aspects, you control them, and I see that the world is a mostly good place.

I see the earth as a bounteous garden that you nurture with love and tenderness, so that out of its vast produce I and all its peoples can be nourished and pleased.

11	You crown the year with your bounty; your wagon tracks overflow with richness.	
12	The pastures of the wilderness overflow, the hills gird themselves with joy,	*Mountains, valleys, plains, and waters shine with you, glow with your love. You provide for me, O Lord, more than I need.*
13	the meadows clothe themselves with flocks, the valleys deck themselves with grain, they shout and sing together for joy.	

Oppressive Thought: I am neglected. *Edifying Thought:* God is generous.

Oppressive Image: Roaring seas *Edifying Image:* A fruitful garden

Forgive me, Lord; renew me. Open my eyes again to your supportive presence. Help me to know again your comfort and love. Restored to your friendship, I am a new person. All is aglow with beauty, goodness, and hope. Bless me, Lord, with such gifts.

PSALM 66

Joy

1	Make a joyful noise to God, all the earth;	*My heart swells with joy, and I see*
2	sing the glory of his name; give to him glorious praise.	*God's wondrous hand in everything. I sing praise to my*
3	Say to God, "How awesome are your deeds! Because of your great power, your enemies cringe before you.	*Lord and hear all creation, every element, from the minuscule to the grandiose, raise in harmony a*
4	All the earth worships you; they sing praises to you, sing praises to your name."	*blessing to our God.*
5	Come and see what God has done: he is awesome in his deeds among mortals.	
6	He turned the sea into dry land; they passed through the river on foot. There we rejoiced in him,	*Out of my trials and terrors, God has made good. Such compassion and wisdom enlivens me, gives me*
7	who rules by his might forever, whose eyes keep watch on the nations— let the rebellious not exalt themselves.	*reassurance and unwavering hope.*

8   Bless our God, O peoples,
    let the sound of his praise be heard,
9   who has kept us among the living,
    and has not let our feet slip.
10 For you, O God, have tested us;
    you have tried us as silver is tried.
11 You brought us into the net;
    you laid burdens on our backs;
12 you let people ride over our heads;
    we went through fire and through water;
    yet you have brought us out to a spacious
        place.
13 I will come into your house with burnt
        offerings;
    I will pay you my vows,
14 those that my lips uttered
    and my mouth promised when I was in
        trouble.
15 I will offer to you burnt offerings of fatlings
    with the smoke of the sacrifice of rams;
    I will make an offering of bulls and goats.
16 Come and hear, all you who fear God,
    and I will tell what he has done for me.
17 I cried aloud to him,
    and he was extolled with my tongue.
18 If I had cherished iniquity in my heart,
    the Lord would not have listened.
19 But truly God has listened;
    he has given heed to the words of my
        prayer.
20 Blessed be God,
    because he has not rejected my prayer
    or removed his steadfast love from me.

At times my trials have been a test, a challenge to give me greater physical and spiritual stamina, an opportunity for me to experience and measure my own virtue and endurance. I have gone through much, but always with a kindly parent, a just and loving God, at my side. Earth offers me no greater gift. And I do not want to ignore such a grace or take it for granted.

Cherishing my God, I put what I am and have, my talents, accomplishments, relationships, and possessions into the divine hands. May all that I am and have be at God's disposal for the working of more wonders. May I become, day by day, a more fitting partner in accomplishing the divine design for bettering our world.

Then I will enjoy a greater assurance that my prayers are efficacious.

Oppressive Thought: The rebellious get their
   way.

Oppressive Image: Ravaging fire

Edifying Thought: God's goodness turns
   sorrow into joy.

Edifying Image: A sweet sacrifice

Let no sorrow, let no pain, O Lord my God, long deter me from the joy of remembering your holy presence. Let me quickly turn to you, the divine font of all that is good, the wellspring of bliss, the foundation of truest contentment. You love so much that you penetrate all things, infusing them with your redeeming, consoling, uplifting, and energizing power. I rejoice in your love.

PSALM 67

Optimism

1 May God be gracious to us and bless us
    and make his face to shine upon us,
2 that your way may be known upon earth,
    your saving power among all nations.
3 Let the peoples praise you, O God;
    let all the peoples praise you.
4 Let the nations be glad and sing for joy,
    for you judge the peoples with equity
    and guide the nations upon earth.
5 Let the peoples praise you, O God;
    let all the peoples praise you.
6 The earth has yielded its increase;
    God, our God, has blessed us.
7 May God continue to bless us;
    let all the ends of the earth revere him.

Every morning report reminds me of the world's great needs. How blessed am I, O Lord! Please continue, dear God, to bless me and those close to me. And keep your loving presence over the entire world. I know you do. For joys are everywhere, even where there are trials and sadness. Yet I ask you this to remind myself, and to remind us all, that accepting your blessings graciously, enjoying without pretense what you have given us, are ways of witnessing to others your glory.

So by a ripple effect, the whole world may come to know you and thus more fully glorify you.

Oppressive Thought: The world is in hopeless misery.

Edifying Thought: God's blessings are everywhere.

Oppressive Image: Depressing news

Edifying Image: God's smiling face

Let me not lose hope, dear Lord, in a world of sadness and pain. Let me look about myself and my world. Let me see the good that is there. And let me be thankful. Renew in me that deep trust in you that is the source of my peace. Let my hope in you inspire me further to do my part in alleviating pain, in bringing encouragement, and in spreading joy.

PSALM 68

The Power of God

1   Let God rise up, let his enemies be scattered;
    let those who hate him flee before him.

2   As smoke is driven away, so drive them away;
    as wax melts before the fire,
    let the wicked perish before God.

3   But let the righteous be joyful;
    let them exult before God;
    let them be jubilant with joy.

4   Sing to God, sing praises to his name;
    lift up a song to him who rides upon the clouds—
  his name is the Lord— be exultant before him.

5   Father of orphans and protector of widows
    is God in his holy habitation.

6   God gives the desolate a home to live in;
    he leads out the prisoners to prosperity,
    but the rebellious live in a parched land.

7   O God, when you went out before your people,
    when you marched through the wilderness,

8   the earth quaked, the heavens poured down rain
    at the presence of God, the God of Sinai,
    at the presence of God, the God of Israel.

9   Rain in abundance, O God, you showered abroad;
    you restored your heritage when it languished;

10   your flock found a dwelling in it;
    in your goodness, O God, you provided for the needy.

11   The Lord gives the command;
    great is the company of those who bore the

God is all-powerful, even in face of stubborn perniciousness. God is my ally as I praise the divine name, as I sing praises to the Lord's glory, to a splendor that shines like sun amid the clouds.

God takes me in like an adoptive parent, full of love, ready to teach and nurture me, anxious to save me from desolation.

You are like thunder, Lord, in your awesome power, like the cool refreshment of driving rain, like the firm hand that generously tends a family.

Against corruption the Lord's words are law.

tidings:
12   "The kings of the armies, they flee, they flee!"
The women at home divide the spoil,
13   though they stay among the sheepfolds—
the wings of a dove covered with silver,
        its pinions with green gold.
14   When the Almighty scattered kings there,
        snow fell on Zalmon.
15   O mighty mountain, mountain of Bashan;
        O many-peaked mountain, mountain of
            Bashan!
16   Why do you look with envy, O many-peaked
            mountain,
        at the mount that God desired for his abode,
    where the Lord will reside forever?
17   With mighty chariotry, twice ten thousand,
        thousands upon thousands,
        the Lord came from Sinai into the holy place.
18   You ascended the high mount,
        leading captives in your train
        and receiving gifts from people,
    even from those who rebel against the Lord
        God's abiding there.
19   Blessed be the Lord,
        who daily bears us up;
        God is our salvation.
20   Our God is a God of salvation,
        and to God, the Lord, belongs escape from
            death.
21   But God will shatter the heads of his enemies,
        the hairy crown of those who walk in their
            guilty ways.
22   The Lord said,
        "I will bring them back from Bashan,
        I will bring them back from the depths of the
            sea,
23   so that you may bathe your feet in blood,
        so that the tongues of your dogs may have
            their share from the foe."
24   Your solemn processions are seen, O God,
        the processions of my God, my King, into the
            sanctuary —

When God drives out wickedness, the good that remains can be savored and shared. There is no use trying to resist once God has taken charge. With God at our lead we have nothing to fear.

Let us commit ourselves to the Lord, to one whose energies surpass all resistance, in order to undo even the greatest harm. By God's wisdom and power, what was once our undoing, what was once poison to us, will become a source of our renewal. We can thus expect a time of rejoicing, a time for celebrating the splendor of our God.

Day after day a succession of events, a series of encounters will—not by chance but by God's design—achieve the unexpected and witness to divine grandeur and love. We call on you, Lord, to renew us in your strength. Stir up in us the power, your kind of power, to defeat what wars against us, what eats away at our peace and security.

25 the singers in front, the musicians last,
      between them girls playing tambourines:
26 "Bless God in the great congregation,
      the Lord, O you who are of Israel's fountain!"
27 There is Benjamin, the least of them, in the
        lead,
      the princes of Judah in a body,
      the princes of Zebulun, the princes of
        Naphtali.
28 Summon your might, O God;
      show your strength, O God, as you have
        done for us before.
29 Because of your temple at Jerusalem
      kings bear gifts to you.
30 Rebuke the wild animals that live among the
        reeds,
      the herd of bulls with the calves of the
        peoples.
      Trample under foot those who lust after tribute;
      scatter the peoples who delight in war.
31 Let bronze be brought from Egypt;
      let Ethiopia hasten to stretch out its hands to
        God.
32 Sing to God, O kingdoms of the earth;
      sing praises to the Lord,
33 O rider in the heavens, the ancient heavens;
      listen, he sends out his voice, his mighty
        voice.
34 Ascribe power to God,
      whose majesty is over Israel;
      and whose power is in the skies.
35 Awesome is God in his sanctuary,
      the God of Israel;
      he gives power and strength to his people.
Blessed be God!

Drive from us, O Lord, all the frenzy, aggression, greed, and hate that spoil us. Let us feel again that you are with us as our God. When God is truly with us, when the Lord is such a mighty protector, we cannot be overly bold.

The divine presence is then clearer to us than the rumbles and flashes of a summer storm.

We thus give to God, our awesome God, all praise that is due.

Oppressive Thought: Evil is more powerful
   than good.

Oppressive Image: A raging bull

Edifying Thought: God overcomes the
   enemy.

Edifying Image: A mighty storm

Your power, O God, is irresistible. Your might is indomitable. Through you I have the power to face the evils plaguing me. By your power I can overcome obstacles to my progress and serenity. Help me, my Lord, to be courageous and strong. Lead me to a day of victory and rejoicing. Sustain me as I live in hope of your enduring fidelity to my every just cause.

PSALM 69

Dishonor

1 Save me, O God,
   for the waters have come up to my neck.
2 I sink in deep mire,
   where there is no foothold;
   I have come into deep waters,
   and the flood sweeps over me.
3 I am weary with my crying;
   my throat is parched.
   My eyes grow dim
   with waiting for my God.
4 More in number than the hairs of my head
   are those who hate me without cause;
   many are those who would destroy me,
   my enemies who accuse me falsely.
   What I did not steal
   must I now restore?
5 O God, you know my folly;
   the wrongs I have done are not hidden from
      you.
6 Do not let those who hope in you be put to
      shame because of me,
   O Lord God of hosts;
   do not let those who seek you be dishonored
      because of me,
   O God of Israel.
7 It is for your sake that I have borne reproach,
   that shame has covered my face.
8 I have become a stranger to my kindred,
   an alien to my mother's children.
9 It is zeal for your house that has consumed me;
   the insults of those who insult you have fallen

I am overwhelmed, O God. I can take no more. My spirit is so stressed that I can hardly cry for help, even to you. It is not fair! It is not just! I do not deserve this! The attacks and enmity from all sides, the rejection from all corners, have little to do with the real me.

Look into my heart, dear God, and see that this is so. I am tempted to question your justice, Lord, and so may others be, seeing my predicament. Can you let this happen when my very trust in you is what brought me to this, what has made me look like a rebel, an eccentric, even to those who know me well? When I tried to defend true virtue and honor, when I sacrificed my own convenience for the sake of sincere religiousness, I was taken for a renegade and a fool.

on me.

10   When I humbled my soul with fasting,
      they insulted me for doing so.

11   When I made sackcloth my clothing,
      I became a byword to them.

12   I am the subject of gossip for those who sit in
      the gate,
      and the drunkards make songs about me.

13   But as for me, my prayer is to you, O Lord.
      At an acceptable time, O God,
      in the abundance of your steadfast love,
      answer me.
    With your faithful help (^{14}) rescue me
      from sinking in the mire;
    let me be delivered from my enemies
      and from the deep waters.

I will not forsake my trust in you, O Lord. I will not forget your generous protective love. Rescue me when you will. Do not let me be defeated by all of this.

15   Do not let the flood sweep over me,
      or the deep swallow me up,
      or the Pit close its mouth over me.

16   Answer me, O Lord, for your steadfast love is
      good;
      according to your abundant mercy, turn to
      me.

Show me your kind face as a first sign of your saving power. You know, my God, what I have suffered. In your heart you have known my sense of defeat and brokenness.

17   Do not hide your face from your servant,
      for I am in distress—make haste to answer
      me.

18   Draw near to me, redeem me,
      set me free because of my enemies.

19   You know the insults I receive,
      and my shame and dishonor;
      my foes are all known to you.

20   Insults have broken my heart,
      so that I am in despair.
    I looked for pity, but there was none;
      and for comforters, but I found none.

You have seen me in my loneliness as my detractors rubbed salt into my wounds. Sometimes I am so disheartened and angry that I want you to crush them all, to make them victims of what they designed for me. How nice it would be if you would repel them all for their impudence and cruelty!

21   They gave me poison for food,
      and for my thirst they gave me vinegar to
      drink.

22   Let their table be a trap for them,
      a snare for their allies.

23   Let their eyes be darkened so that they cannot
      see,

and make their loins tremble continually.

24 Pour out your indignation upon them,
and let your burning anger overtake them.

25 May their camp be a desolation;
let no one live in their tents.

Leave them abandoned; let them suffer nothing but punishments.

26 For they persecute those whom you have
struck down,
and those whom you have wounded, they
attack still more.

27 Add guilt to their guilt;
may they have no acquittal from you.

28 Let them be blotted out of the book of the
living;
let them not be enrolled among the
righteous.

29 But I am lowly and in pain;
let your salvation, O God, protect me.

30 I will praise the name of God with a song;
I will magnify him with thanksgiving.

31 This will please the Lord more than an ox
or a bull with horns and hoofs.

32 Let the oppressed see it and be glad;
you who seek God, let your hearts revive.

33 For the Lord hears the needy,
and does not despise his own that are in
bonds.

34 Let heaven and earth praise him,
the seas and everything that moves in them.

35 For God will save Zion
and rebuild the cities of Judah;
and his servants shall live there and possess it;

36 the children of his servants shall inherit it,
and those who love his name shall live in it.

Yet, as I remember your ways, O God, I beg you to spare me from nagging obsession with such wishes. With a nobler spirit, with heightened consciousness, I turn to God again with praise and thanksgiving. There is no need to convince the Lord of my dedication or of what innocence is mine. Divine justice prevails in the end.

May the glory of God then shine throughout the world. May all the dishonored enjoy new dignity. May the divine love become resplendent among all who have been faithful.

Oppressive Thought: I am sinking into ruin.

Edifying Thought: God is loving and just.

Oppressive Image: Ravaging floods

Edifying Image: An honorable house

Protect me, O Lord, in my innocence. I have done wrong—surely many times—but not in this case. My bad image is not deserved. I have been dishonored unfairly. Let the honest truth, which for now only you know, sustain me. Help me to rest content with the hope that my exoneration will fol-low at a time and in the circumstances that you see as best for all concerned.

PSALM 70

Wanting Vindication

1 Be pleased, O God, to deliver me.
     O Lord, make haste to help me!
2 Let those be put to shame and confusion
     who seek my life.
  Let those be turned back and brought to
     dishonor
     who desire to hurt me.
3 Let those who say, "Aha, Aha!"
     turn back because of their shame.
4 Let all who seek you
     rejoice and be glad in you.
  Let those who love your salvation
     say evermore, "God is great!"
5 But I am poor and needy;
     hasten to me, O God!
  You are my help and my deliverer;
     O Lord, do not delay!

In my helplessness and pain, I cry out for vengeance. May those who mistreat and dishonor me receive what they deserve!

Yet, O Lord, let my words of praise for you ring out above my cries of contempt. You are my greatest con-solation! How do I know who deserves punishment? You are God. Let me never forget that, not for an instant.

Oppressive Thought: I must have revenge.

Oppressive Image: Confusion

Edifying Thought: God is my comforter.

Edifying Image: The greatness of God

Spare me the shame, O Lord my God, of judging anyone erroneously. Help me to know when pro-tecting myself from disdain or harm is more a pitiful act of vengeance and less a respectable attempt to maintain dignity. Support me in trusting your judgment. Let my patience reflect my humble reliance on your help and consolation.

PSALM 71

Wanting Protection

1 In you, O Lord, I take refuge;
  let me never be put to shame.

2 In your righteousness deliver me and rescue
    me;
  incline your ear to me and save me.

3 Be to me a rock of refuge,
  a strong fortress, to save me,
  for you are my rock and my fortress.

4 Rescue me, O my God, from the hand of the
    wicked,
  from the grasp of the unjust and cruel.

5 For you, O Lord, are my hope,
  my trust, O Lord, from my youth.

6 Upon you I have leaned from my birth;
  it was you who took me from my mother's
    womb.
  My praise is continually of you.

7 I have been like a portent to many,
  but you are my strong refuge.

8 My mouth is filled with your praise,
  and with your glory all day long.

9 Do not cast me off in the time of old age;
  do not forsake me when my strength is
    spent.

10 For my enemies speak concerning me,
  and those who watch for my life consult
    together.

11 They say, "Pursue and seize that person
  whom God has forsaken,
  for there is no one to deliver."

12 O God, do not be far from me;
  O my God, make haste to help me!

13 Let my accusers be put to shame and
    consumed;
  let those who seek to hurt me
  be covered with scorn and disgrace.

14 But I will hope continually,

Sometimes I need you, Lord, the way a child needs the strong arms of a father, needs a feeling of utter security and safety.

When I feel attacked or abused, I love to recall what I heard from my youngest years, that you are great and mighty.

Whatever value I am to others, you are the steady source of my merit. It is you who stand behind me. It is you that I proudly proclaim as my constant protection against all wiles, for all the days of my life.

Stay close to me then, Lord. Free me from a sense of dishonor. No matter what is said about me, or no matter what I imagine is said, help me to know the sweet contentment of depending on you, appreciating you, and loving you. In never

and will praise you yet more and more.

15 My mouth will tell of your righteous acts,
   of your deeds of salvation all day long,
   though their number is past my knowledge.

16 I will come praising the mighty deeds of the
      Lord God,
   I will praise your righteousness, yours alone.

ceasing to tell of you, O God, I grow ever more confident of your greatness.

17 O God, from my youth you have taught me,
   and I still proclaim your wondrous deeds.

18 So even to old age and gray hairs,
   O God, do not forsake me,
until I proclaim your might
   to all the generations to come.
Your power (19) and your righteousness, O God,
   reach the high heavens.
You who have done great things,
   O God, who is like you?

Looking back, I can see that you have always been with me, through all my peaks and valleys. Looking ahead, I expect no less security. With all my strength, with all the talents you have given me, I lift up words of praise to you.

20 You who have made me see many troubles and
      calamities
   will revive me again;
from the depths of the earth
   you will bring me up again.

21 You will increase my honor,
   and comfort me once again.

22 I will also praise you with the harp
   for your faithfulness, O my God;
I will sing praises to you with the lyre,
   O Holy One of Israel.

I let my emotions sing of your glory.

23 My lips will shout for joy
   when I sing praises to you;
   my soul also, which you have rescued.

Proclaiming you as my God, enfolded in your arms, I feel invincible.

24 All day long my tongue will talk of your
      righteous help,
for those who tried to do me harm
   have been put to shame, and disgraced.

Oppressive Thought: I have no protection.

Edifying Thought: God has always been there.

Oppressive Image: A cruel hand

Edifying Image: A rock of refuge

123

et me feel your strength, Lord. Let me stand tall. Let me vie courageously against inertia and oppression. Let my sense of valor and might arise from my deeper sense of your protection and encouragement. Let me know and feel secure in your loving care.

PSALM 72

Loving Others

1 Give the king your justice, O God,
   and your righteousness to a king's son.
2 May he judge your people with righteousness,
   and your poor with justice.
3 May the mountains yield prosperity for the
      people,
   and the hills, in righteousness.
4 May he defend the cause of the poor of the
      people,
   give deliverance to the needy,
   and crush the oppressor.

We look for a model of love and sanctity. One whose eminence is praiseworthy is one who is sensitive, kind, and just. One who fosters true prosperity is one who safeguards the poor and oppressed.

5 May he live while the sun endures,
   and as long as the moon, throughout all
      generations.
6 May he be like rain that falls on the mown
      grass,
   like showers that water the earth.

One who lives fully and abundantly is one whose gifts bring refreshment and nurture to countless numbers.

7 In his days may righteousness flourish
   and peace abound, until the moon is no
      more.
8 May he have dominion from sea to sea,
   and from the River to the ends of the earth.
9 May his foes bow down before him,
   and his enemies lick the dust.
10 May the kings of Tarshish and of the isles
      render him tribute,
   may the kings of Sheba and Seba
      bring gifts.
11 May all kings fall down before him,
   all nations give him service.

One of vast influence and renowned sanctity is one whose loving deeds provoke widespread honor, even reverence and devotion.

12 For he delivers the needy when they call,
   he poor and those who have no helper.

A virtuous person cannot forget those in need, especially those

13 He has pity on the weak and the needy, and saves the lives of the needy.	*whose health is failing, or who suf-* *fer from cruel afflictions.*

14   From oppression and violence he redeems their
      life;
      and precious is their blood in his sight.	

15   Long may he live!
      May gold of Sheba be given to him.
    May prayer be made for him continually,
      and blessings invoked for him all day long.
	May such a person be further
	 exalted. May whatever rewards
	 and honor that come with virtue
	 continue unceasingly to redound
	 through love to the good of the
	 whole community.

16   May there be abundance of grain in the land;
      may it wave on the tops of the mountains
      may its fruit be like Lebanon;
    and may people blossom in the cities
      like the grass of the field.	

17   May his name endure forever,
      his fame continue as long as the sun.
    May all nations be blessed in him;
      may they pronounce him happy.	

18 Blessed be the Lord, the God of Israel, who alone does wondrous things.	*All blessings are from our glorious* *God, whose name heaven's chil-* *dren should praise forever.*

19   Blessed be his glorious name forever;
      may his glory fill the whole earth.
           Amen and Amen.	

20 The prayers of David son of Jesse are ended.	

Oppressive Thought: Injustice pays.

Edifying Thought: Great persons are loving instruments of God.

Oppressive Image: Oppression

Edifying Image: Blossoms

Your love for us, O Lord, is limitless. Your kindness abounds for the great and the lowly. Let my love, like yours, go generously to others, especially the wounded, ailing, or poor. Let me learn how best to care. Let my joy be in serving, my respite in contentment for a day well spent.

PSALM 73

Justice

1   Truly God is good to the upright,
     to those who are pure in heart.

2   But as for me, my feet had almost
      stumbled;
     my steps had nearly slipped.

3   For I was envious of the arrogant;
     I saw the prosperity of the wicked.

4   For they have no pain;
     their bodies are sound and sleek.

5   They are not in trouble as others are;
     they are not plagued like other people.

6   Therefore pride is their necklace;
     violence covers them like a garment.

7   Their eyes swell out with fatness;
     their hearts overflow with follies.

8   They scoff and speak with malice;
     loftily they threaten oppression.

9   They set their mouths against heaven,
     and their tongues range over the earth.

10   Therefore the people turn and praise them,
     and find no fault in them.

11   And they say, "How can God know?
     Is there knowledge in the Most High?"

12   Such are the wicked;
     always at ease, they increase in riches.

13   All in vain I have kept my heart clean
     and washed my hands in innocence.

14   For all day long I have been plagued,
     and am punished every morning.

15   If I had said, "I will talk on in this way,"
     I would have been untrue to the circle of
      your children.

16   But when I thought how to understand
      this,
     it seemed to me a wearisome task,

17   until I went into the sanctuary of God;
     then I perceived their end.

Deep in my heart, I know and trust that God blesses the sincere and kindly person. Nevertheless, in my moments of disappointment or confusion, I lose sight of this and begin to think that false pride provokes true honor or that gains of the dishonorable elude all condemnation. They seem to look and feel good while involved in anything but good. Their no-good ways seem to pay, to reward them with pleasures. All the while they are malicious, nasty, and insolent.

Yet the repulsiveness of their smooth ways and words goes undetected, which reinforces their impudence to such a degree that they sin boldly, even defying God.

My virtue has seemed futile. My "rewards" have been pain and affliction.

Fortunately I avoided undermining others' trust in God's justice, even though I hardly found words to express what my heart somehow knew. It was only in moments of prayer, in times of intimate contact with God, that I could sense the futility of vice and sin. Ultimately

18 Truly you set them in slippery places;
   you make them fall to ruin.
19 How they are destroyed in a moment
   swept away utterly by terrors!
20 They are like a dream when one awakes;
   on awaking you despise their phantoms.
21 When my soul was embittered,
   when I was pricked in heart,
22 I was stupid and ignorant;
   I was like a brute beast toward you.
23 Nevertheless I am continually with you;
   you hold my right hand.
24 You guide me with your counsel,
   and afterward you will receive me with
   honor.
25 Whom have I in heaven but you?
   And there is nothing on earth that I
   desire other than you.
26 My flesh and my heart may fail,
   but God is the strength of my heart and
   my portion forever.
27 Indeed, those who are far from you will
   perish;
   you put an end to those who are false to
   you.
28 But for me it is good to be near God;
   I have made the Lord God my refuge,
   to tell of all your works.

there is no hope in them. They are utterly fleeting and worthless.

Only the folly of my own bitterness and irrationality had led me to think otherwise.

Closeness to you, Lord, gives me stability and true insight. You let me feel my own worth deeply.

You let me trust that I am eternally valuable, that you will always have me with you. There are good friends, but none like you. Even in utter weakness, even at my end, you will be there for me. For it is not dishonor but honor that you love. With you at my side, I can proclaim that boldly.

Oppressive Thought: Crime pays.

Edifying Thought: Virtue is rewarded.

Oppressive Image: Stumbling

Edifying Image: Walking confidently

Protect me, Lord, from the destructive assumption that striving for honor or safeguarding my integrity are not worth the effort. Help me to remember that whatever short-term pleasure they bring, laxity and maliciousness poison my soul and lead me ultimately to dread and pain. Renew in me a love of virtue, a dedication to qualities that accord with justice as you determine it and as you reward it.

PSALM 74

Defilement

1 O God, why do you cast us off forever?
   Why does your anger smoke against the
      sheep of your pasture?

2 Remember your congregation, which you
      acquired long ago,
   which you redeemed to be the tribe of your
      heritage.
   Remember Mount Zion, where you came to
      dwell.

3 Direct your steps to the perpetual ruins;
   the enemy has destroyed everything in the
      sanctuary.

4 Your foes have roared within your holy place;
   they set up their emblems there.

5 At the upper entrance they hacked
   the wooden trellis with axes.

6 And then, with hatchets and hammers,
   they smashed all its carved work.

7 They set your sanctuary on fire;
   they desecrated the dwelling place of your
      name,
   bringing it to the ground.

8 They said to themselves, "We will utterly
      subdue them";
   they burned all the meeting places of God in
      the land.

9 We do not see our emblems;
   there is no longer any prophet,
   and there is no one among us who knows
      how long.

10 How long, O God, is the foe to scoff?
   Is the enemy to revile your name forever?

11 Why do you hold back your hand;
   why do you keep your hand in your bosom?

12 Yet God my King is from of old,
   working salvation in the earth.

13 You divided the sea by your might;

How can you abandon me to such sorrow, Lord, when you have shown me that you love me, that I am precious to you? We have been so close!

Yet look at me, wounded to the core! I feel like I have been defiled, like there is no respect for me, my wishes, or my reputation.

My image is shattered, and so may be my self-image.

At times I so burn with rage, am so consumed with shame that there seems to be little room for you in my heart.
It is even hard to believe that we will ever be intimate again.

My wounds seem too great for healing. Why, O God, don't you dispel the perpetrator of my distress?

You are mighty; I know that. You have guided me through treacherous times, saved me from vicious

you broke the heads of the dragons in the
waters.

14 You crushed the heads of Leviathan;
you gave him as food for the creatures of the
wilderness.

15 You cut openings for springs and torrents;
you dried up ever-flowing streams.

16 Yours is the day, yours also the night;
you established the luminaries and the sun.

17 You have fixed all the bounds of the earth;
you made summer and winter.

18 Remember this, O Lord, how the enemy scoffs,
and an impious people reviles your name.

19 Do not deliver the soul of your dove to the wild
animals;
do not forget the life of your poor forever.

20 Have regard for your covenant,
for the dark places of the land are full of the
haunts of violence.

21 Do not let the downtrodden be put to shame;
let the poor and needy praise your name.

22 Rise up, O God, plead your cause;
remember how the impious scoff at you all
day long.

23 Do not forget the clamor of your foes,
the uproar of your adversaries that goes up
continually.

*threats, made a mockery of evil
attacks on me, and protected me
from drowning in iniquity. Such
you did not permit.*

*For in those days, in those times,
you did not permit the beauty of
your creation to be sullied.*

*Repeat your ways, O Lord. Do not
let evil run loose on me.*

*Remember your dedication to me,
how you lifted me up and defended
me.*

*I was so thankful to you then,
Lord, and will be again. For you
will not relent; you will never surrender to the stubborn forces of
evil.*

Oppressive Thought: God has forgotten me.

Edifying Thought: God is a faithful Protector.

Oppressive Image: A ruined sanctuary

Edifying Image: A benevolent ruler

W*hen I am shattered, Lord, when I feel broken and defiled, help me to remember your determination to rescue me, to be my Savior. When my faith is weakened, when I no longer feel I
know you as in times past, renew my confidence in your wisdom. My plans are often folly, but your
providence is unfailing. Help me to be strong in loving what you are.*

PSALM 75

Fairness

1   We give thanks to you, O God;
      we give thanks; your name is near.
   People tell of your wondrous deeds.

2   At the set time that I appoint
      I will judge with equity.

3   When the earth totters, with all its inhabitants,
      it is I who keep its pillars steady.

4   I say to the boastful, "Do not boast,"
      and to the wicked, "Do not lift up your horn;

5   do not lift up your horn on high,
      or speak with insolent neck."

6   For not from the east or from the west
      and not from the wilderness comes lifting
        up;

7   but it is God who executes judgment,
      putting down one and lifting up another.

8   For in the hand of the Lord there is a cup
      with foaming wine, well mixed;
   he will pour a draught from it,
      and all the wicked of the earth
      shall drain it down to the dregs.

9   But I will rejoice forever;
      I will sing praises to the God of Jacob.

10 All the horns of the wicked I will cut off,
      but the horns of the righteous shall be
        exalted.

I can truly be grateful to God, despite all that I have suffered. Closeness to the Lord assures me that fairness reigns eventually, at the divinely appointed time. Things may seem out of balance; but God holds in check the excesses of the haughty, the powers of the malicious. They seem for a time to have their way.

But God, with an eye to ultimate justice, bewilders them so that they finally work toward their own downfall.

My song of joy and hymn of thanks are long overdue. Wickedness never really had a chance.

Oppressive Thought: God ignores fairness.

Edifying Thought: God has a plan.

Oppressive Image: Horns of the wicked

Edifying Image: Steady pillars

When the situation—or life itself—seems unfair, O Lord, I turn again to you for reassurance. Your presence, which I recognize and enjoy by faith, reminds me of your promises to establish justice. Again I see my frustrations and sorrows as transitions to greater satisfaction and joy. My charge is simply to count on you.

PSALM 76

Victory

1. In Judah God is known,
   his name is great in Israel.
2. His abode has been established in Salem,
   his dwelling place in Zion.
3. There he broke the flashing arrows,
   the shield, the sword, and the weapons of
   war.
4. Glorious are you, more majestic
   than the everlasting mountains.
5. The stouthearted were stripped of their spoil;
   they sank into sleep;
   none of the troops
   was able to lift a hand.
6. At your rebuke, O God of Jacob,
   both rider and horse lay stunned.
7. But you indeed are awesome!
   Who can stand before you
   when once your anger is roused?
8. From the heavens you uttered judgment;
   the earth feared and was still
9. when God rose up to establish judgment,
   to save all the oppressed of the earth.
10. Human wrath serves only to praise you,
    when you bind the last bit of your wrath
    around you.
11. Make vows to the Lord your God, and perform
    them;
    let all who are around him bring gifts
    to the one who is awesome,
12. who cuts off the spirit of princes,
    who inspires fear in the kings of the earth.

In my place of worship, in my spiritual community, the Lord is known and blessed.

Our God defied forces of resistance, even forces of evil, and fashioned a people who could recognize the divine majesty in all its awesome dignity and power.

Opponents, enemies from within me or without, may be strong, fearsome, and harmful. But God outdoes them all, proving to be compassionate and just.

By divine wisdom, the greatest threats or evils can work to my good. I need however to commit myself forever to the Lord my Savior.

Oppressive Thought: My opponents will
  succeed.

Edifying Thought: Our Savior reigns.

Oppressive Image: A confused people

Edifying Image: Everlasting mountains

O God, you give us victory over the most fearsome opponents. Let our sense of your power draw our community into greater solidarity and harmony. With you in our midst, let us vie against forces aimed at our harm or destruction. As a group, as a family, we can thus grow in love and dedicate ourselves to you with renewed hearts.

PSALM 77

Desolation

1 I cry aloud to God,
     aloud to God, that he may hear me.
2 In the day of my trouble I seek the Lord;
     in the night my hand is stretched out without
       wearying;
     my soul refuses to be comforted.
3 I think of God, and I moan;
     I meditate, and my spirit faints.
4 You keep my eyelids from closing;
     I am so troubled that I cannot speak.
5 I consider the days of old,
     and remember the years of long ago.
6 I commune with my heart in the night;
     I meditate and search my spirit:
7 "Will the Lord spurn forever,
     and never again be favorable?
8 Has his steadfast love ceased forever?
     Are his promises at an end for all time?
9 Has God forgotten to be gracious?
     Has he in anger shut up his compassion?"
10 And I say, "It is my grief
     that the right hand of the Most High has
      changed."
11 I will call to mind the deeds of the Lord;
     I will remember your wonders of old.
12 I will meditate on all your work,
     and muse on your mighty deeds.
13 Your way, O God, is holy.
     What god is so great as our God?
14 You are the God who works wonders;
     you have displayed your might among the

Though I seek the consolation of the Lord, I do not find it. Though thirsting for God, my desolate spirit is not satisfied. I toss about restlessly and grope for words to express my loss.

Memories of God's former consolations are at first of little help. And their contrast with the present only adds to my grief. Everything looks permanent and hopeless.

Yet by God's grace such memories can inspire the better part of me to trust that what lies ahead is wonderful. By this kind of contrast between the past and future, I can expect that God will display great power.

15 With your strong arm you redeemed your
     people,
    the descendants of Jacob and Joseph.
16 When the waters saw you, O God,
    when the waters saw you, they were afraid;
    the very deep trembled.
17 The clouds poured out water;
    the skies thundered;
    your arrows flashed on every side.
18 The crash of your thunder was in the
     whirlwind;
    your lightnings lit up the world;
    the earth trembled and shook.
19 Your way was through the sea,
    your path, through the mighty waters;
    yet your footprints were unseen.
20 You led your people like a flock
    by the hand of Moses and Aaron.

God will prove that divine holiness works miracles in our lives and turns my people's condition into human holiness. We had been captives to our past. But as an unseen hero and through the work of chosen agents, the Lord set us free. So my soul, whose murky depths resisted the light, opened to God's awesome presence and found new life.

Oppressive Thought: Things will never be
    the same.

Edifying Thought: The past gives me hope.

Oppressive Image: Thirst

Edifying Image: A strong arm

In desolation I long for you, O Lord. Loneliness weighs on me, leaves me empty, renders me aimless. With no vitality, bereft of meaning, I wander and moan. Only gradually does the memory of your work in my life give me hope. Slowly the numbness fades, and I begin to be inspired by images of your power and goodness. You will again prove to be my Savior.

PSALM 78

Rebelliousness

1 Give ear, O my people, to my teaching;
    incline your ears to the words of my mouth.
2 I will open my mouth in a parable;
    I will utter dark sayings from of old,

I would do well to recall from my own history how the Lord has worked, how the wonderful hand of God has touched and sustained

3 things that we have heard and known,
       that our ancestors have told us.
4 We will not hide them from their children;
       we will tell to the coming generation
   the glorious deeds of the Lord, and his might,
       and the wonders that he has done.
5 He established a decree in Jacob,
       and appointed a law in Israel,
   which he commanded our ancestors
       to teach to their children;
6 that the next generation might know them,
       the children yet unborn,
   and rise up and tell them to their children,
7   so that they should set their hope in God,
   and not forget the works of God,
       but keep his commandments;
8 and that they should not be like their
           ancestors,
       a stubborn and rebellious generation,
   a generation whose heart was not steadfast,
       whose spirit was not faithful to God.
9 The Ephraimites, armed with the bow,
       turned back on the day of battle.
10 They did not keep God's covenant,
       but refused to walk according to his law.
11 They forgot what he had done,
       and the miracles that he had shown them.
12 In the sight of their ancestors he worked
           marvels
       in the land of Egypt, in the fields of Zoan.
13 He divided the sea and let them pass through
           it,
       and made the waters stand like a heap.
14 In the daytime he led them with a cloud,
       and all night long with a fiery light.
15 He split rocks open in the wilderness,
       and gave them drink abundantly as from
           the deep.
16 He made streams come out of the rock,
       and caused waters to flow down like rivers.
17 Yet they sinned still more against him,
       rebelling against the Most High in the

me. The memory of God's greatness prepares me for the future by providing lessons in faith for all times.

Even as I learn from my religious heritage, even as I recall how in ages past we were fashioned as a people by God's designs, I should remember how my own formation in my faith has been a work of divine grace. With thanksgiving I take assurance in noting how this better part of me has walked in God's ways.

But another part of me has had its rebellious moments. So I have had my ups and downs. At times I have been so lost in darkness that I have not let my faith sustain me in struggles. I would even refuse to acknowledge God as a force in my life. It was the senseless forgetting, the foolish ignorance, of how divine love had wonderfully brought me to religion in the first place. God had been my guide, light, and nurturer many times.

desert.

18 They tested God in their heart
    by demanding the food they craved.
19 They spoke against God, saying,
    "Can God spread a table in the wilderness?
20 Even though he struck the rock so that water
      gushed out
    and torrents overflowed,
  can he also give bread,
    or provide meat for his people?"
21 Therefore, when the Lord heard, he was full
      of rage;
  a fire was kindled against Jacob,
  his anger mounted against Israel,
22 because they had no faith in God,
    and did not trust his saving power.
23 Yet he commanded the skies above,
    and opened the doors of heaven;
24 he rained down on them manna to eat,
    and gave them the grain of heaven.
25 Mortals ate of the bread of angels;
    he sent them food in abundance.
26 He caused the east wind to blow in the
      heavens,
    and by his power he led out the south
      wind;
27 he rained flesh upon them like dust,
    winged birds like the sand of the seas;
28 he let them fall within their camp,
    all around their dwellings.
29 And they ate and were well filled,
    for he gave them what they craved.
30 But before they had satisfied their craving,
    while the food was still in their mouths,
31 the anger of God rose against them
    and he killed the strongest of them,
    and laid low the flower of Israel.
32 In spite of all this they still sinned;
    they did not believe in his wonders.
33 So he made their days vanish like a breath,
    and their years in terror.
34 When he killed them, they sought for him;

But I blocked that out of my mind and demanded that things go only by my latest decrees. When God did not give in to me, I questioned whether my very Lord had any power at all. God's justice could have dealt with me instantly and given me what, strictly speaking, I deserved.

Yet divine patience prevailed. Not only was I for the moment not punished, but was helped to go on, was sustained on my journey. It was like God was saying, "If this is what you want, take it! If this is what you think you need, enjoy it!"

But, like a good parent, God was just allowing me, sad as it was, to experience the consequences of my own desires. Parts of me, especially my strongest vices, had to go. Even knowing this, I tried to bargain with God and to curry favor.

they repented and sought God earnestly.

35 They remembered that God was their rock,
    the Most High God their redeemer.

36 But they flattered him with their mouths;
    they lied to him with their tongues.

37 Their heart was not steadfast toward him;
    they were not true to his covenant.

38 Yet he, being compassionate,
    forgave their iniquity,
    and did not destroy them;
often he restrained his anger,
    and did not stir up all his wrath.

39 He remembered that they were but flesh,
    a wind that passes and does not come
      again.

40 How often they rebelled against him in the
      wilderness
    and grieved him in the desert!

41 They tested God again and again,
    and provoked the Holy One of Israel.

42 They did not keep in mind his power,
    or the day when he redeemed them from
      the foe;

43 when he displayed his signs in Egypt,
    and his miracles in the fields of Zoan.

44 He turned their rivers to blood,
    so that they could not drink of their
      streams.

45 He sent among them swarms of flies, which
      devoured them,
    and frogs, which destroyed them.

46 He gave their crops to the caterpillar,
    and the fruit of their labor to the locust.

47 He destroyed their vines with hail,
    and their sycamores with frost.

48 He gave over their cattle to the hail,
    and their flocks to thunderbolts.

49 He let loose on them his fierce anger,
    wrath, indignation, and distress,
    a company of destroying angels.

50 He made a path for his anger;
    he did not spare them from death,

When God resisted I pretended to believe by offering hypocritical prayers. Again the Lord was patient and merciful. Human arrogance presumes it is invincible, but divine wisdom sees there fragility and false security. So I continued on my merry way, oblivious that I was playing with fire, while God sighed over my hardness of heart. It meant nothing to me that the Lord preserved me from my self-destructive ways, that by God's designs there were enough distractions from my impudence, enough tasks to occupy my time productively. My great displays of power and talent rightly came to nothing. Unknown to me, God was in charge.

Gradually my pernicious energies began to die away. One by one

but gave their lives over to the plague.

51 He struck all the firstborn in Egypt,
      the first issue of their strength in the tents
        of Ham.
52 Then he led out his people like sheep,
      and guided them in the wilderness like a
        flock.
53 He led them in safety, so that they were not
        afraid;
      but the sea overwhelmed their enemies.
54 And he brought them to his holy hill,
      to the mountain that his right hand had
        won.
55 He drove out nations before them;
      he apportioned them for a possession
      and settled the tribes of Israel in their tents.
56 Yet they tested the Most High God,
      and rebelled against him.
      They did not observe his decrees,
57 but turned away and were faithless like their
        ancestors;
      they twisted like a treacherous bow.
58 For they provoked him to anger with their
        high places;
      they moved him to jealousy with their idols.
59 When God heard, he was full of wrath,
      and he utterly rejected Israel.
60 He abandoned his dwelling at Shiloh,
      the tent where he dwelt among mortals,
61 and delivered his power to captivity,
      his glory to the hand of the foe.
62 He gave his people to the sword,
      and vented his wrath on his heritage.
63 Fire devoured their young men,
      and their girls had no marriage song.
64 Their priests fell by the sword,
      and their widows made no lamentation.
65 Then the Lord awoke as from sleep,
      like a warrior shouting because of wine.
66 He put his adversaries to rout;
      he put them to everlasting disgrace.
67 He rejected the tent of Joseph,

*they fell exhausted. Then I was
ready for a new life, real life.*

*So the Lord led me to finer fields. I
met God afresh and newly sensed
the value of divine commands. I
settled into a becoming lifestyle
and learned appropriate behavior.*

*But even after that—I am ashamed
to say it—I fell again, dishonored
God by even more daring and creative methods of rebellion.*

*Yet I came to see that I am an
inveterate sinner. Scorning my
foibles but nonetheless loving me,
God cast them behind us both.
Away with blasphemy, hatred,
betrayal, obscenity, and idolatry!
God was at my side with palpable
might. Then began the tedious
process of molding me into a new
image.*

he did not choose the tribe of Ephraim;
68 but he chose the tribe of Judah,
Mount Zion, which he loves.
69 He built his sanctuary like the high heavens,
like the earth, which he has founded
forever.
70 He chose his servant David,
and took him from the sheepfolds;
71 from tending the nursing ewes he brought
him
to be the shepherd of his people Jacob,
of Israel, his inheritance.
72 With upright heart he tended them,
and guided them with skillful hand.

God came into my life once more, this time offering a relationship far deeper and lasting. This was a partnership like none before, more like a marriage than an engagement. And God wanted to be true. The Lord provided me with a new home, a rejuvenated sense of belonging. I found new guides, new heroes. At last I was ready to be tended by those who knew profoundly the ways of God.

Oppressive Thought: My past has left me devastated.

Edifying Thought: God has always worked with me.

Oppressive Image: A rebellious generation

Edifying Image: A child skillfully raised

My life, O God, is a catalog of sins, a history of recurrent rebelliousness in face of your designs for me. And I have met your firmness, encountered your discipline. Nonetheless your patience and mercy have been disproportionate to my sins. From my immoral caprices you have led me to constancy and dedication. For this I thank you. Help me never to stray again.

PSALM 79

Upheaval

1 O God, the nations have come into your
inheritance;
they have defiled your holy temple;
they have laid Jerusalem in ruins.
2 They have given the bodies of your servants
to the birds of the air for food,
the flesh of your faithful to the wild animals
of the earth.
3 They have poured out their blood like water

So much has changed, dear God. I feel like a stranger in my own house or a foreigner amid my own people. How much must I change? Until I lose my sense of identity, or forsake the heart of my faith?

all around Jerusalem,
and there was no one to bury them.

4 We have become a taunt to our neighbors,
mocked and derided by those around us.

5 How long, O Lord? Will you be angry forever?
Will your jealous wrath burn like fire?

6 Pour out your anger on the nations
that do not know you,
and on the kingdoms
that do not call on your
name.

7 For they have devoured Jacob
and laid waste his habitation.

8 Do not remember against us the iniquities of our
ancestors;
let your compassion come speedily to meet
us,
for we are brought very low.

9 Help us, O God of our salvation,
for the glory of your name;
deliver us, and forgive our sins,
for your name's sake.

10 Why should the nations say,
"Where is their God?"
Let the avenging of the outpoured blood of your
servants
be known among the nations before our
eyes.

11 Let the groans of the prisoners come before
you;
according to your great power preserve
those doomed to die.

12 Return sevenfold into the bosom of our
neighbors
the taunts with which they taunted you, O
Lord!

13 Then we your people, the flock of your pasture,
will give thanks to you forever;
from generation to generation we will
recount your praise.

These novelties, or these challenges, eat away at me and leave me lifeless, a useless joke to myself and others who need me.

If you are behind this chastisement, O Lord, please relent! Otherwise, if my own ignorance and weakness are the culprits, show your displeasure directly to me so that I might reform my ways and be raised up because of your mercy. Shower us all with your graces. Teach us your ways. Hear my plea for strength and turn my blasphemous doubts into songs of thanksgiving, confidence, and praise.

Then, let us all sing of your glories, let us bless you now and forever.

Oppressive Thought: The changes have ruined me.

Edifying Thought: The challenges have refined me.

Oppressive Image: Rubble

Edifying Image: Eyes of hope

I am so distressed, Lord, that I am not myself. With all the upheaval in my life, I wonder how I fit with those close to me. How much of this have I brought on myself? Show me, Lord, what I must do to retrieve my rightful place, assume my responsibilities, and enjoy the companionship by which you bring added joys to my life.

PSALM 80

Needing Restoration

1 Give ear, O Shepherd of Israel,
　　you who lead Joseph like a flock!
You who are enthroned upon the cherubim,
　　shine forth
2 before Ephraim and Benjamin and
　　　Manasseh.
Stir up your might,
　　and come to save us!
3 Restore us, O God;
　　let your face shine, that we may be saved.
4 O Lord God of hosts,
　　how long will you be angry with your
　　　people's prayers?
5 You have fed them with the bread of tears,
　　and given them tears to drink in full
　　　measure.
6 You make us the scorn of our neighbors;
　　our enemies laugh among themselves.
7 Restore us, O God of hosts;
　　let your face shine, that we may be saved.
8 You brought a vine out of Egypt;
　　you drove out the nations and planted it.
9 You cleared the ground for it;
　　it took deep root and filled the land.
10 The mountains were covered with its shade,

I and my dear community, I and those who are family to me, need you, Lord. We have long cherished your loving guidance. Now we confidently call on you for help in our time of need.

I sometimes feel that you are ignoring our pleas. Are our turmoil and suffering rightful punishments from you, O God? Or are they afflictions for which our darkened minds blame you?

Help us in our dilemma. Let us know your lively presence in all its power. In our earlier years you led us from a lowly, perhaps pitiable, state to a situation of recognition, maybe even grandeur. Our reputation and influence were widespread.

the mighty cedars with its branches;

11 it sent out its branches to the sea,
    and its shoots to the River.

12 Why then have you broken down its walls,
    so that all who pass along the way pluck its
      fruit?

Now, or so it seems, we are not only bereft of honor, but we are being exploited and abused.

13 The boar from the forest ravages it,
    and all that move in the field feed on it.

14 Turn again, O God of hosts;
    look down from heaven, and see;
  have regard for this vine,

15   the stock that your right hand planted.

At this point, Lord, only you have the power it will take to restore us. We are yours. Dispel this crippling disorder of ours!

16 They have burned it with fire,
    they have cut it down;
  may they perish at the rebuke of your
    countenance.

17 But let your hand be upon the one at your
    right hand,
  the one whom you made strong for yourself.

Help us rise anew. Help us prove ourselves a family of true faith. We commit ourselves to you and your truth, to you and your ways. We love you, O Lord, and cherish you as our Savior.

18 Then we will never turn back from you;
    give us life, and we will call on your name.

19 Restore us, O Lord God of hosts;
    let your face shine, that we may be saved.

Oppressive Thought: We are defeated.

Edifying Thought: The Lord will restore us.

Oppressive Image: A smirking enemy

Edifying Image: God's shining face

We seem to be coming apart, O Lord. Our sense of togetherness as a family has waned. The unity we once enjoyed was a complement to the faith we had in you. Now, in our weakness, the bonds of faith and our bonds of love appear to be broken. You, Lord, empower wholeness. You are committed to building up communities. Bring us quickly the glory you have promised those committed to you.

PSALM 81

Obedience

<table>
<tr>
<td>

1   Sing aloud to God our strength;
     shout for joy to the God of Jacob.

2   Raise a song, sound the tambourine,
     the sweet lyre with the harp.

3   Blow the trumpet at the new moon,
     at the full moon, on our festal day.

4   For it is a statute for Israel,
     an ordinance of the God of Jacob.

5   He made it a decree in Joseph,
     when he went out over the land of Egypt.
   I hear a voice I had not known:

6   "I relieved your shoulder of the burden;
     your hands were freed from the basket.

7   In distress you called, and I rescued you;
     I answered you in the secret place of
        thunder;
     I tested you at the waters of Meribah.

8   Hear, O my people, while I admonish you;
     O Israel, if you would but listen to me!

9   There shall be no strange god among you;
     you shall not bow down to a foreign god.

10   I am the Lord your God,
     who brought you up out of the land of
        Egypt.
     Open your mouth wide and I will fill it.

11   "But my people did not listen to my voice;
     Israel would not submit to me.

12   So I gave them over to their stubborn
        hearts,
     to follow their own counsels.

13   O that my people would listen to me,
     that Israel would walk in my ways!

14   Then I would quickly subdue their enemies,
     and turn my hand against their foes.

15   Those who hate the Lord would cringe
        before him,
     and their doom would last forever.

</td>
<td>

When I rejoice, when my soul sings the praises of my God, when I direct my ways according to divine commands, according to impulses of grace, then the days and seasons come alive and ring with sweet music.

Within the melody I can hear God say, in tones new to me: "I have helped you with your burden, relieved you in your pain. While letting you grow, I did not ignore your pleas.

I do no less now, so please believe me. Harken to anything else and you are preferring an idol. I am your God, your Savior and Provider.

You have made the mistake before. You ignored my presence and made your own plans. Following orders devised solely by yourself, you suffered the consequences of your 'clever' designs. Rather than repeat your folly, why do you not discern my will? Have you not had enough self-defeat?

</td>
</tr>
</table>

16 I would feed you with the finest of the wheat, and with honey from the rock I would satisfy you."	*I have nothing but sustenance and security to offer you."*

Oppressive Thought: What I want is always best.

Edifying Thought: Thy will be done.

Oppressive Image: A stubborn heart

Edifying Image: Honey

When I feel your place in my life, O God, when I am confident that I am doing your will, I feel energized and optimistic. The shifting patterns around me provide only signs of your constancy. Help me to remember in every circumstance your promises to sustain and guide me. Help me to be faithful to you, as you are to me.

PSALM 82

Justice

1 God has taken his place in the divine council; in the midst of the gods he holds judgment:	*Ultimately divine justice will prevail.*
2 "How long will you judge unjustly and show partiality to the wicked?	
3 Give justice to the weak and the orphan; maintain the right of the lowly and the destitute.	*Those who rule or exercise authority in God's name can become victims of their own corruption. Such judges are the mainstay of evil. Should I judge, O Lord, let me heed your command to free the deprived and oppressed from malicious exploitation. Let me not contribute to corruption that seeps into the very fabric of creation. Let my actions demonstrate my conviction that privilege of authority will not spare me the just consequences of vile decisions.*
4 Rescue the weak and the needy; deliver them from the hand of the wicked."	
5 They have neither knowledge nor understanding, they walk around in darkness; all the foundations of the earth are shaken.	
6 I say, "You are gods, children of the Most High, all of you;	

7   nevertheless, you shall die like mortals,
       and fall like any prince."
8   Rise up, O God, judge the earth;
       for all the nations belong to you!

For your justice is perfect and universal.

Oppressive Thought: Injustice can be hidden.

Edifying Thought: God's justice is supreme.

Oppressive Image: Hands of the wicked

Edifying Image: Just judges

Help me, my God, to be a good and effective leader. Help me to judge—always by standards that you have set in place—what is right for me and others. Let my sense of direction be the counterpart of my attention to what you have made good and true. Help me not to depend too much on myself. Let me rely in good measure on you.

PSALM 83

Struggle

1   O God, do not keep silence;
       do not hold your peace or be still, O God!
2   Even now your enemies are in tumult;
       those who hate you have raised their heads.
3   They lay crafty plans against your people;
       they consult together against those you protect.
4   They say, "Come, let us wipe them out as a nation;
       let the name of Israel be remembered no more."
5   They conspire with one accord;
       against you they make a covenant—
6   the tents of Edom and the Ishmaelites,
       Moab and the Hagrites,
7   Gebal and Ammon and Amalek,
       Philistia with the inhabitants of Tyre;
8   Assyria also has joined them;

I am at my best, dear God, when I sense your presence, when I know with conviction, when I deeply feel, that you stand by me. Now, as forces gather against me, as characteristics within me appear as devious and destructive characters, I recognize that their greatest power is to undermine my faith in you, to negate my sense that you are forever my Lord. In this tragic drama, even players previously unknown to me, enemies from secret recesses of my soul, have joined in the conspiracy.

they are the strong arm of the children of
Lot.

9 Do to them as you did to Midian,
      as to Sisera and Jabin at the Wadi Kishon,

10 who were destroyed at En-do,
      who became dung for the ground.

11 Make their nobles like Oreb and Zeeb,
      all their princes like Zebah and Zalmunna,

12 who said, "Let us take the pastures of God
      for our own possession."

13 O my God, make them like whirling dust,
      like chaff before the wind.

14 As fire consumes the forest,
      as the flame sets the mountains ablaze,

15 so pursue them with your tempest
      and terrify them with your hurricane.

16 Fill their faces with shame,
      so that they may seek your name, O Lord.

17 Let them be put to shame and dismayed
        forever;
      let them perish in disgrace.

18 Let them know that you alone,
      whose name is the Lord,
      are the Most High over all the earth.

But I rise up in faith. With all my heart I cry to you: Let me see your blessedness. Let me know, O God, that your power in my life renders my enemies weaklings and even repels them like dust in the wind.

With you at my side, I can be so aflame with the fire of your love, so sanctified by your holiness, that I become immune to my enemies' bluffing tactics.

They become forever powerless. And I return to you as my mighty God.

Oppressive Thought: I am doomed.

Oppressive Image: Conspiracy

Edifying Thought: My faith weakens the enemy.

Edifying Image: A purifying breeze

Let me not, O Lord, be oppressed by enemies, especially those from within: the feelings, thoughts, and images that lure me away from my sense of you. My sometimes distressed and untidy soul feels bereft of you while all the while you stand in the wings, anxious for me to find you again, to receive you as the God by whom struggles lead to gain.

PSALM 84

The Dwelling Place of God

1 How lovely is your dwelling place,
   O Lord of hosts!
2 My soul longs, indeed it faints
   for the courts of the Lord;
   my heart and my flesh sing for joy
   to the living God.
3 Even the sparrow finds a home,
   and the swallow a nest for herself,
   where she may lay her young,
   at your altars, O Lord of hosts,
   my King and my God.
4 Happy are those who live in your house,
   ever singing your praise.
5 Happy are those whose strength is in you,
   in whose heart are the highways to Zion.
6 As they go through the valley of Baca
   they make it a place of springs;
   the early rain also covers it with pools.
7 They go from strength to strength;
   the God of gods will be seen in Zion.
8 O Lord God of hosts, hear my prayer;
   give ear, O God of Jacob!
9 Behold our shield, O God;
   look on the face of your anointed.
10 For a day in your courts is better
   than a thousand elsewhere.
   I would rather be a doorkeeper in the house
      of my God
   than live in the tents of wickedness.
11 For the Lord God is a sun and shield;
   he bestows favor and honor.
   No good thing does the Lord withhold
   from those who walk uprightly.
12 O Lord of hosts,
   happy is everyone who trusts in you.

Wherever you dwell, O Lord, I can find your beauty. Whatever your abode—say my heart or family or community or calling—I can name it a holy place, a sanctuary. Your presence transforms me.

I can be struck by your sacredness when I enter a house of prayer. I reverence your abodes, having learned the joy of honoring you according to your prompts and according to the precious traditions you have inspired. So I advance in discovering more fully my joy and strength in you, my God.
Help me then to feel greater security in you, O Lord, and in your appointed servant.

In my occupation I renew my belief that my "accomplishments" are ultimately due to the grace of God's presence, the warmth of divine goodness, the solace of heavenly guidance.

Oppressive Thought: God is nowhere to be found.

Edifying Thought: I treasure God's presence wherever I find it.

Oppressive Image: An arid place

Edifying Image: A happy house

You live, Lord, in so many aspects of my life. Your presence is specially palpable in times, spaces, and places that my faith helps me to name as sacred. Moved according to traditions inspired by you, I approach you with reverence; I spend time in devotion. Tarrying with you, I find my way. Lingering in your dwelling places, I find my true strengths.

PSALM 85

Renewal

1 Lord, you were favorable to your land;
    you restored the fortunes of Jacob.
2 You forgave the iniquity of your people;
    you pardoned all their sin.
3 You withdrew all your wrath;
    you turned from your hot anger.
4 Restore us again, O God of our salvation,
    and put away your indignation toward us.
5 Will you be angry with us forever?
    Will you prolong your anger to all
      generations?
6 Will you not revive us again,
    so that your people may rejoice in you?
7 Show us your steadfast love, O Lord,
    and grant us your salvation.
8 Let me hear what God the Lord will speak,
    for he will speak peace to his people,
    to his faithful, to those who turn to him in
      their hearts.
9 Surely his salvation is at hand for those who
      fear him,
    that his glory may dwell in our land.
10 Steadfast love and faithfulness will meet;
    righteousness and peace will kiss each

I know from experience, Lord, that in due time you relieve me of my plight, even when my own folly reaps horrible consequences for me and those dear to me.

Let your loving kindness shine on us again, dear God, so that we may be spared of sorrows that leave us feeling distant from you.

I open my heart to you, my Lord, to be soothed by your words of comfort. Your wondrous presence lets us be swept into a sweet harmony of love, loyalty, goodness, and tranquility.

other.

11 Faithfulness will spring up from the ground,
  and righteousness will look down from the
    sky.
12 The Lord will give what is good,
  and our land will yield its increase.
13 Righteousness will go before him,
  and will make a path for his steps.

*In your embrace we know security
and dignity. And we can go on,
productively and valiantly.*

Oppressive Thought: I have lost my chances
  for happiness.

Edifying Thought: God renews us.

Oppressive Image: Prolonged anger

Edifying Image: A holy kiss

You do not leave me too long, dear Lord, in my distress. You have taught me of your providence and mercy. However alone I feel, you are with me. You intervene according your wisdom. You enfold me in your love. Your attention becomes my new courage. I am renewed.

PSALM 86

Helplessness

1 Incline your ear, O Lord, and answer me,
  for I am poor and needy.
2 Preserve my life, for I am devoted to you;
  save your servant who trusts in you.
  You are my God; (³) be gracious to me, O
    Lord,
  for to you do I cry all day long.
4 Gladden the soul of your servant,
  for to you, O Lord, I lift up my soul.
5 For you, O Lord, are good and forgiving,
  abounding in steadfast love to all who
    call on you.
6 Give ear, O Lord, to my prayer;
  listen to my cry of supplication.
7 In the day of my trouble I call on you,
  for you will answer me.

*Sometime I do best to confess that
I am utterly helpless, that my sustenance depends entirely upon
God. Turning to divine power then
becomes a continued act of confidence, an admission of my insufficiency in face of God's purifying
and steadying love.*

No one is as reliable as the Lord.

<table>
<tr>
<td>

8   There is none like you among the gods, O
       Lord,
       nor are there any works like yours.

9   All the nations you have made shall come
       and bow down before you, O Lord,
       and shall glorify your name.

</td>
<td>

*I may look to my own qualities or
strengths, even idolize them as
sources of my security. Ultimately,
though, any strength, any dignity,
any marvel, owes its substance to
God.*

</td>
</tr>
</table>

8   There is none like you among the gods, O
         Lord,
         nor are there any works like yours.
9   All the nations you have made shall come
         and bow down before you, O Lord,
         and shall glorify your name.
10   For you are great and do wondrous things;
         you alone are God.
11   Teach me your way, O Lord,
         that I may walk in your truth;
         give me an undivided heart to revere
             your name.
12   I give thanks to you, O Lord my God, with
         my whole heart,
         and I will glorify your name forever.
13   For great is your steadfast love toward me;
         you have delivered my soul from the
             depths of Sheol.
14   O God, the insolent rise up against me;
         a band of ruffians seeks my life,
         and they do not set you before them.
15   But you, O Lord, are a God merciful and
         gracious,
         slow to anger and abounding in
             steadfast love and faithfulness.
16   Turn to me and be gracious to me;
         give your strength to your servant;
         save the child of your serving girl.
17   Show me a sign of your favor,
         so that those who hate me may see it
             and be put to shame,
         because you, Lord, have helped me and
             comforted me.

*I may look to my own qualities or
strengths, even idolize them as
sources of my security. Ultimately,
though, any strength, any dignity,
any marvel, owes its substance to
God.*

*To be helpless in this way is to be
disposed for knowledge and wisdom that only God can impart.
The mind is served by opening the
heart. And the heart is comforted
by the enduring truth the mind
sees. From depths of misery, from
threats of every sort, I can rise to
new heights.*

*However much I may have failed
to see this, in my present helplessness I rest assured of God's
astounding and generous flexibili-
ty. I am renewed in witnessing, to
myself and others, that divine reckoning of faults quickly gives way to
godly compassion and love. I need
only to ask sincerely for help.*

Oppressive Thought: I provide my own
   security.

Oppressive Image: Ruffians

Edifying Thought: There are no ways like
   God's.

Edifying Image: A beloved servant

My weakest moments, O Lord, become occasions of new strength when I turn to you as my only hope. My insufficiency becomes the soil to which you take your nurturing hand. You place in me the kernel of power by which I will gain vitality. You tend to me with compassion and dedication. Helplessness becomes my help.

PSALM 87

Heritage

1 On the holy mount stands the city he
    founded;
2   the Lord loves the gates of Zion
    more than all the dwellings of Jacob.
3 Glorious things are spoken of you,
    O city of God.
4 Among those who know me I mention
    Rahab and Babylon;
    Philistia too, and Tyre, with Ethiopia —
    "This one was born there," they say.
5 And of Zion it shall be said,
    "This one and that one were born in it";
    for the Most High himself will establish
    it.
6 The Lord records, as he registers the
    peoples,
    "This one was born there."
7 Singers and dancers alike say,
    "All my springs are in you."

I love my people, my spiritual family. Through their traditions they have nurtured my faith and helped me to cherish how they live in God's grace. In my heart I feel there is no people like them. Yet I also believe that the Lord, with abundant love for all humanity, looks on countless other places and peoples, blesses them, and names them as children of God.

They all may cherish their spiritual centers, even as I, with a spirit that dances and sings, am sustained by my heritage.

Oppressive Thought: God disdains outsiders.

Oppressive Image: Aliens

Edifying Thought: Love of heritage need not breed haughtiness.

Edifying Image: The City of God

I love my place amid my people, O Lord; I love the traditions by which I find comfort; I love my spiritual home. With my family of faith I thank you for having chosen us and blessed us. With humility and even joy I recognize how other people in places far and near find their ways to you. Help me imitate your love for all humanity.

PSALM 88

Desolation

1 O Lord, God of my salvation,
    when, at night, I cry out in your presence,
2 let my prayer come before you;
    incline your ear to my cry.
3 For my soul is full of troubles,
    and my life draws near to Sheol.
4 I am counted among those who go down to the
       Pit;
    I am like those who have no help,
5 like those forsaken among the dead,
    like the slain that lie in the grave,
like those whom you remember no more,
    for they are cut off from your hand.
6 You have put me in the depths of the Pit,
    in the regions dark and deep.
7 Your wrath lies heavy upon me,
    and you overwhelm me with all your waves.
8 You have caused my companions to shun me;
    you have made me a thing of horror to them.
I am shut in so that I cannot escape;
9   my eye grows dim through sorrow.
Every day I call on you, O Lord;
    I spread out my hands to you.
10 Do you work wonders for the dead?
    Do the shades rise up to praise you?
11 Is your steadfast love declared in the grave,
    or your faithfulness in Abaddon?
12 Are your wonders known in the darkness,
    or your saving help in the land of
       forgetfulness?
13 But I, O Lord, cry out to you;
    in the morning my prayer comes before you.
14 O Lord, why do you cast me off?
    Why do you hide your face from me?
15 Wretched and close to death from my youth up,
    I suffer your terrors; I am desperate.
16 Your wrath has swept over me;

Part of me believes, O Lord, that you are my Savior. So I still dare to address you, even in my present horrid state. I have sunk so low that I feel lifeless, like a corpse in a darkened grave. The pit I inhabit is so bleak and dreary that all seems lost, that I am totally forgotten, even by you, or worse, that I am engulfed by your anger.

In such a depression I even feel that you conspire to make me an outcast from my friends. Though my tears seem to bring me no release, I still turn to you, Lord, and wonder if your goodness, power, and love can touch me in my condition.

My daily prayers then are a collection of confused cries, desperate questions about your motives, interminable complaints about your ways, endless frustration over your will.

151

your dread assaults destroy me.

17 They surround me like a flood all day long;
from all sides they close in on me.

18 You have caused friend and neighbor to shun
me;
my companions are in darkness.

*Crushed and friendless, I see only
the dark.*

Oppressive Thought: I am lost in the depths
of misery.

Edifying Thought: God hears my cries.

Oppressive Image: A deep grave

Edifying Image: Lifted hands

*Without you, O Lord, without a sense of your supportive presence, I am depressed and feel total-
ly alone. Everyone seems to have turned from me, if not turned on me. Even my sense of self
is negative; I attack myself and tear myself down. Reach into this darkness, Lord. I long for life and
light.*

PSALM 89

Confidence

1 I will sing of your steadfast love, O Lord,
forever;
with my mouth I will proclaim your
faithfulness to all generations.

2 I declare that your steadfast love is
established forever;
your faithfulness is as firm as the heavens.

3 You said, "I have made a covenant with my
chosen one,
I have sworn to my servant David:

4 'I will establish your descendants forever,
and build your throne for all generations.'"

5 Let the heavens praise your wonders, O
Lord,
your faithfulness in the assembly of the
holy ones.

6 For who in the skies can be compared to the

*When I know you intimately, O
Lord, when my heart sings of your
constancy and love, your fidelity so
enthralls me that I sense my own
enduring worth. My faith is
renewed.*

*I have fresh confidence in your
commitment to your people, in
your desire to sustain and nurture
all of us, from one generation to
the next. The expanse of our asso-
ciation in your love then appears
to my believing eye so great that I
penetrate your heavens and find
comfort in realizing how many of
our company are with you, now*

Lord?
  Who among the heavenly beings is like
    the Lord,
7 a God feared in the council of the holy ones,
    great and awesome above all that are
    around him?
8 O Lord God of hosts,
    who is as mighty as you, O Lord?
    Your faithfulness surrounds you.
9 You rule the raging of the sea;
    when its waves rise, you still them.
10 You crushed Rahab like a carcass;
    you scattered your enemies with your
    mighty arm.
11 The heavens are yours, the earth also is yours;
    the world and all that is in it—you have
    founded them.
12 The north and the south—you created them;
    Tabor and Hermon joyously praise your
    name.
13 You have a mighty arm;
    strong is your hand, high your right hand.
14 Righteousness and justice are the foundation
    of your throne;
    steadfast love and faithfulness go before
    you.
15 Happy are the people who know the festal
    shout,
    who walk, O Lord, in the light of your
    countenance;
16 they exult in your name all day long,
    and extol your righteousness.
17 For you are the glory of their strength;
    by your favor our horn is exalted.
18 For our shield belongs to the Lord,
    our king to the Holy One of Israel.
19 Then you spoke in a vision to your faithful
    one, and said:
    "I have set the crown on one who is mighty,
    I have exalted one chosen from the people.
20 I have found my servant David;
    with my holy oil I have anointed him;

and forever. Your holiness, your awesome presence and glory, supersedes yet enlivens the entire setting.

Overflowing its celestial heights, your might fills the earth and purifies our world of its threats and miseries.

Transformed by your ardor and light, I see your hand in all things, I recognize the praise of which you are worthy. Wherever I turn—to beauteous nature or a heartened people—power and grace become reflections of your justice and love. An unending "Alleluia!" ascends to you and thus assures continued life and strength.

Our leadership becomes a sign of our own blessedness. Your Anointed One, our Messiah, becomes the focal point of our own consecration to redeemed and sanctified life.

21 my hand shall always remain with him;
     my arm also shall strengthen him.
22 The enemy shall not outwit him,
     the wicked shall not humble him.
23 I will crush his foes before him
     and strike down those who hate him.
24 My faithfulness and steadfast love shall be
       with him;
     and in my name his horn shall be exalted.
25 I will set his hand on the sea
     and his right hand on the rivers.
26 He shall cry to me, 'You are my Father,
     my God, and the Rock of my salvation!'
27 I will make him the firstborn,
     the highest of the kings of the earth.
28 Forever I will keep my steadfast love for him,
     and my covenant with him will stand firm.
29 I will establish his line forever,
     and his throne as long as the heavens
       endure.

Because of your Holy One, we are all fortified against fierce enemies, protected from life's snares. Upholding the honor of the leader, you defeat maliciousness and fortify your people in struggles against iniquity. The one who in our name promises obedience to our mighty God leads the way in finding exultation. For such commitment is but a faint response to God's own immense fidelity. Walking in divine ways, we cannot help attaining life that is innocent and enduring.

30 If his children forsake my law
     and do not walk according to my
       ordinances,
31 if they violate my statutes
     and do not keep my commandments,
32 then I will punish their transgression with
       the rod
     and their iniquity with scourges;
33 but I will not remove from him my steadfast
       love,
     or be false to my faithfulness.

To walk otherwise is to meet obstacles and pitfalls, consequences of our faults in a world well and lovingly designed by God.

34 I will not violate my covenant,
     or alter the word that went forth from my
       lips.
35 Once and for all I have sworn by my holiness;
     I will not lie to David.
36 His line shall continue forever,
     and his throne endure before me like the
       sun.
37 It shall be established forever like the moon,
     an enduring witness in the skies."
38 But now you have spurned and rejected him;

God does not renege on the eternal promise to sustain and to cherish. That is visible in the Messiah. Only the unworthy servant, like a false messiah, is due your wrath, O Lord.

you are full of wrath against your anointed.

39 You have renounced the covenant with your
  servant;
  you have defiled his crown in the dust.
40 You have broken through all his walls;
  you have laid his strongholds in ruins.
41 All who pass by plunder him;
  he has become the scorn of his neighbors.
42 You have exalted the right hand of his foes;
  you have made all his enemies rejoice.
43 Moreover, you have turned back the edge of
  his sword,
  and you have not supported him in battle.
44 You have removed the scepter from his hand,
  and hurled his throne to the ground.
45 You have cut short the days of his youth;
  you have covered him with shame.
46 How long, O Lord? Will you hide yourself
  forever?
  How long will your wrath burn like fire?
47 Remember how short my time is—
  for what vanity you have created all
  mortals!
48 Who can live and never see death?
  Who can escape the power of Sheol?
49 Lord, where is your steadfast love of old,
  which by your faithfulness you swore to
  David?
50 Remember, O Lord, how your servant is
  taunted;
  how I bear in my bosom the insults of the
  peoples,
51 with which your enemies taunt, O Lord,
  with which they taunted the footsteps of
  your anointed.
52 Blessed be the Lord forever.
  Amen and Amen.

And here I must humbly caution myself against smug security. In my rebelliousness or impudence I can be brought low, I can be defeated soundly and publicly. All that I thought was settled can suffer upheaval. I can grow powerless and pitiable. My sense of security can mock my own feebleness and render enduring life a fearsome prospect.

In such a state I would no longer know you, dear God, no longer rejoice in a divine countenance that has looked upon me, looked into me, with eternal love. Then I would feel like the mortal of mortals, duped by the lies of the flesh, cut off from your reassuring companionship.

May I be spared such a fate. May I forever revel in your blessings, my Lord and my God!

Oppressive Thought: I am in danger.

Edifying Thought: God's faithfulness is firm.

Oppressive Image: A carcass

Edifying Image: A throne

My faith in you, O God, is so reassuring. With you and through you I feel confident in face of fearsome challenges. I remember how your protection and comfort have endured throughout the history of my people. I see how you have been among us and empowered us. Let my gratitude for your many graces never turn to presumption. Strengthen me in the commitments that are part of my faith.

PSALM 90

Wanting Rejuvenation

1   Lord, you have been our dwelling place
       in all generations.
2   Before the mountains were brought forth,
       or ever you had formed the earth and the
           world,
       from everlasting to everlasting you are God.
3   You turn us back to dust,
       and say, "Turn back, you mortals."
4   For a thousand years in your sight
       are like yesterday when it is past,
       or like a watch in the night.
5   You sweep them away; they are like a dream,
       like grass that is renewed in the morning;
6   in the morning it flourishes and is renewed;
       in the evening it fades and withers.
7   For we are consumed by your anger;
       by your wrath we are overwhelmed.
8   You have set our iniquities before you,
       our secret sins in the light of your
           countenance.
9   For all our days pass away under your wrath;
       our years come to an end like a sigh.
10 The days of our life are seventy years,

Your presence among mortals, O God, let alone your bond to our universe through your creative energies, affects a vast expanse of time and history. Compared with these innumerable centuries, our brief lives on earth seem, at least for this moment, insignificant, like daylilies that fade with the night. The flower at least glories from dawn to dark.

In my present plight I feel that insult has been added to injury. On my few years hang as well the burdensome consequences of my sins. I may pass from this world having known nothing but misery.

or perhaps eighty, if we are strong;
even then their span is only toil and trouble;
they are soon gone, and we fly away.

11 Who considers the power of your anger?
Your wrath is as great as the fear that is
due you.

Where I have failed, I acknowledge my guilt.

12 So teach us to count our days
that we may gain a wise heart.

13 Turn, O Lord! How long?
Have compassion on your servants!

Grant us wisdom, O God, to make the most of our remaining days. Sustain us in your love that we may know in life the joys of your compassion and protection. Diminish our sorrow. Give fair proportion to our gladness.

14 Satisfy us in the morning with your steadfast
love,
so that we may rejoice and be glad all our
days.

15 Make us glad as many days as you have
afflicted us,
and as many years as we have seen evil.

16 Let your work be manifest to your servants,
and your glorious power to their children.

Favor us with new life, life in you that yields abundant goodness!

17 Let the favor of the Lord our God be upon us,
and prosper for us the work of our hands—
O prosper the work of our hands!

Oppressive Thought: Life is essentially burdensome.

Edifying Thought: God gives me new energy.

Oppressive Image: Wilted plants

Edifying Image: Productivity

As with seemingly increasing speed, O Lord, my days and years pass; I feel the weight of time. My burdensome mistakes add to my sense that so many moments flee before they can be grasped, before I can accomplish all that I desire. Give me new life, at least by knowing that what good I do through you is far more than good enough.

PSALM 91

Sincerity

1 You who live in the shelter of the Most High,
who abide in the shadow of the Almighty,

How comforting it is to snuggle up to God, like nestling in a mother's

2   will say to the Lord, "My refuge and my
        fortress;
      my God, in whom I trust."
3   For he will deliver you from the snare of the
        fowler
      and from the deadly pestilence;
4   he will cover you with his pinions,
      and under his wings you will find refuge;
      his faithfulness is a shield and buckler.
5   You will not fear the terror of the night,
      or the arrow that flies by day,
6   or the pestilence that stalks in darkness,
      or the destruction that wastes at noonday.
7   A thousand may fall at your side,
      ten thousand at your right hand,
      but it will not come near you.
8   You will only look with your eyes
      and see the punishment of the wicked.
9   Because you have made the Lord your refuge,
      the Most High your dwelling place,
10   no evil shall befall you,
      no scourge come near your tent.
11   For he will command his angels concerning
        you
      to guard you in all your ways.
12   On their hands they will bear you up,
      so that you will not dash your foot against a
        stone.
13   You will tread on the lion and the adder,
      the young lion and the serpent you will
        trample under foot.
14   Those who love me, I will deliver;
      I will protect those who know my name.
15   When they call to me, I will answer them;
      I will be with them in trouble,
      I will rescue them and honor them.
16   With long life I will satisfy them,
      and show them my salvation.

arms, where one is swaddled in solace and security. How reassuring it is to sense safety, like knowing that a courageous father defies every assailant.

One can feel bold, think brave thoughts, convinced and content that her fidelity and his heroism are absolutely unshakable. Let the battle rage! Let the whirlwind touch whatever needs ravaging! I am immune! Threats and horrors can weaken one's defenses, like cracking or crumbling walls of a house. But even for this, God has provided.

Heavenly powers help one who trusts in God to rise above the fray, to become faithful and heroic in one's own right.

It is love that works such wonders, human love given, divine love shared, empowering love, ennobling love, love that lasts forever.

Oppressive Thought: I am in danger.   *Edifying Thought:* God is my security.

Oppressive Image: Battle   *Edifying Image:* In the arms of an angel

*I*know, O Lord, that we all suffer and that I too will have my share of pain. But I also believe you when you promise protection against harm, when you assure immunity from infectious strife, when you guarantee security in dangerous circumstances. You allot each of us a generous portion of such protection. I count on your loving kindness.

PSALM 92

Strength

1	It is good to give thanks to the Lord, to sing praises to your name, O Most High;	*When I thank you, Lord, for all that you have done, music rises in my soul. All day long my very being resonates with your loving deeds, the marvels you have worked, for me and for others.*
2	to declare your steadfast love in the morning, and your faithfulness by night,	
3	to the music of the lute and the harp, to the melody of the lyre.	
4	For you, O Lord, have made me glad by your work; at the works of your hands I sing for joy.	
5	How great are your works, O Lord! Your thoughts are very deep!	*My sights are so restricted, my understanding so contained, that your wondrous deeds at times escape my notice. I do not see that your exalted wisdom and justice are at work, that your powers are obscured by my erroneous, even sinful, expectations.*
6	The dullard cannot know, the stupid cannot understand this:	
7	though the wicked sprout like grass and all evildoers flourish, they are doomed to destruction forever,	
8	but you, O Lord, are on high forever.	
9	For your enemies, O Lord, for your enemies shall perish; all evildoers shall be scattered.	
10	But you have exalted my horn like that of the wild ox; you have poured over me fresh oil.	*Yet in moments of clarity, in the comforting light of your grace, I do know your power and feel it within me.*
11	My eyes have seen the downfall of my enemies; my ears have heard the doom of my evil	

assailants.

12 The righteous flourish like the palm tree,
    and grow like a cedar in Lebanon.
13 They are planted in the house of the Lord;
    they flourish in the courts of our God.
14 In old age they still produce fruit;
    they are always green and full of sap,
15 showing that the Lord is upright;
    he is my rock, and there is no
    unrighteousness in him.

Then I know that my own gifts will work to the benefit of us all, that what you have begun in me will reach its proper end. I find you anew, my God, as the source of my creative energies, as the might by which I am strong, all the days of my life.

Oppressive Thought: Everything is out of control.

Edifying Thought: God works more wonders than I know.

Oppressive Image: Pervasive crime

Edifying Image: A flourishing tree

My greatest power, O God, comes with relying on you. In my distraction and haste, I too often overlook what you are accomplishing in my life and in the larger currents of history. Yet, when I recognize your almighty hand, I am strengthened through confidence in your designs. With you in my world, I have new courage.

PSALM 93

Optimism

1 The Lord is king, he is robed in majesty;
    the Lord is robed, he is girded with strength.
  He has established the world; it shall never be
    moved;
2 your throne is established from of old;
    you are from everlasting.
3 The floods have lifted up, O Lord,
    the floods have lifted up their voice;
    the floods lift up their roaring.
4 More majestic than the thunders of mighty
    waters,
    more majestic than the waves of the sea,
    majestic on high is the Lord!

When I truly glory in the Lord, when I sense God's awesome majesty, I rest secure in knowing that all is well.

Despite all threats and hurts, whether from nature or society, the loving, kindly rule of God holds sway. Evil itself becomes a coward.

5 Your decrees are very sure;
   holiness befits your house,
   O Lord, forevermore.

*God commands goodness, and
compliance follows. God is holy.
So, by and large, is the world.*

Oppressive Thought: It is a losing battle.

Edifying Thought: God is a kindly ruler.

Oppressive Image: Roaring floods

Edifying Image: Divine majesty

Sorrow and tragedy, evident as they are, pale in face of divine grandeur, O Lord. Your power keeps our lives and nature's courses so in hand that the world largely remains a place of joy and promise. Sustained by you, I remain staunchly optimistic. Much is already well; and in your time all good will reach perfection.

PSALM 94

Punishment

1 O Lord, you God of vengeance,
   you God of vengeance, shine forth!
2 Rise up, O judge of the earth;
   give to the proud what they deserve!
3 O Lord, how long shall the wicked,
   how long shall the wicked exult?
4 They pour out their arrogant words;
   all the evildoers boast.
5 They crush your people, O Lord,
   and afflict your heritage.
6 They kill the widow and the stranger,
   they murder the orphan,
7 and they say, "The Lord does not see;
   the God of Jacob does not perceive."
8 Understand, O dullest of the people;
   fools, when will you be wise?
9 He who planted the ear, does he not hear?
   He who formed the eye, does he not see?
10 He who disciplines the nations,
   he who teaches knowledge to humankind,

*I believe, O Lord, in your goodness
and justice. By your awesome universal power you restore your children to order. You heal them and
uplift them according to your wonderful designs. Though we have
become wounded, not only by evil
but also by our own misguided
choices, you do not permit maliciousness, whether of nature or
humanity, to endure too long.*

*Because your design for us has
been so loving, ways that resist and
oppose your plan suffer by their
own degeneracy. So often it*

does he not chastise?

11 The Lord knows our thoughts,
   that they are but an empty breath.

12 Happy are those whom you discipline, O
   Lord,
   and whom you teach out of your law,

13 giving them respite from days of trouble,
   until a pit is dug for the wicked.

14 For the Lord will not forsake his people;
   he will not abandon his heritage;

15 for justice will return to the righteous,
   and all the upright in heart will follow it.

16 Who rises up for me against the wicked?
   Who stands up for me against
   evildoers?

17 If the Lord had not been my help,
   my soul would soon have lived in the
   land of silence.

18 When I thought, "My foot is slipping,"
   your steadfast love, O Lord, held me up.

19 When the cares of my heart are many,
   your consolations cheer my soul.

20 Can wicked rulers be allied with you,
   those who contrive mischief by statute?

21 They band together against the life of the
   righteous,
   and condemn the innocent to death.

22 But the Lord has become my stronghold,
   and my God the rock of my refuge.

23 He will repay them for their iniquity
   and wipe them out for their wickedness;
   the Lord our God will wipe them out.

appears that ruthlessness prevails, that horrors we concoct are vindicated by your tolerance. Should I be sorry to say, O God, that I want to see you demonstrate your justice? My sorrow is such that I long to see the evils of my world repulsed forever. There are wrongs, O Lord, iniquities that I have brought upon myself, or in which I have participated to others' grief, or which have been heaped upon me.

In such affliction you are our support, O God. By your power may such bleakness be dispelled.

May the world come to its senses. May hearts and minds be renewed. Help us to rejoice again in your designs. May all people confess from the depths of their spirits that you are a just and loving God.

Oppressive Thought: Evil goes unpunished.

Oppressive Image: Evildoers

Edifying Thought: God's discipline is loving.

Edifying Image: A cheered heart

Let me not forget, O Lord my God, that my wrongdoing brings its own punishment and, as necessary, requital by you. Let my longing for the hasty penalization of others' offenses spring from the deeper sentiment of confidence in the designs by which you effectively and justly prepare us to refashion our lives. Let me long for justice by steadfastly imitating your ways of love.

PSALM 95

The Majesty of God

1   O come, let us sing to the Lord;
      let us make a joyful noise to the rock of
        our salvation!

2   Let us come into his presence with
        thanksgiving;
      let us make a joyful noise to him with
        songs of praise!

3   For the Lord is a great God,
      and a great King above all gods.

4   In his hand are the depths of the earth;
      the heights of the mountains are his also.

5   The sea is his, for he made it,
      and the dry land, which his hands have
        formed.

6   O come, let us worship and bow down,
      let us kneel before the Lord, our Maker!

7   For he is our God,
      and we are the people of his pasture,
      and the sheep of his hand.
    O that today you would listen to his voice!

8   Do not harden your hearts, as at
        Meribah,
    as on the day at Massah in the
        wilderness,

9   when your ancestors tested me,
      and put me to the proof, though they had
        seen my work.

10   For forty years I loathed that generation
      and said, "They are a people whose
        hearts go astray,
    and they do not regard my ways."

11   Therefore in my anger I swore,
      "They shall not enter my rest."

How good it is to sing God's praises, to let my heart soar in joyful thanksgiving for all that my Lord has done for me! The melody of my soul resonates with the song of creation as divine breath suffuses the entire assemblage, all the lows and highs, from canyons and ocean depths to shores and mountaintops, from the secret recesses of my spirit to the heights of my passion and fervor.

In such song I know in my heart that God, great and kindly, provides for all my needs.

The words of the Lord are loving and firm. They alert me forcefully to divine power and care.

I must count myself among those who had forgotten how to sing. No more though! I want to know the bliss that brings true serenity.

Oppressive Thought: God does not care.

Edifying Thought: God's majesty is every-where.

Oppressive Image: Wilderness

Edifying Image: Beautiful Earth

When my heart sings, O Lord, when my soul rejoices, my faith reminds me of your majesty and goodness. When I cannot sing, when my heart sinks, when I turn from you, my soul tastes the sadness that must somehow signal your own repugnance for disloyalty. How much I prefer the song!

PSALM 96

Renewal

1 O sing to the Lord a new song; sing to the Lord, all the earth.	*It is a new day! I see the world, I see my life, as wondrously differ-*
2 Sing to the Lord, bless his name; tell of his salvation from day to day.	*ent. God has entered. I want to proclaim God's goodness to all,*

3   Declare his glory among the nations,
    his marvelous works among all the
    peoples.
	God's Lordship over all. Divine power to heal and renew evokes in me a song of praise, a melody I

4   For great is the Lord, and greatly to be
    praised;
    he is to be revered above all gods.
	have not known for so long a time. I cannot contain my joyful spirit. I must confess and proclaim that in

5 For all the gods of the peoples are idols, but the Lord made the heavens.	*all the corners of my world, in the very fabric of history, the grace of*

6   Honor and majesty are before him;
    strength and beauty are in his
    sanctuary.
	God is active. The Lord is supreme, the essence of all that is good. To

7   Ascribe to the Lord, O families of the
    peoples,
    ascribe to the Lord glory and strength.
	have missed the glory of God is to have missed the beauty of life. To recognize the font of all holiness is

8   Ascribe to the Lord the glory due his
    name;
    bring an offering, and come into his
    courts.
	also to tap my own wellspring of sanctity.

9 Worship the Lord in holy splendor; tremble before him, all the earth.	
10 Say among the nations, "The Lord is king!	

The world is firmly established; it shall
    never be moved.
He will judge the peoples with equity."

11 Let the heavens be glad, and let the earth
    rejoice;
    let the sea roar, and all that fills it;

12   let the field exult, and everything in it.
Then shall all the trees of the forest sing
    for joy

13 before the Lord; for he is coming,
    for he is coming to judge the earth.
He will judge the world with
    righteousness,
    and the peoples with his truth.

*Thank you, Lord, for your patience
with me, for not withdrawing as
my heart and mind wandered aim-
lessly, forgetting you. Now I know
that even if my song should dwin-
dle, you are always ready to renew
it, to lighten my days and bring
them harmony.*

Oppressive Thought: It is the same old
    world.

Edifying Thought: I can see things
    differently.

Oppressive Image: Barren fields

Edifying Image: Budding trees

My heart overflows with a melody of you, O God. The world is glorious as my ecstatic soul responds to your grandeur. Let me not lose the song. Let my words and actions always blend in witness to your unending excellence. Let my renewal be for good.

PSALM 97

The Forcefulness of God

1 The Lord is king! Let the earth rejoice;
    let the many coastlands be glad!

2 Clouds and thick darkness are all around
    him;
    righteousness and justice are the
    foundation of his throne.

3 Fire goes before him,
    and consumes his adversaries on every
    side.

4 His lightnings light up the world;

*How wholesome it is to welcome a
rightful display of forcefulness.
Resistance to good is far flung and
momentous, is so tenacious that in
some instances only might and
genuine authority can insure order
and propriety. God dwells in mystery, yet reveals divine love as discipline and justice. They are displayed with the rush of a*

the earth sees and trembles.

5 The mountains melt like wax
 before the Lord, before the Lord of all the
  earth.

6 The heavens proclaim his righteousness;
 and all the peoples behold his glory.

7 All worshipers of images are put to shame,
 those who make their boast in worthless
  idols;
 all gods bow down before him.

8 Zion hears and is glad,
 and the towns of Judah rejoice,
 because of your judgments, O God.

9 For you, O Lord, are most high over all the
  earth;
 you are exalted far above all gods.

10 The Lord loves those who hate evil;
 he guards the lives of his faithful;
 he rescues them from the hand of the
  wicked.

11 Light dawns for the righteous,
 and joy for the upright in heart.

12 Rejoice in the Lord, O you righteous,
 and give thanks to his holy name!

firestorm, the steadiness of flowing lava, or the calm of burning candle wax.

Hearts and spirits everywhere who have known such love, who have been raised with it, who have profited from it, acknowledge its worth. They discount the benighted claims of anyone who would discount it as useless or even harmful. To obey heavenly decrees or to acknowledge divine punishments is to accept God's love in its entirety.

Oppressive Thought: God does not discipline.

Oppressive Image: Weakness

Edifying Thought: God's authority is loving.

Edifying Image: A just and honored king

The proclamation of your love, dear Lord, soothes a soul wounded by inordinate fear of your punishments. Yet you reveal firm determination to reproach and chasten in accord with heavenly justice. Such forcefulness is reconciled with your faithful parental love that exhorts and reproves as well as comforts and forgives. May I revere every aspect of your devoted attention to me.

PSALM 98

Transformation

1 O sing to the Lord a new song,
    for he has done marvelous things
His right hand and his holy arm
    have gotten him victory.
	When I feel the refreshing touch of God, my life is so transformed that I see with new eyes. In places far and near, in areas I would not have explored until now, God's guiding hand is apparent. The love of the Lord that now lifts me up shows in the lives of other persons and other nations.

1 O sing to the Lord a new song,
　　for he has done marvelous things
His right hand and his holy arm
　　have gotten him victory.
2 The Lord has made known his victory;
　　he has revealed his vindication in the
　　　　sight of the nations.
3 He has remembered his steadfast love and
　　faithfulness
　　to the house of Israel.
All the ends of the earth have seen
　　the victory of our God.

When I feel the refreshing touch of God, my life is so transformed that I see with new eyes. In places far and near, in areas I would not have explored until now, God's guiding hand is apparent. The love of the Lord that now lifts me up shows in the lives of other persons and other nations.

4 Make a joyful noise to the Lord, all the earth
　　break forth into joyous song and sing
　　　　praises.
5 Sing praises to the Lord with the lyre,
　　with the lyre and the sound of melody.
6 With trumpets and the sound of the horn
　　make a joyful noise before the King, the
　　　　Lord.

God is surely praiseworthy! A song of joy and thanks fills my heart. I proclaim in spirited melodies the glories of the Lord. In my renewed condition, in my new life of grace, I experience my song blending with many more.

7 Let the sea roar, and all that fills it;
　　the world and those who live in it.
8 Let the floods clap their hands;
　　let the hills sing together for joy

Nature forms a chorus.

9 at the presence of the Lord, for he is coming
　　to judge the earth.
He will judge the world with righteousness,
　　and the peoples with equity.

And God is proclaimed as all peoples' gracious Lord.

Oppressive Thought: God's influence is
　　restricted.

Edifying Thought: I can see God's action in
　　new ways.

Oppressive Image: Defeat

Edifying Image: A chorus of praise

I love, O God, those precious times when I feel close to you and transformed. My eyes are opened to the deep abiding goodness, your very life, that permeates all things. The creation of which you are Lord becomes a sacrament of your glory. I blend with countless voices—nature's wonder and humanity's excellence—to sing your praise.

PSALM 99

Divine Authority

<table>
<tr>
<td>1</td>
<td>The Lord is king; let the peoples tremble!
    He sits enthroned upon the cherubim; let the
      earth quake!</td>
<td>*The Lord's authority extends to all, to every place and people under the heavens.*</td>
</tr>
<tr>
<td>2</td>
<td>The Lord is great in Zion;
    he is exalted over all the peoples.</td>
<td></td>
</tr>
<tr>
<td>3</td>
<td>Let them praise your great and awesome name.
    Holy is he!</td>
<td rowspan="2">*We do well to recall that living in God's love means conforming to God's ways. Obedience to a righteous and holy Lord should be esteemed as a virtue everywhere. God does not let justice be long ignored.*</td>
</tr>
<tr>
<td>4</td>
<td>Mighty King, lover of justice,
    you have established equity;
you have executed justice
    and righteousness in Jacob.</td>
</tr>
<tr>
<td>5</td>
<td>Extol the Lord our God;
    worship at his footstool.
    Holy is he!</td>
<td></td>
</tr>
<tr>
<td>6</td>
<td>Moses and Aaron were among his priests,
    Samuel also was among those who called on
      his name.
    They cried to the Lord, and he
      answered them.</td>
<td rowspan="2">*Prophets and priests, those whose leadership we admire, have respected the limits of the Creator's tolerance. And God responded to their dutifulness with constancy and compassion.*</td>
</tr>
<tr>
<td>7</td>
<td>He spoke to them in the pillar of cloud;
    they kept his decrees,
    and the statutes that he gave them.</td>
</tr>
<tr>
<td>8</td>
<td>O Lord our God, you answered them;
    you were a forgiving God to them,
    but an avenger of their wrongdoings.</td>
<td></td>
</tr>
<tr>
<td>9</td>
<td>Extol the Lord our God,
    and worship at his holy mountain;
    for the Lord our God is holy.</td>
<td>*May praise of God's holiness include thanks for divine justice.*</td>
</tr>
</table>

Oppressive Thought: God does not punish.

Edifying Thought: God loves and has expectations.

Oppressive Image: Fainthearted authority

Edifying Image: An imposing mountain

I need never regret your justice, O God, for it always attends to my uniqueness, always respects my dignity. Your authority over me and all your children sets rightful limits on us and directs us toward our own good. May my desires and prayers conform to your sacred designs.

PSALM 100

Joy

1 Make a joyful noise to the Lord, all the earth.
2 Worship the Lord with gladness;
   come into his presence with singing.
3 Know that the Lord is God.
   It is he that made us, and we are his;
   we are his people, and the sheep of his pasture.
4 Enter his gates with thanksgiving,
   and his courts with praise.
   Give thanks to him, bless his name.
5 For the Lord is good;
   his steadfast love endures forever,
   and his faithfulness to all generations.

If all peoples at every moment offered joyful prayers of praise to God, how wonderful the world would be. Exultant souls would find comfort and security, sure that a wise creator protects and loves them. An enduring song of thanksgiving would swell before the Lord.

God's eternal goodness would be forever cherished in every heart. It would be heaven on earth. Let it be.

Oppressive Thought: Optimism must be strictly controlled.

Edifying Thought: Joy can be infectious.

Oppressive Image: Alone in a pasture

Edifying Image: A happy world

Let me dream, O Lord, of a happy world, of a world renewed by love of you. Accept my dream as an act of hope. Let my hope, dear God, bring me peace. In my tranquil soul let there swell the joy of knowing the full expanse of your grandeur. Let my exultation inspire me to love more greatly you and your creation.

PSALM 101

Integrity

1 I will sing of loyalty and of justice;
      to you, O Lord, I will sing.
2 I will study the way that is blameless.
      When shall I attain it?
   I will walk with integrity of heart
      within my house;
3 I will not set before my eyes
      anything that is base.
   I hate the work of those who fall away;
      it shall not cling to me.
4 Perverseness of heart shall be far from me
      I will know nothing of evil.
5 One who secretly slanders a neighbor
      I will destroy.
   A haughty look and an arrogant heart
      I will not tolerate.
6 I will look with favor on the faithful in the land,
      so that they may live with me;
   whoever walks in the way that is blameless
      shall minister to me.
7 No one who practices deceit
      shall remain in my house;
   no one who utters lies
      shall continue in my presence.
8 Morning by morning I will destroy
      all the wicked in the land,
   cutting off all evildoers
      from the city of the Lord.

I aspire, O Lord, to what I know you love—innocence and integrity. Though I make mistakes, I want to do my best, day by day, to do what is good, to be upright and honorable.

Knowing that my judgments of others, how they appear in my eyes, can be more truly a reflection of what I myself am and do, I will look for good instead of evil.

When I see wrongdoing, when I am offended by what appears as misguided or destructive, I shall first wonder if I, more truly, am the malfactor. And I will try to change.

Oppressive Thought: They need to be corrected.

Edifying Thought: I need to be corrected.

Oppressive Image: Liars

Edifying Image: A pure heart

Let me aim for my own integrity, O Lord, before I campaign for other people's reform. Help me to find in my environment those exemplars of virtue who inspire me to aim higher, to complete my mission of dispelling evil from my own life, of abandoning my sins, of embracing your truth, of developing every capacity you have given me.

PSALM 102

Hope Wavering

1 Hear my prayer, O Lord;
     let my cry come to you.

2 Do not hide your face from me
     in the day of my distress.
   Incline your ear to me;
     answer me speedily in the day when I call.

3 For my days pass away like smoke,
     and my bones burn like a furnace.

4 My heart is stricken and withered like grass;
     I am too wasted to eat my bread.

5 Because of my loud groaning
     my bones cling to my skin.

6 I am like an owl of the wilderness,
     like a little owl of the waste places.

7 I lie awake;
     I am like a lonely bird on the housetop.

8 All day long my enemies taunt me;
     those who deride me use my name for a
       curse.

9 For I eat ashes like bread,
     and mingle tears with my drink,

10 because of your indignation and anger;
     for you have lifted me up and thrown me
       aside.

11 My days are like an evening shadow;
     I wither away like grass.

12 But you, O Lord, are enthroned forever;
     your name endures to all generations.

13 You will rise up and have compassion on Zion,
     for it is time to favor it;
       the appointed time has come.

When I sorrow or am afflicted, when I sense keenly my own immortality, I long for you, Lord. But in my distress I hear your voice, see your face, feel your presence only off and on. Consolation and desolation circle one another, playfully and tragically. A fever manifests my parched spirit. Listlessness reveals the fatigue of my soul. My body and mind wither. Who will nurse a bird, alone and cold, fallen from its nest? Who will console me as I mourn my own destiny? Who?

God, who lives forever! You have had compassion on your people before, O Lord.

171

14 For your servants hold its stones dear, and have pity on its dust.	*We have known the joy of your power in our midst. Before many others we have witnessed your glory.*
15 The nations will fear the name of the Lord, and all the kings of the earth your glory.	
16 For the Lord will build up Zion; he will appear in his glory.	
17 He will regard the prayer of the destitute, and will not despise their prayer.	*From your heaven you love us. Out of your compassion you have chosen to stand by us. You are here, Lord, and I love you. Spare me now. Do not let me lose you again.*

18 Let this be recorded for a generation to come,
  so that a people yet unborn may praise the
    Lord:	

19 that he looked down from his holy height, from heaven the Lord looked at the earth,	
20 to hear the groans of the prisoners, to set free those who were doomed to die;	

21 so that the name of the Lord may be declared
    in Zion,
  and his praise in Jerusalem,	

22 when peoples gather together, and kingdoms, to worship the Lord.	
23 He has broken my strength in midcourse; he has shortened my days.	*I cling to you as I cling to life. And I long for security.*

24 "O my God," I say, "do not take me away
  at the mid-point of my life,
you whose years endure
  throughout all generations."	

25 Long ago you laid the foundation of the earth, and the heavens are the work of your hands.	*My heart assures me that no hand is as reliable as yours. Like a loving parent you are steady in your protection and nurture.*

26 They will perish, but you endure;
  they will all wear out like a garment.
You change them like clothing, and they
    pass away;	

27 but you are the same, and your years have no end.	

28 The children of your servants shall live secure;
  their offspring shall be established in your
    presence.
	I am your child forever.

Oppressive Thought: I am nothing but prey.   *Edifying Thought:* God does not forget us.

Oppressive Image: A lost fledgling   *Edifying Image:* A loved child

When my afflicted soul feels dry, dear Lord, when I hunger for more life, let me not relinquish fond memories of your consolations. My backward glances on your kindness remind me of your fidelity. Then, in my unsteady state, I find firm ground. You become again my hope and my sustenance. You love me into a finer mood.

PSALM 103

Divine Mercy

1 Bless the Lord, O my soul,
      and all that is within me,
         bless his holy name.
2 Bless the Lord, O my soul,
      and do not forget all his benefits —
3 who forgives all your iniquity,
      who heals all your diseases,
4 who redeems your life from the Pit,
      who crowns you with steadfast love and
         mercy,
5 who satisfies you with good as long as you live
      so that your youth is renewed like the eagle's.
6 The Lord works vindication
      and justice for all who are oppressed.
7 He made known his ways to Moses,
      his acts to the people of Israel.
8 The Lord is merciful and gracious,
      slow to anger and abounding in steadfast
         love.
9 He will not always accuse,
      nor will he keep his anger forever.
10 He does not deal with us according to our sins,
      nor repay us according to our iniquities.
11 For as the heavens are high above the earth,
      so great is his steadfast love toward those
         who fear him;
12 as far as the east is from the west,
      so far he removes our transgressions from
         us.
13 As a father has compassion for his children,
      so the Lord has compassion for those who

God gives me such new life that I want, with all my being, to raise toward heaven a song of thanks and praise. There are times when my body manifests through health and agility that I have been transformed from within, renewed through and through, healed of inner hurts, freed from serious faults, forgiven of terrible misdeeds. My spirit soars, witnessing that God is full of compassion and love. For the Lord, like a dutiful parent, not only makes demands, not only disciplines, but is lenient at times and in ways that truly benefit all of us.

The expanse of divine mercy is incalculable, and so is the debt of my sins. In my repentance I can find peace. I can feel assured that God no longer measures my debt but gazes into my heart, touches my depths with kindness and affection.

fear him.

14 For he knows how we were made;
   he remembers that we are dust.
15 As for mortals, their days are like grass;
   they flourish like a flower of the field;
16 for the wind passes over it, and it is gone,
   and its place knows it no more.
17 But the steadfast love of the Lord is from
       everlasting to everlasting
       on those who fear him,
   and his righteousness to children's children,
18 to those who keep his covenant
   and remember to do his commandments.
19 The Lord has established his throne in the
       heavens,
   and his kingdom rules over all.
20 Bless the Lord, O you his angels,
   you mighty ones who do his bidding,
   obedient to his spoken word.
21 Bless the Lord, all his hosts,
   his ministers that do his will.
22 Bless the Lord, all his works,
   in all places of his dominion.
   Bless the Lord, O my soul.

God has made us achievers but knows what obstacles we face. The Lord gives us new life but sees that we are fragile.

I therefore entrust myself to divine ways with confidence that my own children, or all the generations that follow mine, will find the wisdom to do the same.

Thus will unending praise redound to God, whose dominion is over every time and place.

Oppressive Thought: God is unrelenting.

Edifying Thought: God is lenient.

Oppressive Image: Wilted grass

Edifying Image: A forgiving parent

My faith in your mercy, O Lord my God, frees me from oppressive monotony. My spirit, at times even my physical energy, is renewed through delighting in your loving acceptance. I strive never to toy with your compassion by languishing in my sin and presumptuously counting on your good will. I desire only to be lifted up by your kind godly attention.

PSALM 104

Providence

1 Bless the Lord, O my soul.
   O Lord my God, you are very great.
You are clothed with honor and majesty,
2   wrapped in light as with a garment.
You stretch out the heavens like a tent,
3   you set the beams of your chambers on the
        waters,
you make the clouds your chariot,
   you ride on the wings of the wind,
4 you make the winds your messengers,
   fire and flame your ministers.
5 You set the earth on its foundations,
   so that it shall never be shaken.
6 You cover it with the deep as with a garment;
   the waters stood above the mountains.
7 At your rebuke they flee;
   at the sound of your thunder they take to
      flight.
8 They rose up to the mountains, ran down to
      the valleys
   to the place that you appointed for them.
9 You set a boundary that they may not pass,
   so that they might not again cover the
      earth.
10 You make springs gush forth in the valleys;
   they flow between the hills,
11 giving drink to every wild animal;
   the wild asses quench their thirst.
12 By the streams the birds of the air have their
      habitation;
   they sing among the branches.
13 From your lofty abode you water the
      mountains;
   the earth is satisfied with the fruit of your
      work.
14 You cause the grass to grow for the cattle,
   and plants for people to use,

How refreshed I am, O Lord, by opening my eyes to the beauty of your creation, by sensing again your power as it extends generously from heaven and penetrates all the earth.

In my daily routine, with eyes and ears dulled to the fullness of life, I simply assume that nature takes its course. But when I see the light, when your wonders ignite my soul, the joy of seeing your hand everywhere renews me. In this world of yours, order prevails. Nature may here and there raise its head rebelliously, but overall, as days come and go, as seasons turn, as ages pass, your design is the rule.

Running waters nurture life. Vegetation, green and luxuriant, provides food, havens, and shelter. All parts of nature, the whole environment, Earth's vast store of elements reach out to one another in harmony, support one another in sacred unison. All who can know you in their hearts, like those who also pray, are part of the arrangement. So the human heart receives as blessings from your hand nature's favorite gifts.

to bring forth food from the earth,
15   and wine to gladden the human heart
oil to make the face shine,
    and bread to strengthen the human heart.
16 The trees of the Lord are watered
       abundantly,
    the cedars of Lebanon that he planted.
17 In them the birds build their nests;
    the stork has its home in the fir trees.
18 The high mountains are for the wild goats;
    the rocks are a refuge for the coneys.
19 You have made the moon to mark the
       seasons;
    the sun knows its time for setting.
20 You make darkness, and it is night,
    when all the animals of the forest come
       creeping out.
21 The young lions roar for their prey
    seeking their food from God.
22 When the sun rises, they withdraw
    and lie down in their dens.
23 People go out to their work
    and to their labor until the evening.
24 O Lord, how manifold are your works!
    In wisdom you have made them all;
    the earth is full of your creatures.
25 Yonder is the sea, great and wide,
    creeping things innumerable are there,
    living things both small and great.
26 There go the ships,
    and Leviathan that you formed to sport in
      it.
27 These all look to you
    to give them their food in due season;
28 when you give to them, they gather it up;
    when you open your hand, they are filled
      with good things.
29 When you hide your face, they are dismayed;
    when you take away their breath, they die
    and return to their dust.
30 When you send forth your spirit, they are
      created;

Everything has its proper time and place, times for growth and pleasure, times for rest and renewal. And all because of you, my God. While we are secure in our tended world, the distant stars and planets fulfill their missions in the vast expanses of your cosmos.

Infinite in your power, boundless in your presence, you are nonetheless nearby. You draw close and in a whisper offer care. We need only to turn to you, to open our hearts to you, to know your dedication and your remarkable generosity. It is to our shame and to our loss not to recognize your divine goodness. Your energy, your own life-giving breath, shapes and refashions the entire habitation that, by your Word, has become ours.

and you renew the face of the ground.

31 May the glory of the Lord endure forever;
   may the Lord rejoice in his works—

32 who looks on the earth and it trembles,
   who touches the mountains and they
     smoke.

33 I will sing to the Lord as long as I live;
   I will sing praise to my God while I have
     being.

34 May my meditation be pleasing to him,
   for I rejoice in the Lord.

35 Let sinners be consumed from the earth,
   and let the wicked be no more.
   Bless the Lord, O my soul.
   Praise the Lord!

*How well I do then to praise you,
Lord. I desire for my soul the luster
of joy, the reflection of your own
brilliance in what you have made.*

*May I know darkness no more in
knowing you above all.*

Oppressive Thought: Life is dull.

Edifying Thought: God empowers all
   creation.

Oppressive Image: A dreary day

Edifying Image: A new Earth

*Wake my soul, O Lord, to the vastness of your plan for us. Refresh me with a keener sense of
your boundless providence. Calm me through a broader vision of your designs for our world,
for indeed the entire universe. Forgetting how you work everywhere, I am prey to pessimism.
Remembering your infinite wisdom, I am endued with hope.*

PSALM 105

Thankfulness

1 O give thanks to the Lord, call on his name,
   make known his deeds among the
     peoples.

2 Sing to him, sing praises to him;
   tell of all his wonderful works.

3 Glory in his holy name;
   let the hearts of those who seek the
     Lord rejoice.

*When I feel far from God and
somewhat down, I find it uplifting
to recall thankfully all that God
has done in my life. This helps me
find my way back to that divine
Presence by which I have lived,
and by which I am strong.*

4   Seek the Lord and his strength;
        seek his presence continually.
5   Remember the wonderful works he has
            done,
        his miracles, and the judgments he
            uttered,
6   O offspring of his servant Abraham,
        children of Jacob, his chosen ones.
7   He is the Lord our God;
        his judgments are in all the earth.
8   He is mindful of his covenant forever,
        of the word that he commanded, for a
            thousand generations,
9   the covenant that he made with Abraham,
        his sworn promise to Isaac,
10   which he confirmed to Jacob as a statute,
        to Israel as an everlasting covenant,
11   saying, "To you I will give the land of
            Canaan
        as your portion for an inheritance."
12   When they were few in number,
        of little account, and strangers in it,
13   wandering from nation to nation,
        from one kingdom to another people,
14   he allowed no one to oppress them;
        he rebuked kings on their account,
15   saying, "Do not touch my anointed ones;
        do my prophets no harm."
16   When he summoned famine against the
            land,
        and broke every staff of bread,
17   he had sent a man ahead of them,
        Joseph, who was sold as a slave.
18   His feet were hurt with fetters,
        his neck was put in a collar of iron;
19   until what he had said came to pass,
        the word of the Lord kept testing him.
20   The king sent and released him;
        the ruler of the peoples set him free.
21   He made him lord of his house,
        and ruler of all his possessions,
22   to instruct his officials at his pleasure,

How glad I am, first of all, that I learned of God from my elders, from my parents and all those who took charge of me. I was taught that God is everywhere, faithfully watching over all peoples throughout history. Yet, from such a large group God could single me out for special blessings and special protection. How secure that made me feel! How wonderful it is to have learned that! How glad I am that I believed it! All of that was good. And I am grateful.

I came to depend on God's presence, to believe that I was being cared for, to expect that my needs would be met. That too was good. And I am grateful.

As I encountered difficulties, even early in my life, I learned to trust that the Lord was seeing me through them. That too was good. And I am grateful. In my youth I often felt captive to ways that were strange, to expectations that others had of me. Though I would rebel, I came to learn that God's wisdom took all things into account, so that no matter what, I could still trust in the Lord's power to have things come out well. That too was good. And I am grateful.

and to teach his elders wisdom.

23 Then Israel came to Egypt;
    Jacob lived as an alien in the land of
        Ham.
24 And the Lord made his people very
        fruitful,
    and made them stronger than their foes,
25 whose hearts he then turned to hate his
        people,
    to deal craftily with his servants.
26 He sent his servant Moses,
    and Aaron whom he had chosen.
27 They performed his signs among them,
    and miracles in the land of Ham.
28 He sent darkness, and made the land dark;
    they rebelled against his words.
29 He turned their waters into blood,
    and caused their fish to die.
30 Their land swarmed with frogs,
    even in the chambers of their kings.
31 He spoke, and there came swarms of flies,
    and gnats throughout their country.
32 He gave them hail for rain,
    and lightning that flashed through their
        land.
33 He struck their vines and fig trees,
    and shattered the trees of their country.
34 He spoke, and the locusts came,
    and young locusts without number;
35 they devoured all the vegetation in their
        land,
    and ate up the fruit of their ground.
36 He struck down all the firstborn in their
        land,
    the first issue of all their strength.
37 Then he brought Israel out with silver and
        gold,
    and there was no one among their tribes
        who stumbled.
38 Egypt was glad when they departed,
    for dread of them had fallen upon it.
39 He spread a cloud for a covering,

As a young adult and ready to conquer the world, I was rather productive. But the joys of success were regularly tempered by the normal stresses of life.

Yet I was not alone. At each time of need, someone was there to help, to give support, to dissuade me from succumbing to the darkness of self-pity, to help my tears be cleansing rather than embittering, to incite me to cast out oppressive thoughts, ideas that worked against me and my serenity. I came to believe that God sent such helpers. That too was good. And I am grateful.

Even when I was plagued by illnesses or had to face alone the darkness under the surgeon's knife, I learned the value of trusting God and knowing all would be well. That too was good. And I am grateful.

and fire to give light by night.

40 They asked, and he brought quails,
and gave them food from heaven in
abundance.
41 He opened the rock, and water gushed out;
it flowed through the desert like a river.
42 For he remembered his holy promise,
and Abraham, his servant.
43 So he brought his people out with joy,
his chosen ones with singing.
44 He gave them the lands of the nations,
and they took possession of the wealth
of the peoples,
45 that they might keep his statutes
and observe his laws.
Praise the Lord!

I learned to rejoice that God was so wise that even a dreaded situation could be made to work for my good. I saw that God, though often unobserved, was able to guide my course, sustain me, and revive me. That too was good. And I am grateful. I have indeed had my sad or desperate times. But I have always been able to return to what joy this earth has for me. I have learned that God always provides. That too is good. And I am truly grateful!

Oppressive Thought: I am helpless.

Edifying Thought: God has always been
there for me.

Oppressive Image: Plagues

Edifying Image: A new land

Give me, my God, the grace to survey my life with an eye to your blessings. Help me assay the sadder times without being so intent on them that I am enfeebled by remorse. Stir in me excitement for a broader vision of the finer things, the wonderful things, that have enriched my days and made them fruitful. Thankful for all you have done, I look to the future with energizing expectancy.

PSALM 106

Confession

1 Praise the Lord!
O give thanks to the Lord, for he is good;
for his steadfast love endures forever.
2 Who can utter the mighty doings of the Lord,
or declare all his praise?
3 Happy are those who observe justice,
who do righteousness at all times.

God has been so kind to me that I cannot recount every blessing. I praise my Lord, however, and strive for that supreme peace that comes with living by divine designs. Help me, Lord, to do what is right, to rejoice in your graces,

4 Remember me, O Lord, when you show favor
    to your people;
  help me when you deliver them;
5 that I may see the prosperity of your chosen
    ones,
    that I may rejoice in the gladness of your
    nation,
    that I may glory in your heritage.
6 Both we and our ancestors have sinned;
    we have committed iniquity, have done
    wickedly.
7 Our ancestors, when they were in Egypt,
    did not consider your wonderful works;
  they did not remember the abundance of your
    steadfast love,
    but rebelled against the Most High at the
    Red Sea.
8 Yet he saved them for his name's sake,
    so that he might make known his mighty
    power.
9 He rebuked the Red Sea, and it became dry;
    he led them through the deep as through a
    desert.
10 So he saved them from the hand of the foe,
    and delivered them from the hand of the
    enemy.
11 The waters covered their adversaries;
    not one of them was left.
12 Then they believed his words;
    they sang his praise.
13 But they soon forgot his works;
    they did not wait for his counsel.
14 But they had a wanton craving in the
    wilderness,
    and put God to the test in the desert;
15 he gave them what they asked,
    but sent a wasting disease among them.
16 They were jealous of Moses in the camp,
    and of Aaron, the holy one of the Lord.
17 The earth opened and swallowed up Dathan,
    and covered the faction of Abiram.
18 Fire also broke out in their company;

*to experience all that comes with
living in your love.*

*I have not always done what is
good in your sight; that I confess.
As a sinner I have imitated or
instigated behaviors that bring
shame on your people, that have
impaired spiritual progress. But
you were always there, Lord, a
companion on my journey.*

*You saw me through harrowing
times despite my weaknesses. I was
able, thanks to you, to move
beyond some hardened tendencies.
My later falls came with attempts
to advance alone, neglecting my
relationship with you.*

*In trying your patience, Lord, I
squandered precious time and
reaped what I deserved.*

*I thought so little of myself that I
did not welcome others' distinctive
gifts. I was consumed by my own
false humility, insatiably trying to
be what I was not. I turned to the*

the flame burned up the wicked.
19   They made a calf at Horeb
         and worshiped a cast image.
20   They exchanged the glory of God
         for the image of an ox that eats grass.
21   They forgot God, their Savior,
         who had done great things in Egypt,
22   wondrous works in the land of Ham,
         and awesome deeds by the Red Sea.
23   Therefore he said he would destroy them—
         had not Moses, his chosen one,
      stood in the breach before him,
         to turn away his wrath from destroying
            them.
24   Then they despised the pleasant land,
         having no faith in his promise.
25   They grumbled in their tents,
         and did not obey the voice of the Lord.
26   Therefore he raised his hand and swore to
            them
         that he would make them fall in the
            wilderness,
27   and would disperse their descendants among
            the nations,
         scattering them over the lands.
28   Then they attached themselves to the Baal of
            Peor,
         and ate sacrifices offered to the dead;
29   they provoked the Lord to anger with their
            deeds,
         and a plague broke out among them.
30   Then Phinehas stood up and interceded,
         and the plague was stopped.
31   And that has been reckoned to him as
            righteousness
         from generation to generation forever.
32   They angered the Lord at the waters of
            Meribah,
         and it went ill with Moses on their account;
33   for they made his spirit bitter,
         and he spoke words that were rash.
34   They did not destroy the peoples,

wrong places for security. Rather than finding my peace, first and foremost, in knowing you, my God, I sought things that only looked important, that deceived me with their allure. You were kind enough, however, not to let me totally degenerate through such idolatry.

When I failed to trust you, when I rebelled against your plans for me, it became clear that I was only hurting myself, contributing to my own undoing. I was associating with the wrong people, participating in activities that poisoned both my soul and body.

But you sent the right person at the right time to spare me substantial damage.

Nonetheless, I was frequently enough a bad influence. My own misbehavior had its effect on others. Rather than work at rooting out my vices, I was content to live with them.

as the Lord commanded them,
35 but they mingled with the nations
and learned to do as they did.
36 They served their idols,
which became a snare to them.
37 They sacrificed their sons
and their daughters to the demons;
38 they poured out innocent blood,
the blood of their sons and daughters,
whom they sacrificed to the idols of Canaan;
and the land was polluted with blood.
39 Thus they became unclean by their acts,
and prostituted themselves in their doings.
40 Then the anger of the Lord was kindled
against his people,
and he abhorred his heritage;
41 he gave them into the hand of the nations,
so that those who hated them ruled over
them.
42 Their enemies oppressed them,
and they were brought into subjection
under their power.
43 Many times he delivered them,
but they were rebellious in their purposes,
and were brought low through their
iniquity.
44 Nevertheless he regarded their distress
when he heard their cry.
45 For their sake he remembered his covenant,
and showed compassion according to the
abundance of his steadfast love.
46 He caused them to be pitied
by all who held them captive.
47 Save us, O Lord our God,
and gather us from among the nations,
that we may give thanks to your holy name
and glory in your praise.
48 Blessed be the Lord, the God of Israel,
from everlasting to everlasting.
And let all the people say, "Amen."
Praise the Lord!

They trapped me, and I became addicted to what I thus unhealthily craved. I was uncaring enough to let the younger ones observe and even imitate my foul ways. They thus became victims of my own deviance. Such wretchedness rebounded on me as multiplication of my shame and as punishment for my wrongdoing. So I had even less possession of myself, even less occasion to experience dignity.

Even when you were merciful to me, Lord, when you gave me opportunities to see the light, I stubbornly refused them. Yet in your steadfast love, you persisted, you pursued.

When you had me, or when I saw that you did, I fell humbly before you, weeping in sorrow. Help me, O God, always to remember this confession. Give me the grace to know my errors, to be thankful for your forgiveness, and to thrive forever in your love.

Oppressive Thought: My sins are hidden
  and harmless.

Edifying Thought: God lovingly awaits my
  confession.

Oppressive Image: Dark depths of the earth

Edifying Image: A gladdened nation

Lord, I am so vulnerable to the allurements of idols, to the temptations of things or places or persons that harmfully distract me from you. You are with me always, but I am too often distant from you. I am so sorry, my God, to have failed you. I will make up for my deficiency. I will strive to turn my life once and for all toward you. The "rewards" of my sins are so deceptive. The sweetness of knowing you is genuine and lasting.

PSALM 107

Thankfulness

1 O give thanks to the Lord, for he is good;
    for his steadfast love endures forever.
2 Let the redeemed of the Lord say so,
    those he redeemed from trouble
3 and gathered in from the lands,
    from the east and from the west,
    from the north and from the south.
4 Some wandered in desert wastes,
    finding no way to an inhabited town;
5 hungry and thirsty,
    their soul fainted within them.
6 Then they cried to the Lord in their trouble,
    and he delivered them from their
      distress;
7 he led them by a straight way,
    until they reached an inhabited town.
8 Let them thank the Lord for his steadfast
      love,
    for his wonderful works to humankind.
9 For he satisfies the thirsty,
    and the hungry he fills with good things.
10 Some sat in darkness and in gloom,
    prisoners in misery and in irons,

God's love is constant. With my life now changed, I recognize how often the Lord has touched me, how divine energy brought the varied aspects of my past into an impressive harmony.

At times I was lonely, in a strange place with no guide or friend. Longing for companionship, I turned to God and was given comfort. God's spirit led me; kindly people reached out to me.

Thank you, Lord, for your kindness. You were there with what I needed at just the right time. At times I was depressed, brought low, and shackled by expectations that were not being met. They could not be met because they were adverse

11 for they had rebelled against the words of
      God,
        and spurned the counsel of the Most
          High.

12 Their hearts were bowed down with hard
      labor;
        they fell down, with no one to help.

13 Then they cried to the Lord in their trouble,
        and he saved them from their distress;

14 he brought them out of darkness and
      gloom,
        and broke their bonds asunder.

15 Let them thank the Lord for his steadfast
      love,
        for his wonderful works to humankind.

16 For he shatters the doors of bronze,
        and cuts in two the bars of iron.

17 Some were sick through their sinful ways,
        and because of their iniquities endured
          affliction;

18 they loathed any kind of food,
        and they drew near to the gates of death.

19 Then they cried to the Lord in their trouble,
        and he saved them from their distress;

20 he sent out his word and healed them,
        and delivered them from destruction.

21 Let them thank the Lord for his steadfast
      love,
        for his wonderful works to humankind.

22 And let them offer thanksgiving sacrifices,
        and tell of his deeds with songs of joy.

23 Some went down to the sea in ships,
        doing business on the mighty waters;

24 they saw the deeds of the Lord,
        his wondrous works in the deep.

25 For he commanded and raised the stormy
      wind,
        which lifted up the waves of the sea.

26 They mounted up to heaven, they went
      down to the depths;
        their courage melted away in their
          calamity;

to God's will, to the divine plan for my life. I held fast to these longings, however, and thus struggled against my nature.

When I prayed for help, the Lord let me see my irrationality, showed me goals that were attainable.

How thankful I am for the new joys I found, and the new freedom. At times my body revealed my excesses: too much work or too much pleasure that led to sluggishness, infection, and loss of appetite, sometimes the appetite for life itself.

I could not help but pray. My words were a cry of anguish. God's soothing touch brought me good health, and I could again give thanks for the Lord's wondrous care.

At times I overextended myself, took on a sea of responsibilities that I could not maintain. God did not stop me but let me become engulfed. I reeled under the pressure and grew so fainthearted that I nearly despaired. Again, though, when I prayed, the Lord led the way.

27 they reeled and staggered like drunkards,
    and were at their wits' end.
28 Then they cried to the Lord in their trouble,
    and he brought them out from their
    distress;
29 he made the storm be still,
    and the waves of the sea were hushed.
30 Then they were glad because they had
    quiet,
    and he brought them to their desired
    haven.
31 Let them thank the Lord for his steadfast
    love,
    for his wonderful works to humankind.
32 Let them extol him in the congregation of
    the people,
    and praise him in the assembly of the
    elders.

Many of the tasks no longer looked so urgent. I could survey the scene with tranquility and discretion. How thankful I am for such moments of grace. May others who still feel overwhelmed turn to God for guidance and peace.

33 He turns rivers into a desert,
    springs of water into thirsty ground,
34 a fruitful land into a salty waste,
    because of the wickedness of its
    inhabitants.
35 He turns a desert into pools of water,
    a parched land into springs of water.
36 And there he lets the hungry live,
    and they establish a town to live in;
37 they sow fields, and plant vineyards,
    and get a fruitful yield.
38 By his blessing they multiply greatly,
    and he does not let their cattle decrease.

God gives us new life when we feel dried up, adds spice to our bland days. To neglect the Lord is to instigate our own undoing. How wise it is then to relish God's ways, to seek divine nurture above all. There is no surer recipe for freshness and productivity.

39 When they are diminished and brought low
    through oppression, trouble, and sorrow,
40 he pours contempt on princes
    and makes them wander in trackless
    wastes;
41 but he raises up the needy out of distress,
    and makes their families like flocks.
42 The upright see it and are glad;
    and all wickedness stops its mouth.
43 Let those who are wise give heed to these
    things,

Whatever may befall us, whoever may attack, whatever griefs may plague us, God will not give them free reign. Their maliciousness will be undone. By the Lord's plan our deepest desires, our real needs, will be met. And we will rejoice again. God's love is constant. No matter what, it will always show itself.

and consider the steadfast love of the
    Lord.

Oppressive Thought: Everything goes from
    bad to worse.

Edifying Thought: I have much for which to
    be thankful.

Oppressive Image: Desert

Edifying Image: Fruitful vineyards

Dear God, how grateful I am that the ups and downs of my life are no gauge of your commit-ment to me and all your children. You have repeatedly sustained me in sorrows and helped to free me from constraints. Thank you for your constancy. With my hope in you renewed, my self-confidence is restored.

PSALM 108

Renewal

1 My heart is steadfast, O God, my heart is
      steadfast;
    I will sing and make melody.
    Awake, my soul!
2 Awake, O harp and lyre!
    I will awake the dawn.
3 I will give thanks to you, O Lord, among the
      peoples,
    and I will sing praises to you among the
      nations.
4 For your steadfast love is higher than the
      heavens,
    and your faithfulness reaches to the clouds.
5 Be exalted, O God, above the heavens,
    and let your glory be over all the earth.
6 Give victory with your right hand, and answer
      me,
    so that those whom you love may be
      rescued.
7 God has promised in his sanctuary:
    "With exultation I will divide up Shechem,

How I cherish the moments when I feel strong, when God's presence gives me new vigor. I am renewed from within and want to announce it to the world.

The Lord's power is great, extending from the heavens to every corner of the earth.

Let your might work everywhere, Lord; save us from all strife and sorrow.

When I feel close to God, when my faith is truly alive, I know with

and portion out the Vale of Succoth.

8 Gilead is mine; Manasseh is mine;
    Ephraim is my helmet;
    Judah is my scepter.
9 Moab is my washbasin;
    on Edom I hurl my shoe;
    over Philistia I shout in triumph."
10 Who will bring me to the fortified city?
    Who will lead me to Edom?
11 Have you not rejected us, O God?
    You do not go out, O God, with our armies.
12 O grant us help against the foe,
    for human help is worthless.
13 With God we shall do valiantly;
    it is he who will tread down our foes.

clarity that my weaknesses are ephemeral. Divine grace penetrates every part of me. My body, mind, and spirit harmonize while my trust in the Lord carries me forward.

As in the past, my faith will at times falter. But with God at my side I rally, revived by new hope.

Oppressive Thought: Renewal is only temporary.

Edifying Thought: Revival will come.

Oppressive Image: A defeated nation

Edifying Image: A steadfast heart

*Y*ou are my life, O Lord. By your grace, by your favor and support, my soul advances in virtue and becomes continually renewed. From my recurrent falls you lift me to new heights. My mind sees truth; my heart knows love; I nearly swoon with happiness. Living for you, I live fully.

PSALM 109

Needing Perspective

1 Do not be silent, O God of my praise.
2 For wicked and deceitful mouths are opened
      against me,
    speaking against me with lying tongues.
3 They beset me with words of hate,
    and attack me without cause.
4 In return for my love they accuse me,
    even while I make prayer for them.
5 So they reward me evil for good,

When I feel downtrodden, I need you, my wonderful Lord, to help me take lightly all that sounds unfair and abusive, or to identify and correct what seem to be insults of others but which are more my own oppressive self-accusations. I try to be loving and kind, but what I hear is that I

and hatred for my love.

6   They say, "Appoint a wicked man against
        him;
        let an accuser stand on his right.

7   When he is tried, let him be found guilty;
        let his prayer be counted as sin.

8   May his days be few;
        may another seize his position.

9   May his children be orphans,
        and his wife a widow.

10 May his children wander about and beg;
        may they be driven out of the ruins they
        inhabit.

11 May the creditor seize all that he has;
        may strangers plunder the fruits of his
        toil.

12 May there be no one to do him a kindness,
        nor anyone to pity his orphaned children.

13 May his posterity be cut off;
        may his name be blotted out in the
        second generation.

14 May the iniquity of his father be
        remembered before the Lord,
        and do not let the sin of his mother be
        blotted out.

15 Let them be before the Lord continually,
        and may his memory be cut off from the
        earth.

16 For he did not remember to show kindness,
        but pursued the poor and needy
        and the brokenhearted to their death.

17 He loved to curse; let curses come on him.
        He did not like blessing; may it be far from
        him.

18 He clothed himself with cursing as his coat,
        may it soak into his body like water,
        like oil into his bones.

19 May it be like a garment that he wraps
        around himself,
        like a belt that he wears every day."

20 May that be the reward of my accusers from
        the Lord,

*deserve recrimination and condem-
nation.*

*In their words I even hear a death
wish, so that I will have no more
responsibility, will no longer have
to sacrifice myself, for those given
into my care. They seem to want
me to lose anything that defines
me as a unique person and to be
deprived of any admiration,
whether of my contemporaries or
my descendants.*

*They want me to think, or so it
appears, that I can put blame for
my failings on my parents and thus
escape responsibility that is truly
my own.*

*They seem to find gratification in
depicting me as so malicious that I
bring on myself nothing but the
negative fruits of such deviance.
They therefore appear to wish that
I become thoroughly poisoned by
it.*

*Whatever devil provokes such
wishes, O Lord—be it a darkness*

of those who speak evil against my life.

21 But you, O Lord my Lord,
    act on my behalf for your name's sake;
    because your steadfast love is good,
      deliver me.

22 For I am poor and needy,
    and my heart is pierced within me.

23 I am gone like a shadow at evening;
    I am shaken off like a locust.

24 My knees are weak through fasting;
    my body has become gaunt.

25 I am an object of scorn to my accusers;
    when they see me, they shake their
      heads.

26 Help me, O Lord my God!
    Save me according to your steadfast love.

27 Let them know that this is your hand;
    you, O Lord, have done it.

28 Let them curse, but you will bless.
    Let my assailants be put to shame; may
      your servant be glad.

29 May my accusers be clothed with dishonor;
    may they be wrapped in their own shame
      as in a mantle.

30 With my mouth I will give great thanks to
      the Lord;
    I will praise him in the midst of the
      throng.

31 For he stands at the right hand of the needy,
    to save them from those who would
      condemn them to death.

within me or an evil influence on those I hear—let its destiny be as fatal as its designs for me. Let your love evoke in me a proper sense of my own worth. In my isolation from you, God, I lose perspective, and others rightly observe that I am something less than my true self.

Let your love so shine in me that the horrid accusations no longer ring true, to me or those I hear. Let my sense of dignity appear as a blessing that comes with acceptance by you, that dispels wrongful disdain and everywhere displays its falsity.

Such new life would please me, Lord. For the very hope of it I thank you with all my heart.

Oppressive Thought: The accusations are
    totally true.

Edifying Thought: God gives me proper
    perspective.

Oppressive Image: A gaunt body

Edifying Image: Praying for assailants

When *other seem to be degrading me, or when I take their words as degradation, I am plagued by darkness and suspicion. I lose my way amid judgments and accusations that sting and pierce, and at times bring me down. Be there for me, O Lord. Be the light by which I see, the glow by which I am warmed. Through you I humbly face the truth.*

PSALM 110

The Messiah

1 The Lord says to my lord,
  "Sit at my right hand until I make
  your enemies your footstool."
2 The Lord sends out from Zion
  your mighty scepter.
  Rule in the midst of your foes.
3 Your people will offer themselves willingly
  on the day you lead your forces
  on the holy mountains.
  From the womb of the morning,
  like dew, your youth will come to you.
4 The Lord has sworn and will not change his
    mind,
  "You are a priest forever
    according to the order of Melchizedek."
5 The Lord is at your right hand;
  he will shatter kings on the day of his wrath.
6 He will execute judgment among the nations,
  filling them with corpses;
  he will shatter heads
  over the wide earth.
7 He will drink from the stream by the path;
  therefore he will lift up his head.

God made our Lord and King, our Messiah, an instrument of our security and serenity. One with him through faith and loyalty, we can rise above our failings and rejoice that all enemies are rendered ultimately helpless.

Our Messiah is thus a priest linking us with heaven and revealing our dignity as God's protected children.

No threat can take from us this assurance that God has chosen to bless us forever.

Oppressive Thought: I am alone.

Oppressive Image: A corpse

Edifying Thought: My Lord saves me.

Edifying Image: A scepter

You have anointed one for us, O God. You have designated him our Messiah. Through him we know your faithful love. In him we see heaven triumph over powers of evil in every place and every heart. Our Lord and Messiah stands by his people and prevails. We are one with him in your victory over sin.

PSALM 111

Blessings

1 Praise the Lord!
 I will give thanks to the Lord with my
  whole heart,
   in the company of the upright, in the
   congregation.
2 Great are the works of the Lord,
  studied by all who delight in them.
3 Full of honor and majesty is his work,
  and his righteousness endures forever.
4 He has gained renown by his wonderful
   deeds;
   the Lord is gracious and merciful.
5 He provides food for those who fear him;
  he is ever mindful of his covenant.
6 He has shown his people the power of his
   works,
   in giving them the heritage of the
   nations.
7 The works of his hands are faithful and just;
  all his precepts are trustworthy.
8 They are established forever and ever,
  to be performed with faithfulness and
  uprightness.
9 He sent redemption to his people;
  he has commanded his covenant forever.
  Holy and awesome is his name.
10 The fear of the Lord is the beginning of
   wisdom;
   all those who practice it have a good
   understanding.
   His praise endures forever.

God's blessings are at times so manifest that I want to proclaim my thanks publicly and loudly.

Exceeding fragile human plans, the Lord's ways should be pondered. What God achieves is honorable, exalted, and of enduring value. Divine kindness and compassion combine with faithful care to demonstrate God's loving designs. We need only look around to see the Lord rewarding virtue. We need only trust that what God asks of us will lead to peace and joy.

The Lord has acted on our behalf with godly determination. To honor the divine plan for us, to let praise and thanksgiving be mutually eliciting, is to attain uncommon wisdom.

Oppressive Thought: God is not active in my life.

Edifying Thought: God's works are numerous.

Oppressive Image: A divided heart

Edifying Image: A whole heart

Your bounty, Lord, is revealed through the countless blessings that touch my life. The challenge is to recognize them. Circumstances, incidents, and fortune may appear as occasions of spontaneous convergence. On prayerful reconsideration, on examination with an eye of faith, they disclose your generous gifts. Help me, Lord, to find more.

PSALM 112

Authority

1 Praise the Lord!
Happy are those who fear the Lord,
 who greatly delight in his commandments.
2 Their descendants will be mighty in the
  land;
 the generation of the upright will be
  blessed.
3 Wealth and riches are in their houses,
 and their righteousness endures forever.
4 They rise in the darkness as a light for the
  upright;
 they are gracious, merciful, and
  righteous.
5 It is well with those who deal generously
  and lend,
 who conduct their affairs with justice.
6 For the righteous will never be moved;
 they will be remembered forever.
7 They are not afraid of evil tidings;
 their hearts are firm, secure in the Lord.
8 Their hearts are steady, they will not be
  afraid;
 in the end they will look in triumph on
  their foes.

To heed admirable authority is to profit from wise direction and to experience accomplishments. To exert authority admirably is to foster stability in the subject or in the next generation. Obedience to God is thus no burden but an occasion for rejoicing, like gratitude for a parent who combined love with discipline. One trained and nurtured in this way is spiritually fortified, exhibits with ease the virtues of kindness, compassion, generosity, and fairness.

Such a person is a prized example for others. Torn by isolation and rage, those who have not learned obedience, have not known proper authority, are unsure and fearful.

193

9   They have distributed freely, they have
        given to the poor;
      their righteousness endures forever;
      their horn is exalted in honor.
10 The wicked see it and are angry;
      they gnash their teeth and melt away;
      the desire of the wicked comes to
        nothing.

Their hearts long for the security of feeling loved and guided.

Oppressive Thought: Authority is harmful.

Edifying Thought: Admirable authority is fortifying.

Oppressive Image: An angry child

Edifying Image: A happy child

Help me, O God, in my appreciation of rightful authority. By your lordship over me, I am blessed with sound directives. Your Word is the way of truth. Open my eyes to trustworthy ways in the sway of civil and religious leadership. Stand by as I direct all those, young and old, who are accountable to me. I love you as my Lord and Master.

PSALM 113

Providence

1   Praise the Lord!
    Praise, O servants of the Lord;
      praise the name of the Lord.
2   Blessed be the name of the Lord
      from this time on and forevermore.
3   From the rising of the sun to its setting
      the name of the Lord is to be praised.
4   The Lord is high above all nations,
      and his glory above the heavens.
5   Who is like the Lord our God,
      who is seated on high,
6   who looks far down
      on the heavens and the earth?
7   He raises the poor from the dust,
      and lifts the needy from the ash heap,

May God be praised without limit in every place and time. May the world rejoice in the protection and compassion of our heavenly Lord.

The design for all creation springs from divine love. Who can imitate God's kindness? To what extent must we?

In due course the needy will be rescued and ennobled.

8   to make them sit with princes,
       with the princes of his people.
9   He gives the barren woman a home,
       making her the joyous mother of children.
     Praise the Lord!
	The unfruitful will become productive. And God will be rightly praised by dutiful servants.

<table>
<tr><td>Oppressive Thought: It is a sad world.</td><td>Edifying Thought: Praise God for all the world's good things.</td></tr>
<tr><td>Oppressive Image: An ash heap</td><td>Edifying Image: The rising sun</td></tr>
</table>

Fortify my soul, O Lord, by trust in your providence. Dispel the world's fear through greater reliance on your universal power. May I dutifully adapt my plans and actions to your wise designs. For you are God of the earth.

PSALM 114

Rejuvenation

1   When Israel went out from Egypt,
       the house of Jacob from a people of strange
         language,
	When I came out of my crisis, God was with me in a new and closer way.

2 Judah became God's sanctuary, Israel his dominion.	
3 The sea looked and fled; Jordan turned back.	*The grief and terror that had flooded my being were swept back and replaced by divine grace.*
4 The mountains skipped like rams, the hills like lambs.	
5 Why is it, O sea, that you flee? O Jordan, that you turn back?	*The obstacles that had appeared insurmountable were transfigured into settings of God's revelation.*
6 O mountains, that you skip like rams? O hills, like lambs?	
7 Tremble, O earth, at the presence of the Lord, at the presence of the God of Jacob,	*Such miracles, the effects of the Lord's love, are our inexhaustible sources of true life.*
8 who turns the rock into a pool of water, the flint into a spring of water.	

Oppressive Thought: There is no way out.

Oppressive Image: Bondage

Edifying Thought: God brings new life.

Edifying Image: Spring water

Turn me again and again, O Lord, to the wellspring of all that is good. Bring me to the source of my surest sustenance. Bring me anew to yourself. Stay me in your favor. Soothe my pain. Free me from uncertainty. Touch me through your wondrous deeds. Bless me with renewed vitality.

PSALM 115

Grace

1 Not to us, O Lord, not to us, but to your name
  give glory,
  for the sake of your steadfast love and your
  faithfulness.
2 Why should the nations say,
  "Where is their God?"
3 Our God is in the heavens;
  he does whatever he pleases.
4 Their idols are silver and gold,
  the work of human hands.
5 They have mouths, but do not speak;
  eyes, but do not see.
6 They have ears, but do not hear;
  noses, but do not smell.
7 They have hands, but do not feel;
  feet, but do not walk;
  they make no sound in their throats.
8 Those who make them are like them;
  so are all who trust in them.
9 O Israel, trust in the Lord!
  He is their help and their shield.
10 O house of Aaron, trust in the Lord!
  He is their help and their shield.
11 You who fear the Lord, trust in the Lord!
  He is their help and their shield.
12 The Lord has been mindful of us; he will bless

When I acknowledge God's heavenly glory, the constancy of divine love is impressed on me anew. My praise gives visible testimony of my faith that divinity is essentially something beyond me and beyond this world.

To believe otherwise would be to risk idolatry and the forfeiture of divine blessings. In such error and loss, the godliness in which I share, the grace by which I am transformed, is mistaken for a quality that is essentially mine.

Then I forget that whatever I say, see, hear, or sense serves me truly and fully because it is activated and guided by the Spirit of my Lord.

us;
>   he will bless the house of Israel;
>   he will bless the house of Aaron;

13 he will bless those who fear the Lord,
>   both small and great.

14 May the Lord give you increase,
>   both you and your children.

15 May you be blessed by the Lord,
>   who made heaven and earth.

16 The heavens are the Lord's heavens,
>   but the earth he has given to human beings.

17 The dead do not praise the Lord,
>   nor do any that go down into silence.

18 But we will bless the Lord
>   from this time on and forevermore.
>   Praise the Lord!

Any action or journey contributes to my life of peace and love because true divinity ennobles my mere humanness. Without this grace my life is empty and ultimately futile. In trusting God more than myself, I find security, growth, productivity, and a heavenly future.

Oppressive Thought: I do not need God.

Edifying Thought: God is my life.

Oppressive Image: An idol

Edifying Image: Heaven

Let me not, O God, make an idol of myself. Let my self-esteem be spiritually edifying. Let me not in weakness and sin take excessive credit for any good I do. Let my life acknowledge my faith in your godliness. Let my gratitude for your support, my joy in your grace, bespeak honor of you. Let what I say and do proclaim that you are my God.

PSALM 116

The Power of Prayer

1 I love the Lord, because he has heard
>   my voice and my supplications.

2 Because he inclined his ear to me,
>   therefore I will call on him as long as I live.

3 The snares of death encompassed me;
>   the pangs of Sheol laid hold on me;
>   I suffered distress and anguish.

4 Then I called on the name of the Lord:

The Lord that I love is totally reliable. My God's unwavering compassion is my lifelong consolation. From depths of misery and defeat I have prayed for help and have always been heard.

"O Lord, I pray, save my life!"

5   Gracious is the Lord, and righteous;
      our God is merciful.

6   The Lord protects the simple;
      when I was brought low, he saved me.

7   Return, O my soul, to your rest,
      for the Lord has dealt bountifully with you.

8   For you have delivered my soul from death,
      my eyes from tears,
      my feet from stumbling.

9   I walk before the Lord
      in the land of the living.

10   I kept my faith, even when I said,
      "I am greatly afflicted";

11   I said in my consternation,
      "Everyone is a liar."

12   What shall I return to the Lord
      for all his bounty to me?

13   I will lift up the cup of salvation
      and call on the name of the Lord,

14   I will pay my vows to the Lord
      in the presence of all his people.

15   Precious in the sight of the Lord
      is the death of his faithful ones.

16   O Lord, I am your servant;
      I am your servant, the child of your serving
        girl.
      You have loosed my bonds.

17   I will offer to you a thanksgiving sacrifice
      and call on the name of the Lord.

18   I will pay my vows to the Lord
      in the presence of all his people,

19   in the courts of the house of the Lord,
      in your midst, O Jerusalem.
      Praise the Lord!

The Lord reaches out with a parent's tender hand, offering me security and comfort. Held by God, I know ineffable peace. I have never been vanquished by threats to my life, attacks on my body, or assaults on my character.

Such onslaughts have been numerous and serious. Yet my faith kept me sure of God's constant and boundless mercy.

My prayer now is for a life that glorifies the Lord, for a spirit that radiates the kind of warmth and goodness that have come to me from God. I relinquish my trivial designs and place my life again in the hands of the Lord, who is generous, wise, and benevolent.

This is my public witness to the greatness of my God. This is my thanksgiving and Alleluia.

Oppressive Thought: God does not hear me.

Oppressive Image: A deaf ear

Edifying Thought: God answers all prayers.

Edifying Image: A kind parent

You have answered so many of my prayers, O Lord, not always immediately and not always as I wished. Yet your attendance to my pleas has been, for my growing faith, evidence enough that prayer is effective. Your words and deeds convince me, O God, that you want me to pray and that you reward me for persistence. You inspire me to confidence in you.

PSALM 117

Praise

1 Praise the Lord, all you nations!
    Extol him, all you peoples!
2 For great is his steadfast love toward us,
    and the faithfulness of the Lord endures
       forever.
   Praise the Lord!

My heart is so open to the Lord's devoted love that I see all people everywhere united in an unceasing song to our great God!

Oppressive Thought: God is largely ignored.

Edifying Thought: God is praised everywhere.

Oppressive Image: A silent nation

Edifying Image: A united world

My vision, Lord, of multitudes praising you corresponds to the love you have demonstrated to me. Your love is boundless. In your infinite goodness you love me and every other person wholly. You gift us with the power to celebrate your holiness universally. May we one day know such heavenly joy.

PSALM 118

Courage

1 O give thanks to the Lord, for he is good;
    his steadfast love endures forever!
2 Let Israel say,
    "His steadfast love endures forever."
3 Let the house of Aaron say,
    "His steadfast love endures forever."

Of all that is, of all that is within me and without, there is nothing more reliable than the steady, inexhaustible love of God. My heart inclining to worship assures me of this. So does my mind accounting

4	Let those who fear the Lord say,
		"His steadfast love endures forever."
5	Out of my distress I called on the Lord;
		the Lord answered me and set me in a
			broad place.
6	With the Lord on my side I do not fear.
		What can mortals do to me?
7	The Lord is on my side to help me;
		I shall look in triumph on those who
			hate me.
8	It is better to take refuge in the Lord
		than to put confidence in mortals.
9	It is better to take refuge in the Lord
		than to put confidence in princes.
10	All nations surrounded me;
		in the name of the Lord I cut them off!
11	They surrounded me, surrounded me on
			every side;
		in the name of the Lord I cut them off!
12	They surrounded me like bees;
		they blazed like a fire of thorns;
		in the name of the Lord I cut them off!
13	I was pushed hard, so that I was falling,
		but the Lord helped me.
14	The Lord is my strength and my might;
		he has become my salvation.
15	There are glad songs of victory in the
			tents of the righteous:
	"The right hand of the Lord does
			valiantly;
16		the right hand of the Lord is exalted;
		the right hand of the Lord does
			valiantly."
17	I shall not die, but I shall live,
		and recount the deeds of the Lord.
18	The Lord has punished me severely,
		but he did not give me over to death.
19	Open to me the gates of righteousness,
		that I may enter through them
		and give thanks to the Lord.
20	This is the gate of the Lord;
		the righteous shall enter through it.

for my sins.

In turmoil and discouragement I have sought divine help. And God lovingly and wisely put the sources of my pain far from me. In the depths of my soul rests the conviction that no consolation is as great as this. At times I have doubted, have looked to other persons or other things as my supreme good, desiring them as though they were all my heart's need.

But as I was besieged by diverse enemies, as inner doubts or unruly passions pressed upon me, I resisted valiantly, standing them off by the power of God, knowing how divine love enriched and strengthened me.

I may stumble or fall, but I will not succumb to permanent helplessness, not with the Lord as my Protector and Savior. The strength of God is the heart of my courage.

Fear of ultimate loss is foreign to my soul when I remember, when I rely upon, the goodness that the Lord works in me. Even death's fearsome threats become feeble whimpers in face of God's awesome might. The moments of consolation, the very real joys, the many blessings, the little tastes of

21 I thank you that you have answered me
    and have become my salvation.
22 The stone that the builders rejected
    has become the chief cornerstone.
23 This is the Lord's doing;
    it is marvelous in our eyes.
24 This is the day that the Lord has made;
    let us rejoice and be glad in it.
25 Save us, we beseech you, O Lord!
    O Lord, we beseech you, give us
      success!
26 Blessed is the one who comes in the
    name of the Lord.
    We bless you from the house of the
      Lord.
27 The Lord is God,
    and he has given us light.
    Bind the festal procession with branches,
    up to the horns of the altar.
28 You are my God, and I will give thanks to
    you;
    you are my God, I will extol you.
29 O give thanks to the Lord, for he is good,
    for his steadfast love endures forever.

the kingdom of God that I enjoy from time to time are fleeting signs of the heavenly realm that awaits me. The little losses that I suffer, the little deaths from which I rise, are reliable portents of that which God's marvelous love has designed for my eternal delight. In me, O Lord, in my life, which by many measures is small and insignificant, you have demonstrated the great truth of your redeeming love. For this I rejoice; for this I thank you with all my heart.

In the name of God, by the power of divine love, I thus make my journey through life. With praise and thanksgiving I approach by earthly steps the very heart of heaven.

Oppressive Thought: I am abandoned.

Edifying Thought: God's steadfast love
    endures forever.

Oppressive Image: Surrounded by bees

Edifying Image: The cornerstone

Knowing you, O God, gives me courage. Accepting your demonstrations of support sustains me in my struggles. Believing in your power fortifies my soul. You are my companion in every battle. I accept my charge with determination. Though I may someday fall, I will surely rise again with great might.

PSALM 119

The Law of God

1   Happy are those whose way is blameless,
     who walk in the law of the Lord.

2   Happy are those who keep his decrees,
     who seek him with their whole heart,

3   who also do no wrong,
     but walk in his ways.

4   You have commanded your precepts
     to be kept diligently.

5   O that my ways may be steadfast
     in keeping your statutes!

6   Then I shall not be put to shame,
     having my eyes fixed on all your
       commandments.

7   I will praise you with an upright heart,
     when I learn your righteous ordinances.

8   I will observe your statutes;
     do not utterly forsake me.

9   How can young people keep their way pure?
     By guarding it according to your word.

10   With my whole heart I seek you;
     do not let me stray from your
       commandments.

11   I treasure your word in my heart,
     so that I may not sin against you.

12   Blessed are you, O Lord;
     teach me your statutes.

13   With my lips I declare
     all the ordinances of your mouth.

14   I delight in the way of your decrees
     as much as in all riches.

15   I will meditate on your precepts,
     and fix my eyes on your ways.

16   I will delight in your statutes;
     I will not forget your word.

17   Deal bountifully with your servant,
     so that I may live and observe your word.

18   Open my eyes, so that I may behold

A heart that is innocent is happy, for it is in tune with God, the source of all goodness and joy. So attuned, the heart resonates with divine ways, not perfectly perhaps, but at least in sincerely seeking to learn anew and follow more faithfully the Lord's commands.

Blamelessness then becomes steadfast contentment, the pleasure of obedience to a God whose will becomes an inspiration, whether secretly, touching depths of the soul, or publicly, as a revelation. Listening to your Word, O Lord, I commit myself to you and count on your fidelity. May your Word be my guide. May you help me see what wisdom is contained in your commands. May my dutiful observance of them enrich my life. May they lead me from sin and direct my steps more toward you.

wondrous things out of your law.

19 I live as an alien in the land;
   do not hide your commandments from me.

20 My soul is consumed with longing
   for your ordinances at all times.

21 You rebuke the insolent, accursed ones,
   who wander from your commandments;

22 take away from me their scorn and contempt,
   for I have kept your decrees.

23 Even though princes sit plotting against me,
   your servant will meditate on your statutes.

24 Your decrees are my delight,
   they are my counselors.

25 My soul clings to the dust;
   revive me according to your word.

26 When I told of my ways, you answered me;
   teach me your statutes.

27 Make me understand the way of your
      precepts,
   and I will meditate on your wondrous
      works.

28 My soul melts away for sorrow;
   strengthen me according to your word.

29 Put false ways far from me;
   and graciously teach me your law.

30 I have chosen the way of faithfulness;
   I set your ordinances before me.

31 I cling to your decrees, O Lord;
   let me not be put to shame.

32 I run the way of your commandments,
   for you enlarge my understanding.

33 Teach me, O Lord, the way of your statutes,
   and I will observe it to the end.

34 Give me understanding, that I may keep your
      law
   and observe it with my whole heart.

35 Lead me in the path of your commandments,
   for I delight in it.

36 Turn my heart to your decrees,
   and not to selfish gain.

37 Turn my eyes from looking at vanities;
   give me life in your ways.

To discover your ways, O Lord, is at times to be set apart, to become alienated from one's culture or times, to aspire to what by prevailing norms, by the dictates of those deemed to be experts, is foolish or false.

Help me, Lord, in adverse conditions to be true to you and thus to myself. I know that I bring sorrow to myself when I fail to heed your Word. Save me, Lord, from such foolishness; for by your grace, by the light you give to my soul, I choose you and your ways.

Thus I am a constant learner. And you, my God, are the faithful Master. You instruct me in your mysteries and so transform me, ever anew, into my true self, the fullness of my being, in accord with the gifts with which you have endowed me. You have promised newness of life to those who are faithful to you.

38 Confirm to your servant your promise,
  which is for those who fear you.
39 Turn away the disgrace that I dread,
  for your ordinances are good.
40 See, I have longed for your precepts;
  in your righteousness give me life.
41 Let your steadfast love come to me, O Lord,
  your salvation according to your promise.
42 Then I shall have an answer for those who
    taunt me,
  for I trust in your word.
43 Do not take the word of truth utterly out of my
    mouth,
  for my hope is in your ordinances.
44 I will keep your law continually,
  forever and ever.
45 I shall walk at liberty,
  for I have sought your precepts.
46 I will also speak of your decrees before kings,
  and shall not be put to shame;
47 I find my delight in your commandments,
  because I love them.
48 I revere your commandments, which I love,
  and I will meditate on your statutes.
49 Remember your word to your servant,
  in which you have made me hope.
50 This is my comfort in my distress,
  that your promise gives me life.
51 The arrogant utterly deride me,
  but I do not turn away from your law.
52 When I think of your ordinances from of old,
  I take comfort, O Lord.
53 Hot indignation seizes me because of the
    wicked,
  those who forsake your law.
54 Your statutes have been my songs
  wherever I make my home.
55 I remember your name in the night, O Lord,
  and keep your law.
56 This blessing has fallen to me,
  for I have kept your precepts.
57 The Lord is my portion;

I desire, O Lord—with all my heart!—to be among the faithful ones. May your love ever support me and encourage me in my fidelity. Let my unfailing obedience so renew me that my life, as a testimony to your wisdom, refutes the claims of anyone—even the so-called experts—who would have me live otherwise.

In doing your will, O God, I savor your goodness, your precious spirit, and my soul finds joy in you. Such delight bears me through many troubles, especially the pain of thinking I need something other than what you have designed for me. Sustained in your ways, I realize that my own insistence amounts to arrogance. Your rule, O Lord, your law over me, becomes a shelter, a sure refuge from the ravages of false guides and my own unruliness.

From your many gifts, Lord, I

I promise to keep your words.

58 I implore your favor with all my heart;
    be gracious to me according to your
      promise.

59 When I think of your ways,
    I turn my feet to your decrees;

60 I hurry and do not delay
    to keep your commandments.

61 Though the cords of the wicked ensnare me,
    I do not forget your law.

62 At midnight I rise to praise you,
    because of your righteous ordinances.

63 I am a companion of all who fear you,
    of those who keep your precepts.

64 The earth, O Lord, is full of your steadfast
      love;
    teach me your statutes.

65 You have dealt well with your servant,
    O Lord, according to your word.

66 Teach me good judgment and knowledge,
    for I believe in your commandments.

67 Before I was humbled I went astray,
    but now I keep your word.

68 You are good and do good;
    teach me your statutes.

69 The arrogant smear me with lies,
    but with my whole heart I keep your
      precepts.

70 Their hearts are fat and gross,
    but I delight in your law.

71 It is good for me that I was humbled,
    so that I might learn your statutes.

72 The law of your mouth is better to me
    than thousands of gold and silver pieces.

73 Your hands have made and fashioned me;
    give me understanding that I may learn your
      commandments.

74 Those who fear you shall see me and rejoice,
    because I have hoped in your word.

75 I know, O Lord, that your judgments are right,
    and that in faithfulness you have humbled
      me.

cherish above all the bequest of yourself. I accept you first and foremost. With a thankful heart I ask you for graces to persevere according to your designs. Help me to find supportive company. Let me sing your praises, even in uncommon circumstances.

You have taught me the hard lesson that your will for me, despite my obstinate resistance, is good. In step with you, Lord, the source of all good, I am at times out of step with those who are presumptuous about their own perceptions of good and bad, right and wrong. Nevertheless I rejoice in having finally come to treasure your will, your law for my life.

Now, with your help, I can live what I understand. With you at my side I can be an example to those who have their own lessons to learn. And when I stumble, when I fail to conform to rules for my own happiness, support me and forgive me. Renew me by your

76 Let your steadfast love become my comfort
   according to your promise to your servant.

77 Let your mercy come to me, that I may live;
   for your law is my delight.

78 Let the arrogant be put to shame,
   because they have subverted me with guile;
   as for me, I will meditate on your precepts.

79 Let those who fear you turn to me,
   so that they may know your decrees.

80 May my heart be blameless in your statutes,
   so that I may not be put to shame.

81 My soul languishes for your salvation;
   I hope in your word.

82 My eyes fail with watching for your promise;
   I ask, "When will you comfort me?"

83 For I have become like a wineskin in the
   smoke,
   yet I have not forgotten your statutes.

84 How long must your servant endure?
   When will you judge those who persecute
   me?

85 The arrogant have dug pitfalls for me;
   they flout your law.

86 All your commandments are enduring;
   I am persecuted without cause; help me!

87 They have almost made an end of me on earth;
   but I have not forsaken your precepts.

88 In your steadfast love spare my life,
   so that I may keep the decrees of your
   mouth.

89 The Lord exists forever;
   your word is firmly fixed in heaven.

90 Your faithfulness endures to all generations;
   you have established the earth, and it
   stands fast.

91 By your appointment they stand today,
   for all things are your servants.

92 If your law had not been my delight,
   I would have perished in my misery.

93 I will never forget your precepts,
   for by them you have given me life.

94 I am yours; save me,

goodness and constancy.

Slow learner that I am, my folly can nonetheless become a source of wisdom. Having made mistakes from which I have learned, I can better counsel myself and others. In times of turmoil and resistance, when the support of others is meager, when I feel alone or lost, let my trust in you and your law be my assurance and comfort. Let me not be misled by thinking it would be better to proceed by another law or another desire. For another way would be my downfall.

Your ways renew my life. You, Lord, are my greatest good. To know you is to know heaven, my eternal delight. Submission to your law is submission to your generosity and providence. May your law never become for me something taken for granted. May I ever penetrate your designs in order to marvel more fully in your love and majesty. For my perceptions are limited and far exceeded by your

for I have sought your precepts.

95 The wicked lie in wait to destroy me,
   but I consider your decrees.

96 I have seen a limit to all perfection,
   but your commandment is exceedingly
      broad.

97 Oh, how I love your law!
   It is my meditation all day long.

98 Your commandment makes me wiser than my
      enemies,
   for it is always with me.

99 I have more understanding than all my
      teachers,
   for your decrees are my meditation.

100 I understand more than the aged,
    for I keep your precepts.

101 I hold back my feet from every evil way,
    in order to keep your word.

102 I do not turn away from your ordinances,
    for you have taught me.

103 How sweet are your words to my taste,
    sweeter than honey to my mouth!

104 Through your precepts I get understanding;
    therefore I hate every false way.

105 Your word is a lamp to my feet
    and a light to my path.

106 I have sworn an oath and confirmed it,
    to observe your righteous ordinances.

107 I am severely afflicted;
    give me life, O Lord, according to your
       word.

108 Accept my offerings of praise, O Lord,
    and teach me your ordinances.

109 I hold my life in my hand continually,
    but I do not forget your law.

110 The wicked have laid a snare for me,
    but I do not stray from your precepts.

111 Your decrees are my heritage forever;
    they are the joy of my heart.

112 I incline my heart to perform your statute
    forever, to the end.

113 I hate the double-minded,

greater plan.

Even a brilliant teacher cannot give me what I must learn from you alone, my God. Generations of human learning are no substitute for the richness of divine wisdom. Unless they suggest your grace and guiding hand, unless they benefit this world, I am wary of human directives and decrees.

Above all else, you are my guiding light. My allegiance to you is my greatest surety. I must hold fast to this belief even in times of sorrow. I must not succumb to wayward darkness and its snares. Your commands, I must remember, are nurture and invigoration now and forever.

Help me to be sincere in my

but I love your law.

114 You are my hiding place and my shield;
  I hope in your word.
115 Go away from me, you evildoers,
    that I may keep the commandments of my
      God.
116 Uphold me according to your promise, that I
    may live,
    and let me not be put to shame in my
      hope.
117 Hold me up, that I may be safe
    and have regard for your statutes
      continually.
118 You spurn all who go astray from your
      statutes;
    for their cunning is in vain.
119 All the wicked of the earth you count as
      dross;
    therefore I love your decrees.
120 My flesh trembles for fear of you,
    and I am afraid of your judgments.
121 I have done what is just and right;
    do not leave me to my oppressors.
122 Guarantee your servant's well-being;
    do not let the godless oppress me.
123 My eyes fail from watching for your salvation,
    and for the fulfillment of your righteous
      promise.
124 Deal with your servant according to your
      steadfast love,
    and teach me your statutes.
125 I am your servant; give me understanding,
    so that I may know your decrees.
126 It is time for the Lord to act,
    for your law has been broken.
127 Truly I love your commandments
    more than gold, more than fine gold.
128 Truly I direct my steps by all your precepts;
    I hate every false way.
129 Your decrees are wonderful;
    therefore my soul keeps them.
130 The unfolding of your words gives light;

reliance on your law. Let me not be tempted to break it because the rewards of my obedience are not immediate. Let me hope in your goodness be my support in times of temptation. How sad I would be, Lord, cut off from you because of my false cunning and distorted values. You would rightly allow me to endure the due consequences of poor and rebellious judgment. I fear such weakness in myself and respect you enough, my God, not to dare suppose that your compassion will cancel out your justice.

You are as fearsome as a firm and loving father. At times I feel oppressed by an endless waiting for the rewards of my obedience. My desires thus fuel judgmental attitudes—regarding you, my God! Such haughtiness on my part! Let me never forget who is Master here and who is servant, whose Word is golden compared with my vain discourse.

Your commands are nurture for my soul and wisdom for my mind. If my fidelity to you, Lord, could be

it imparts understanding to the simple.

131 With open mouth I pant,
because I long for your commandments.

132 Turn to me and be gracious to me,
as is your custom toward those who love
your name.

133 Keep my steps steady according to your
promise,
and never let iniquity have dominion over
me.

134 Redeem me from human oppression,
that I may keep your precepts.

135 Make your face shine upon your servant,
and teach me your statutes.

136 My eyes shed streams of tears
because your law is not kept.

137 You are righteous, O Lord,
and your judgments are right.

138 You have appointed your decrees in
righteousness
and in all faithfulness.

139 My zeal consumes me
because my foes forget your words.

140 Your promise is well tried,
and your servant loves it.

141 I am small and despised,
yet I do not forget your precepts.

142 Your righteousness is an everlasting
righteousness,
and your law is the truth.

143 Trouble and anguish have come upon me,
but your commandments are my delight.

144 Your decrees are righteous forever;
give me understanding that I may live.

145 With my whole heart I cry; answer me, O
Lord.
I will keep your statutes.

146 I cry to you; save me,
that I may observe your decrees.

147 I rise before dawn and cry for help;
I put my hope in your words.

148 My eyes are awake before each watch of the

only a fraction of yours for me, I would be secure.

Tears confess my resistance to your prompts. In foolishness I have spurned your directives and support. Your laws, O Lord—whether revealed through your sacred Word, or in nature, or as the proper directives of my conscience—are an expression of your goodness. You declare to be right what conforms with your righteousness.

My reliance on your wisdom is my greatest security and comfort. In times of confusion, when my soul sighs in distress, your will for me seems obscure. I move about in darkness and trust that patience will bear me steadily to a new day's light. Let me not be doomed,

night,
    that I may meditate on your promise.

149 In your steadfast love hear my voice;
    O Lord, in your justice preserve my life.

150 Those who persecute me with evil purpose
    draw near;
    they are far from your law.

151 Yet you are near, O Lord,
    and all your commandments are true.

152 Long ago I learned from your decrees
    that you have established them forever.

153 Look on my misery and rescue me,
    for I do not forget your law.

154 Plead my cause and redeem me;
    give me life according to your promise.

155 Salvation is far from the wicked,
    for they do not seek your statutes.

156 Great is your mercy, O Lord;
    give me life according to your justice.

157 Many are my persecutors and my
    adversaries,
    yet I do not swerve from your decrees.

158 I look at the faithless with disgust,
    because they do not keep your commands.

159 Consider how I love your precepts;
    preserve my life according to your
    steadfast love.

160 The sum of your word is truth;
    and every one of your righteous ordinances
    endures forever.

161 Princes persecute me without cause,
    but my heart stands in awe of your words.

162 I rejoice at your word
    like one who finds great spoil.

163 I hate and abhor falsehood,
    but I love your law.

164 Seven times a day I praise you
    for your righteous ordinances.

165 Great peace have those who love your law;
    nothing can make them stumble.

166 I hope for your salvation, O Lord,
    and I fulfill your commandments.

dear God, because of resistance to your truths. Let me live, forever anchored in your steadfast love.

Save me, Lord, from my own folly. Stand up for me against insidious suggestions—from myself or others—that the ways of God are not worth my attention and trust. Help me to be faithful, mindful of your justice, even as I find peace in knowing of your wondrous mercy. Your love is strong and tender, Lord, challenging and unconditional.

In face of criticism and rebuke from those who claim influence in my life, I turn to your Word for guidance and truth. I thus gain ever-deepening insights into your magnificent wisdom and the truth by which you rule your people and your creation.

167 My soul keeps your decrees;
    I love them exceedingly.

168 I keep your precepts and decrees,
    for all my ways are before you.

169 Let my cry come before you, O Lord;
    give me understanding according to your
        word.

170 Let my supplication come before you;
    deliver me according to your promise.

171 My lips will pour forth praise,
    because you teach me your statutes.

172 My tongue will sing of your promise,
    for all your commandments are right.

173 Let your hand be ready to help me,
    for I have chosen your precepts.

174 I long for your salvation, O Lord,
    and your law is my delight.

175 Let me live that I may praise you,
    and let your ordinances help me.

176 I have gone astray like a lost sheep; seek out
        your servant,
    for I do not forget your commandments.

You are a loving lawgiver, Lord; I love all that you have accomplished and will accomplish in my life and in my world. Hear my word of praise, O Lord, and let me repeat with accuracy and insight all that you have taught me. Lead me in your truth so that I, and all those for whom I am responsible, may find our rewards in you. Let your firm and loving guidance be my permanent surety.

Oppressive Thought: God's directives are a
    burden.

Oppressive Image: Snares

Edifying Thought: I delight in the Lord's
    decrees.

Edifying Image: A lighted path

You guide me, dear Lord, benevolently and wisely. Through your manifest Word, through your appointed servants, or through your hushed prompts within me, you speak life-giving words of truth. To follow them is to find happiness. To ignore them is to invite disaster. Help me to recognize your law and not be fooled by its counterfeits. Having tasted your goodness, let me always prefer it above all else.

PSALM 120

Needing Self-Evaluation

1 In my distress I cry to the Lord,
    that he may answer me:
2 "Deliver me, O Lord,
    from lying lips, from a deceitful tongue."
3 What shall be given to you?
    And what more shall be done to you, you
      deceitful tongue?
4 A warrior's sharp arrows,
    with glowing coals of the broom tree!
5 Woe is me, that I am an alien in Meshech,
    that I must live among the tents of Kedar.
6 Too long have I had my dwelling
    among those who hate peace.
7 I am for peace;
    but when I speak,
    they are for war.

Help me, Lord, to be fairer to myself. Too often I hear the words of others as devaluations of me and my accomplishments. Confidence in your love sharpens my wit so that I can distinguish constructive criticism from mindless chatter.

I do not need to prolong the folly of multiplying my stress by ranking myself among the opposition.

Oppressive Thought: All of their barbs are
    true.

Edifying Thought: I calmly accept only
    rightful criticism.

Oppressive Image: Sharp arrows

Edifying Image: A peace treaty

Teach me, Lord, to be friendly to myself without being self-indulgent. At times my guilt is evoked more through my fear of inadequacy than by others' due criticism. Help me listen humbly. Spare me self-deceit. Bless me with truthful self-awareness.

PSALM 121

Trust

1 I lift up my eyes to the hills—
    from where will my help come?
2 My help comes from the Lord,

Like a child I look up to the Lord. God's greatness and power appear as the unmistakable source of all

who made heaven and earth.
3 He will not let your foot be moved;
  he who keeps you will not slumber.
4 He who keeps Israel
  will neither slumber nor sleep.
5 The Lord is your keeper;
  the Lord is your shade at your right hand.
6 The sun shall not strike you by day,
  nor the moon by night.
7 The Lord will keep you from all evil;
  he will keep your life.
8 The Lord will keep
  your going out and your coming in
  from this time on and forevermore.

that is essential in my world. Such grandeur tells me that I am secure, that my Lord in heaven will never abandon me, never cease to provide for me.

God will guide and instruct me, not let me wander needlessly amid alien elements that can dishearten or ravage me.

Oppressive Thought: God has little time for
  me.

Edifying Thought: God is a faithful
  provider.

Oppressive Image: Sunburn

Edifying Image: Cool shade

When you touch me, Lord, your strong comforting presence assuages my fears. You provide and protect with divine surety. Relying on you, I am calm, even bold. My soul is robed in your edifying grace. I trust you above all.

PSALM 122

Peace

1 I was glad when they said to me,
  "Let us go to the house of the Lord!"
2 Our feet are standing
  within your gates, O Jerusalem.
3 Jerusalem—built as a city
  that is bound firmly together.
4 To it the tribes go up,
  the tribes of the Lord,
  as was decreed for Israel,
  to give thanks to the name of the Lord.

How blessed I am to have been raised in my faith, to have been shown a way to heaven. To know my God, to trust my Lord, and love divine ways is to know already something of joys to come, something of my heavenly home. All peoples are drawn to God, the Lord who has created them and will endow them with their greatest

5 For there the thrones for judgment were set
   up,
      the thrones of the house of David.
6 Pray for the peace of Jerusalem:
      "May they prosper who love you.
7 Peace be within your walls,
      and security within your towers."
8 For the sake of my relatives and friends
      I will say, "Peace be within you."
9 For the sake of the house of the Lord our
   God,
      I will seek your good.

honors.

May love and respect ever be the dearest companions of every faith. May all God's peoples long for peace, the solidarity that inspires hope, the love that is a foretaste of heaven's wonders.

Oppressive Thought: We cannot get along.

Edifying Thought: God leads us to peace.

Oppressive Image: A ruined city

Edifying Image: A prospering city

When I feel your presence, Lord, I know the deep peace that you have promised to those who are your own. May more people, nations, and continents be drawn to you. May their sense of your peace draw them into greater unanimity. May earthly fellowship begin to manifest the peace that is heavenly.

PSALM 123

Wanting Comfort

1 To you I lift up my eyes,
      O you who are enthroned in the heavens!
2 As the eyes of servants
      look to the hand of their master,
   as the eyes of a maid
      to the hand of her mistress,
   so our eyes look to the Lord our God,
      until he has mercy upon us.
3 Have mercy upon us, O Lord, have mercy upon
   us,
      for we have had more than enough of
         contempt.
4 Our soul has had more than its fill

I turn to you, my God of heaven, in need of your gentle hand, longing for your compassion, ready for your support.

The neglect or disdain that I feel from others has left me overflowing with pain. Touch me, Lord, with your holy comfort.

of the scorn of those who are at ease,
of the contempt of the proud.

Oppressive Thought: Such contempt will be
my undoing.

Edifying Thought: God overflows with
compassion.

Oppressive Image: A scornful smile

Edifying Image: God's gentle hand

When I hurt, O Lord my God, you are my solace. Barbs afflict me. Disappointment ravages me. Pain overtakes my body and soul. But you relieve and comfort me. I look to you for mercy.

PSALM 124

Safety

1 If it had not been the Lord who was on our
        side
    —let Israel now say—
2 if it had not been the Lord who was on our
        side,
        when our enemies attacked us,
3 then they would have swallowed us up alive,
        when their anger was kindled against us;
4 then the flood would have swept us away,
        the torrent would have gone over us;
5 then over us would have gone
        the raging waters.
6 Blessed be the Lord,
        who has not given us
        as prey to their teeth.
7 We have escaped like a bird
        from the snare of the fowlers;
    the snare is broken,
        and we have escaped.
8 Our help is in the name of the Lord,
        who made heaven and earth.

There have been those terrible times, those oppressive periods when I have felt engulfed by saddening, frightful, repulsive forces. Some were assailants out for my ruin. Others were terrors of my own making—belittling, discouraging, or condemnatory judgments that I heaped upon myself. They all have shown their fearsome faces.

I have learned however that my salvation is safety in God's faithful care. Without my Lord, I would come to nothing or be destroyed.

Oppressive Thought: I am destroyed.

Edifying Thought: God is my rescuer.

Oppressive Image: Torrential rains

Edifying Image: A bird set free

Who is my most fearsome adversary, Lord—the callous rival or my own unmerciful mind? If I am suffering unjust attack, or if I am plaguing myself with undue self-judgment, help me to remember your mercy. You love me with proven fidelity. Your holiness ultimately shields me from every destructive power.

PSALM 125

Commitment to God

1 Those who trust in the Lord are like Mount
    Zion,
        which cannot be moved, but abides
            forever.
2 As the mountains surround Jerusalem,
        so the Lord surrounds his people,
        from this time on and forevermore.
3 For the scepter of wickedness shall not rest
        on the land allotted to the righteous,
    so that the righteous might not stretch out
        their hands to do wrong.
4 Do good, O Lord, to those who are good,
        and to those who are upright in their
            hearts.
5 But those who turn aside to their own
        crooked ways
    the Lord will lead away with evildoers
    Peace be upon Israel!

I commit to you, O Lord, my whole life.

I submit to your loving protection all those who count on me, whether near or far. They should know, dear God, that whatever benefit I am to them is but a pale reflection of the wondrous and magnanimous care you provide for us all.

Only in reckless abandon could we trust anyone else more. You reward virtue. You are our source of utter peace.

Oppressive Thought: I am content without
    that distant God.

Edifying Thought: God leads us in the ways
    of peace.

Oppressive Image: A treacherous path

Edifying Image: Mountains around
    Jerusalem

Why, why, O God, have I abandoned you? What impertinence impelled me to turn elsewhere for my prime support? I retract my decision. My firm commitment is to you. I welcome you into my life. You provide for my welfare. You revive my soul.

PSALM 126

Joy Restored

1 When the Lord restored the fortunes of Zion, we were like those who dream.	*Times of great joy, when my spirit is rapturous and I feel greatly blessed, seem too good to be true. But the deepest part of my soul, that secret space where faith brings me to God, recognizes such moments as supremely true.*

1 When the Lord restored the fortunes of Zion,
    we were like those who dream.
2 Then our mouth was filled with laughter,
    and our tongue with shouts of joy;
  then it was said among the nations,
    "The Lord has done great things for them."
3 The Lord has done great things for us,
    and we rejoiced.
4 Restore our fortunes, O Lord,
    like the watercourses in the Negeb.
5 May those who sow in tears
    reap with shouts of joy.
6 Those who go out weeping,
    bearing the seed for sowing,
  shall come home with shouts of joy,
    carrying their sheaves.

Times of great joy, when my spirit is rapturous and I feel greatly blessed, seem too good to be true. But the deepest part of my soul, that secret space where faith brings me to God, recognizes such moments as supremely true.

Enriched again by sunshine and mirth, I bear new fruit through the love of my Lord.

Oppressive Thought: My struggle will never
    end.

Edifying Thought: God turns mourning
    into laughter.

Oppressive Image: A ravaged crop

Edifying Image: An abundant harvest

In your kindness, O Lord, you do not leave me long in sorrow. Responding to my tears, you draw me closer to yourself. I feel once more the vibrancy of believing in you. My freshened soul celebrates. I become innovative and productive again. You are the fullness of my joy.

PSALM 127

Help from God

1 Unless the Lord builds the house,
    those who build it labor in vain.
  Unless the Lord guards the city,
    the guard keeps watch in vain.
2 It is in vain that you rise up early
    and go late to rest,
  eating the bread of anxious toil;
    for he gives sleep to his beloved.
3 Sons are indeed a heritage from the
    Lord,
    the fruit of the womb a reward.
4 Like arrows in the hand of a warrior
    are the sons of one's youth.
5 Happy is the man who has
    his quiver full of them.
  He shall not be put to shame
    when he speaks with his enemies in
      the gate.

A fine household, a community enriched by security and joy, is not fashioned simply by human energy. Surely one provides strenuously for it or faithfully nurtures those who belong to it. But such efforts, especially when tainted by workaholism and worry, can easily become counterproductive. They require a steady faith that finds support and direction from God so that those in one's care become blessings who provide many seasons of contentment and pride.

Oppressive Thought: My family relies on me alone.

Edifying Thought: God is a dedicated partner.

Oppressive Image: Endless toil

Edifying Image: Children graciously helping

Spare me, Lord, the curse of working so hard that I hardly enjoy those entrusted to my care. Temper my productive energies with reliance on your help. Let me savor communal life. Those who are mine, my family, my community, are the sunshine you provide. They are scarcely perfect. But they are warmth and light. Bless us all.

218

PSALM 128

Happiness

1 Happy is everyone who fears the Lord,
    who walks in his ways.
2 You shall eat the fruit of the labor of your
        hands;
    you shall be happy, and it shall go well
        with you.
3 Your wife will be like a fruitful vine
        within your house;
    your children will be like olive shoots
        around your table.
4 Thus shall the man be blessed
    who fears the Lord.
5 The Lord bless you from Zion.
    May you see the prosperity of
        Jerusalem
    all the days of your life.
6 May you see your children's children.
    Peace be upon Israel!

To respect the ways of God, to discern the divine will, and to live by it is to find true happiness. The joy of living according to the Lord's plan resembles the joy of parenting. A responsible mother or father is productively occupied with nurturing, training, and caring for children.

In joining ourselves to God, we accept a destiny that shares in abundant divine love, providence that never ceases, an eternal heavenly peace.

Oppressive Thought: My productivity is
    entirely my own doing.

Edifying Thought: I trust God's designs for
    my life.

Oppressive Image: Pretentious swagger

Edifying Image: Strolling in God's company

Help me find my happiness, Lord, in conforming to your will. Let me shudder at the very thought of doing otherwise. Let me gladly accept partnership in your plan to sustain and better our world. Give me the joy of love that resembles yours, love that is generous and fruitful.

PSALM 129

Indignation

1 "Often have they attacked me from my
        youth"
    —let Israel now say—
2 "often have they attacked me from my
        youth,
    yet they have not prevailed against
        me.
3 The plowers plowed on my back;
    they made their furrows long."
4 The Lord is righteous;
    he has cut the cords of the wicked.
5 May all who hate Zion
    be put to shame and turned
        backward.
6 Let them be like the grass on the
        housetops
    that withers before it grows up,
7 with which reapers do not fill their
        hands
    or binders of sheaves their arms,
8 while those who pass by do not say,
    "The blessing of the Lord be upon
        you!
    We bless you in the name of the
        Lord!"

As children we can be wounded by inconsideration, defamation, mistreatment, or abuse.

Though God's grace can bring healing, behaviors such as these manifest evil. They should be abhorred and deterred. Harmful words or deeds—whether expressions of maliciousness, weakness, or ignorance—have power to leave enduring scars on the personality as well as the body. Meriting righteous indignation, abuses should not be ignored in the name of politeness or pacification. Good-willed persons try responsibly to discern appropriate and effective ways to diminish harm and to heal its victims and perpetrators.

Oppressive Thought: Keep the peace; look
    the other way.

Oppressive Image: "Good will" that abets
    abuse

Edifying Thought: In face of some wrongs,
    toughness is more loving than leniency.

Edifying Image: A firm and loving discipli-
    narian

May I not become insensitive, dear Lord, to any encroaching evil. May I not hide behind unfit compassion when misconduct or degeneracy challenges me to confront it. May I be strong in safeguarding everyone, especially the impressionable and vulnerable, from reckless hurt. Enlighten me to your righteousness and help me act accordingly.

PSALM 130

Discouragement

1 Out of the depths I cry to you, O Lord.
2   Lord, hear my voice!
  Let your ears be attentive
    to the voice of my supplications!
3 If you, O Lord, should mark iniquities,
    Lord, who could stand?
4 But there is forgiveness with you,
    so that you may be revered.
5 I wait for the Lord, my soul waits,
    and in his word I hope;
6 my soul waits for the Lord
    more than those who watch for the
      morning,
    more than those who watch for the
      morning.
7 O Israel, hope in the Lord!
    For with the Lord there is steadfast
      love,
    and with him is great power to
      redeem.
8 It is he who will redeem Israel
    from all its iniquities.

When I am utterly discouraged, if not depressed, without felt comfort I reach beyond a last fond dream. I grope past the darkness; I stretch my mind and heart. I wring my soul for light, reaching toward you, my Lord. In your compassion you turn to me, though the gloom that grips me has resulted from my own wrongful choices and deeds. Your forgiveness becomes a day of deliverance on which I can love you more deeply and, learning new trust, be properly disciplined.

My ways are tempered, refined according to your designs for me and those whom I love.

Oppressive Thought: There is only darkness.

Oppressive Image: Endless waiting

Edifying Thought: God is here to help me.

Edifying Image: Dawn

When my soul is downcast, dear God, when I long for the feeling of your presence, I reach beyond my desolation. Clinging to a thread of hope, I find you anew. Your generous response sheds light on the gloom that is, at least in part, a product of my sin. Upon my confession, your forgiveness reassures me of your constancy. You are always there for me.

PSALM 131

Security

1 O Lord, my heart is not lifted up,
 my eyes are not raised too high;
 I do not occupy myself with things
 too great and too marvelous for me.
2 But I have calmed and quieted my soul,
 like a weaned child with its mother;
 my soul is like the weaned child that is
 with me.
3 O Israel, hope in the Lord
 from this time on and forevermore.

No grandiose speculation or intricate theology uplifts me. At this moment my deepest sense is the peace of resting in God. Like a child snuggled in its mother's arms, my inner self, my soul, is secure in my tranquility.

May all of us be so blessed.

Oppressive Thought: I must think and plot.

Oppressive Image: Great piles of books and
 lists

Edifying Thought: Closeness to God is
 deeply calming.
Edifying Image: Mother and child

Never let my mind, O Lord, undo my peace of soul. Never let my thoughts and programs become a barrier to you. Help my insights and pursuits to flow from a tranquil spirit. My deeper sense of your calming presence nurtures me most. The finest schemes reflect your godly wisdom.

PSALM 132

Expectation

1 O Lord, remember in David's favor
 all the hardships he endured;
2 how he swore to the Lord
 and vowed to the Mighty One of Jacob,
3 "I will not enter my house
 or get into my bed;
4 I will not give sleep to my eyes
 or slumber to my eyelids,
5 until I find a place for the Lord,

There was a special time, O Lord, that precious season of knowing you, that moment of newness and closeness, the honeymoon of my faith. I had struggled toward it, and it finally came, exceeding my expectations.

a dwelling place for the Mighty One of
　　Jacob."

6　We heard of it in Ephrathah;
　　we found it in the fields of Jaar.

7　"Let us go to his dwelling place;
　　let us worship at his footstool."

8　Rise up, O Lord, and go to your resting place,
　　you and the ark of your might.

9　Let your priests be clothed with
　　　righteousness,
　　and let your faithful shout for joy.

10　For your servant David's sake
　　do not turn away the face of your anointed
　　　one.

11　The Lord swore to David a sure oath
　　　from which he will not turn back:
　　"One of the sons of your body
　　　I will set on your throne.

12　If your sons keep my covenant
　　　and my decrees that I shall teach them,
　　their sons also, forevermore,
　　　shall sit on your throne."

13　For the Lord has chosen Zion;
　　he has desired it for his habitation:

14　"This is my resting place forever;
　　here I will reside, for I have desired it.

15　I will abundantly bless its provisions;
　　I will satisfy its poor with bread.

16　Its priests I will clothe with salvation,
　　and its faithful will shout for joy.

17　There I will cause a horn to sprout up for
　　　David;
　　I have prepared a lamp for my anointed
　　　one.

18　His enemies I will clothe with disgrace,
　　but on him, his crown will gleam."

Bless me, Lord, as I hold that memory, not that I may linger there in complacency, but that what I knew there, what I felt there, what I drank of deeply there, may remain in your grace. May the memory glimmer as a sign of hope for what is to come as I walk expectantly with you, as you become increasingly the life of my life.

Help me be ready at every moment to receive your Anointed One, the Son of David, our Messiah, on the day your Word has promised. Let me share this joyous hope with my brothers and sisters in the faith. Let us work together to be faithful to you, to show how greatly we appreciate your blessings.

Supported by you, we will await responsibly and receive commendably your glorious Messiah, our anointed King.

Oppressive Thought: I can rest content in
　　the past.

Edifying Thought: My hope for the future
　　can be energizing.

Oppressive Image: A lifeless relationship

Edifying Image: Waiting for our Messiah

I remember fondly, Lord, that time when I first related to you in a deep and personal way. Your grace brought me new joy and security. Holding this memory dear, I continue my journey of faith. Though I periodically falter, the hope awakened in the past moves me to greater expectation. Accepting your Word, I await the dawn of your eternal kingdom.

PSALM 133

Companionship

1 How very good and pleasant it is
    when kindred live together in unity!
2 It is like the precious oil on the head,
    running down upon the beard,
on the beard of Aaron,
    running down over the collar of his
      robes.
3 It is like the dew of Hermon,
    which falls on the mountains of Zion.
For there the Lord ordained his blessing,
    life forevermore.

Bless all my relationships, Lord.

Let me experience in them the sweetness of love and joyous companionship. Help me to foster unity, to be overcome and engulfed by your Spirit, to be strengthened and refreshed by the caresses of enduring love.

Oppressive Thought: Reconciliation is
    impossible.

Edifying Thought: The Spirit of God nurtures fellowship.

Oppressive Image: Dark valleys

Edifying Image: A happy family

You have created us for one another, Lord. Through fellowship and intimacy we find this earth our welcome habitation. Love is the sweet balm of our souls. You, who are eternally loving, incline us to find happiness in solidarity. As we respond to your blessings, you draw us closer and make us one.

PSALM 134

Blessings

1 Come, bless the Lord, all you servants of the
    Lord,
    who stand by night in the house of the Lord!
2 Lift up your hands to the holy place,
    and bless the Lord.
3 May the Lord, maker of heaven and earth,
    bless you from Zion.

The constancy of our fellowship in the Lord has called for much dedication. Let us offer praise together, accepting the generous blessings of our Creator and Protector.

Oppressive Thought: Our accomplishment is solely our own.

Edifying Thought: God's blessings have sustained us.

Oppressive Image: Arms smugly folded

Edifying Image: Hands lovingly outstretched

Our community of faith, dear God, offers praise to you in many ways. We worship in the sanctuary. We worship in responding to need anywhere. However we praise or glorify you, we act because of your support, encouragement, and direction. Your blessings give us true life.

PSALM 135

Providence

1 Praise the Lord!
    Praise the name of the Lord;
    give praise, O servants of the Lord,
2 you that stand in the house of the Lord,
    in the courts of the house of our God.
3 Praise the Lord, for the Lord is good;
    sing to his name, for he is gracious.
4 For the Lord has chosen Jacob for himself,
    Israel as his own possession.
5 For I know that the Lord is great;

Everyone in our circle, our cherished community, should praise our God, the Holy One who dwells close to us and whose blessings we enjoy. For what we are, what we have accomplished, and what we are attaining are sustained by the graciousness and generosity of the divine hand.

      our Lord is above all gods.

6 Whatever the Lord pleases he does,
      in heaven and on earth,
      in the seas and all deeps.

7 He it is who makes the clouds rise at the end of
        the earth;
      he makes lightnings for the rain
      and brings out the wind from his
        storehouses.

8 He it was who struck down the firstborn of
        Egypt,
      both human beings and animals;

9 he sent signs and wonders
      into your midst, O Egypt,
      against Pharaoh and all his servants.

God never deceives us with false hopes or with goals that become idols. His loving designs suffuse all our interests and occupations, directing them to ways that are proper, virtuous, and godly.

10 He struck down many nations
      and killed mighty kings—

11 Sihon, king of the Amorites,
      and Og, king of Bashan,
      and all the kingdoms of Canaan—

12 and gave their land as a heritage,
      a heritage to his people Israel.

Only the forces of ignorance, weakness, or maliciousness that rule us—at times intensely—divert us from the blessedness of our destinies.

13 Your name, O Lord, endures forever,
      your renown, O Lord, throughout all ages.

14 For the Lord will vindicate his people,
      and have compassion on his servants.

When we are true to our truest selves, and thus to our true God, providence gently but firmly guides us, nurtures us, and rewards us.

15 The idols of the nations are silver and gold,
      the work of human hands.

16 They have mouths, but they do not speak;
      they have eyes, but they do not see;

17 they have ears, but they do not hear,
      and there is no breath in their mouths.

18 Those who make them
      and all who trust them
      shall become like them.

19 O house of Israel, bless the Lord!
      O house of Aaron, bless the Lord!

20 O house of Levi, bless the Lord!
      You that fear the Lord, bless the Lord!

21 Blessed be the Lord from Zion,
      he who resides in Jerusalem.
      Praise the Lord!

With great joy let us praise this God of ours, ours forevermore!

Oppressive Thought: One path is as good as another.

Edifying Thought: God leads me to blessedness and joy.

Oppressive Image: A road to nowhere

Edifying Image: The divine heart of our community

I am awestruck, O Lord, by the wisdom of your ways. How shortsighted I am to rely unduly on my own pathways and goals. When they divert me from you, they are idols. They provide nothing. Your providence towers over my senseless errors. You become my surest way and truest life.

PSALM 136

God's Love

1 O give thanks to the Lord, for he is good, 　　for his steadfast love endures forever.	*God loves us without restraint, without hesitance, without cessation. Thanksgiving is our due and heartfelt response.*
2 O give thanks to the God of gods, 　　for his steadfast love endures forever.	
3 O give thanks to the Lord of lords, 　　for his steadfast love endures forever;	
4 who alone does great wonders, 　　for his steadfast love endures forever;	*For divine love showers us with miracles of every sort. Vast cosmic spaces yet to be explored, expanses of land and sea still to be tended, mysteries of sun and moon as yet unfathomed are the issue of this love.*
5 who by understanding made the heavens, 　　for his steadfast love endures forever;	
6 who spread out the earth on the waters, 　　for his steadfast love endures forever;	
7 who made the great lights, 　　for his steadfast love endures forever;	
8 the sun to rule over the day, 　　for his steadfast love endures forever;	
9 the moon and stars to rule over the night, 　　for his steadfast love endures forever;	
10 who struck Egypt through their firstborn, 　　for his steadfast love endures forever;	
11 and brought Israel out from among them, 　　for his steadfast love endures forever;	
12 with a strong hand and an outstretched arm, 　　for his steadfast love endures forever;	*God's enduring love defends us, supports us, works for us, saves us,*

13 who divided the Red Sea in two,
  for his steadfast love endures forever;
14 and made Israel pass through the midst of it,
  for his steadfast love endures forever;
15 but overthrew Pharaoh and his army in the Red Sea,
  for his steadfast love endures forever;
16 who led his people through the wilderness,
  for his steadfast love endures forever;
17 who struck down great kings,
  for his steadfast love endures forever;
18 and killed famous kings,
  for his steadfast love endures forever;
19 Sihon, king of the Amorites,
  for his steadfast love endures forever;
20 and Og, king of Bashan,
  for his steadfast love endures forever;
21 and gave their land as a heritage,
  for his steadfast love endures forever;
22 a heritage to his servant Israel,
  for his steadfast love endures forever.
23 It is he who remembered us in our low estate
  for his steadfast love endures forever;
24 and rescued us from our foes,
  for his steadfast love endures forever;
25 who gives food to all flesh,
  for his steadfast love endures forever.
26 O give thanks to the God of heaven,
  for his steadfast love endures forever.

protects us, guides us, heals us, uplifts us, provides for us, nurtures us.

Let our thanks, mundane and meager as it may seem, issue from sincerest hearts as a poor but true love for our God, whose love for us is boundless and enduring.

Oppressive Thought: There are no signs of God's love.

Edifying Thought: We are overwhelmed by God's love.

Oppressive Image: A thankless heart

Edifying Image: A grateful heart

No love, Lord, approaches yours. It abounds to our favor, gently and remarkably encompassing our lives. In and beyond our sight, fulfilling yet promising, commonplace but miraculous, your love penetrates our hearts and beckons us toward your mystery. As your love overflows, our souls thirst to love you more.

PSALM 137

Grief

1   By the rivers of Babylon—
      there we sat down and there we wept
      when we remembered Zion.
 2   On the willows there
      we hung up our harps.
 3   For there our captors
      asked us for songs,
    and our tormentors asked for mirth, saying,
      "Sing us one of the songs of Zion!"
	In our grief we shed tears together, unable to find joy in life. We were tempted to deny our loss, to pretend that our former happiness was now a pleasant memory that we have let go.

4   How could we sing the Lord's song
      in a foreign land?
 5   If I forget you, O Jerusalem,
      let my right hand wither!
 6   Let my tongue cling to the roof of my mouth,
      if I do not remember you,
    if I do not set Jerusalem
      above my highest joy.
	But that would have been blasphemous, a repudiation of a blessing once truly enjoyed.

7   Remember, O Lord, against the Edomites
      the day of Jerusalem's fall,
    how they said, "Tear it down! Tear it down!
      Down to its foundations!"
	May our remembrance of such blessedness at once rebuke despair and summon hope.

8   O daughter Babylon, you devastator!
      Happy shall they be who pay you back
      what you have done to us!
 9   Happy shall they be who take your little ones
      and dash them against the rock!
	May the ravages of dark grief not propagate their spite but become the heralds of light and new life.

Oppressive Thought: We can ignore our loss.

Edifying Thought: Our grief prepares us for hope.

Oppressive Image: A mask of joy

Edifying Image: Harps readied for playing

When grief, O God, becomes the master of my soul, I become a victim of bitterness and anger. Yet my darker moods become the passages through which my spirit finds hope. Preciousness lost reminds me of blessings once given. I wail for vengeance and—though not quite rightly—trust enough to pray.

PSALM 138

Thankfulness

1   I give you thanks, O Lord, with my whole
      heart;
    before the gods I sing your praise;

2   I bow down toward your holy temple
    and give thanks to your name for your
      steadfast love and your faithfulness
    for you have exalted your name and your
      word
    above everything.

3   On the day I called, you answered me,
    you increased my strength of soul.

4   All the kings of the earth shall praise you, O
      Lord,
    for they have heard the words of your
      mouth.

5   They shall sing of the ways of the Lord,
    for great is the glory of the Lord.

6   For though the Lord is high, he regards the
      lowly;
    but the haughty he perceives from far
      away.

7   Though I walk in the midst of trouble,
    you preserve me against the wrath of my
      enemies;
  you stretch out your hand,
    and your right hand delivers me.

8   The Lord will fulfill his purpose for me;
    your steadfast love, O Lord, endures
      forever.
    Do not forsake the work of your hands.

When my heart swells with thanks to you, O Lord, I realize how great you are, how loving and true. All else that I am tempted to regard as ultimately important pales before your grandeur.

You have always been there for me, something I only fully realized when I needed you most and asked for your help. You have charge of the world, O Lord, and charge of my life.

You treat us all, out of your overflowing glory, with compassion and generosity. Your unconditional love is complemented by your making our humility, our appropriate obedience, a condition for certain future blessings.

May your closeness, O God, protect me, above all from my own weaknesses.

Oppressive Thought: God is not important.

Edifying Thought: A loving God is in charge of my life.

Oppressive Image: Haughty laughter

Edifying Image: Holding God's hand

Your abundant blessings and graces, Lord, appear more fully when I am thankful. My distraction veils the splendor of your goodness and attempts to seduce me into dark, haughty indifference. So, familiar with your warmth, I strive through gratitude to know you more intimately. You are my soul's bliss.

PSALM 139

Life in God

1 O Lord, you have searched me and known
    me.
2 You know when I sit down and when I rise
    up;
    you discern my thoughts from far away.
3 You search out my path and my lying down,
    and are acquainted with all my ways.
4 Even before a word is on my tongue,
    O Lord, you know it completely.
5 You hem me in, behind and before,
    and lay your hand upon me.
6 Such knowledge is too wonderful for me;
    it is so high that I cannot attain it.
7 Where can I go from your spirit?
    Or where can I flee from your presence?
8 If I ascend to heaven, you are there;
    if I make my bed in Sheol, you are there.
9 If I take the wings of the morning
    and settle at the farthest limits of the sea,
10 even there your hand shall lead me,
    and your right hand shall hold me fast.
11 If I say, "Surely the darkness shall cover me,
    and the light around me become night,"
12 even the darkness is not dark to you;
    the night is as bright as the day,
    for darkness is as light to you.
13 For it was you who formed my inward parts;
    you knit me together in my mother's womb.
14 I praise you, for I am fearfully and
    wonderfully made.
    Wonderful are your works;

I deprive myself of so much comfort, assurance and hope when I fail to hold firmly to what my faith, in moments of composure and insight, reveals to me: that all is well. God is with me. Divine grace filling me, permeating my body and soul, touches me intimately and supports me.

My mind may wander. My heart may lose touch with God's holiness. But the mind of God is ever on me. The divine heart of love is ever faithful to me. My mind may be darkened or my emotions parched, but God recognizes such shadows and aridity as nothing. They become no deterrent to God's commitment and devotion to me.

Boundlessly more than a mother or father, God has nurtured me, directed me, molded me.

that I know very well.

15 My frame was not hidden from you,
when I was being made in secret
intricately woven in the depths of the
earth.

16 Your eyes beheld my unformed substance
In your book were written
all the days that were formed for me,
when none of them as yet existed.

17 How weighty to me are your thoughts, O
God!
How vast is the sum of them!

18 I try to count them—they are more than the
sand;
I come to the end—I am still with you.

19 O that you would kill the wicked, O God,
and that the bloodthirsty would depart
from me—

20 those who speak of you maliciously,
and lift themselves up against you for evil!

21 Do I not hate those who hate you, O Lord?
And do I not loathe those who rise up
against you?

22 I hate them with perfect hatred;
I count them my enemies.

23 Search me, O God, and know my heart;
test me and know my thoughts.

24 See if there is any wicked way in me,
and lead me in the way everlasting.

If what I have become is less than what I should be by God's designs, it is because of my resistance, my negligence, my hardness of heart, my disobedience. These traits of mine—roots and products of my self-defeating ignorance—are my greatest enemies.

When my faith revives, when divine truth awakens my soul, I find myself again with God. May the Lord of my life, my true life, help conquer my enemies. May I see more clearly what they are and scorn them. May I rest anew in the heart of God.

Oppressive Thought: I am hidden from God.

Edifying Thought: God knows my every thought and desire.

Oppressive Image: Shadows of the night

Edifying Image: Wings at dawn

Enlighten my soul, O Lord. Shine on me those rays of divine truth that illuminate my life revealed in its fullest measure. Let me see how, at my worst, I ignore or reject you. Guide me in discovering anew, at a depth that revives my soul, how faithful you are to me, how generous you are in your support, how encompassing you are in your love.

PSALM 140

Needing Self-Esteem

1 Deliver me, O Lord, from evildoers;
    protect me from those who are violent,
2 who plan evil things in their minds
    and stir up wars continually.
3 They make their tongue sharp as a snake's,
    and under their lips is the venom of vipers.
4 Guard me, O Lord, from the hands of the
      wicked;
    protect me from the violent
    who have planned my downfall.
5 The arrogant have hidden a trap for me,
    and with cords they have spread a net,
    along the road they have set snares for me.
6 I say to the Lord, "You are my God;
    give ear, O Lord, to the voice of my
      supplications."
7 O Lord, my Lord, my strong deliverer,
    you have covered my head in the day of
      battle.
8 Do not grant, O Lord, the desires of the
      wicked;
    do not further their evil plot.
9 Those who surround me lift up their heads;
    let the mischief of their lips overwhelm
      them!
10 Let burning coals fall on them!
    Let them be flung into pits, no more to
      rise!
11 Do not let the slanderer be established in the
      land;
    let evil speedily hunt down the violent!
12 I know that the Lord maintains the cause of
      the needy,
    and executes justice for the poor.
13 Surely the righteous shall give thanks to
      your name;
    the upright shall live in your presence.

Grant me, O Lord, the wisdom to see through the impudence and onslaughts of those who appear to be dangerous to me, those who malign me, those who seek to hurt me, those who aspire to ruin me.

Help me to realize that my imagination can render them far more fearsome than they really are. Protect me and everyone from the truly violent. Yet let me also be freed from falsehoods of my own making, from frivolous fears rooted in my lack of that proper esteem whereby I appreciate my genuine gifts and all the graces that come from you. Help me to realize that the hatred I see in "enemies" is often a disdain I have for myself. My false sense of selfhood then becomes my greatest foe. Let it shrivel away, melt to nothing.

By you, O God, my inner eye sees aright. With you as my friend, Lord, I can rightfully befriend myself.

Oppressive Thought: Many are against me.

Edifying Thought: I am more lovable than their attitude indicates.

Oppressive Image: Attackers

Edifying Image: A constant friend

When I feel under attack, dear God, when I find others reviling or wounding me, give me the wisdom to distinguish truth from my own false judgments. Grant me the sense to refrain from adding to their irritation by overestimating their worth. Help me to be honest about myself, to be grateful for the gifts and talents I enjoy, and to praise you in thanksgiving for all that you are in my life.

PSALM 141

Wanting Self-Discipline

1 I call upon you, O Lord; come quickly to me;
   give ear to my voice when I call to you.
2 Let my prayer be counted as incense before
      you,
   and the lifting up of my hands as an
      evening sacrifice.
3 Set a guard over my mouth, O Lord;
   keep watch over the door of my lips.
4 Do not turn my heart to any evil,
   to busy myself with wicked deeds
in company with those who work iniquity;
   do not let me eat of their delicacies.
5 Let the righteous strike me;
   let the faithful correct me.
Never let the oil of the wicked anoint my
      head,
   for my prayer is continually against their
      wicked deeds.
6 When they are given over to those who
      shall condemn them,
   then they shall learn that my words
      were pleasant.
7 Like a rock that one breaks apart and

At times, O Lord, I need your help instantly. Temptation comes quickly as a force by which, if I succumb, I will turn from your designs, from the path of enduring happiness. I would then choose that which gives but fleeting gratification and dulls my appetite for knowing you more.

Give me the grace, dear God, to discipline myself the way a wise master or loving parent would discipline me. Grant that I might find vice futile and depravity destructive, that I might find sin repugnant, that I might grow strong in virtue, content and peaceful in deepening my relationship with you.

shatters on the land,
    so shall their bones be strewn at the
       mouth of Sheol.

8 But my eyes are turned toward you, O God,
      my Lord;
    in you I seek refuge; do not leave me
      defenseless.

9 Keep me from the trap that they have laid for
      me,
    and from the snares of evildoers.

10 Let the wicked fall into their own nets,
    while I alone escape.

*I look to you with love, expecting
your kind protection.*

*When I am firmly at your side,
temptation is the loser.*

Oppressive Thought: I am a victim of temp-
    tation.

Oppressive Image: A shattered rock

Edifying Thought: God fortifies me.

Edifying Image: A strong heart

Keep me alert and wise, O Lord. Arm me against the sudden, sometimes forceful onslaught of temptation. Safeguard me from the wiles of those allurements that appeal to my weaker side, that gratify my misguided desires. By the power of your grace, that godly force always available to me, let me scorn false attractions and walk steadily toward you and your eternal goodness.

PSALM 142

Needing Comfort

1 With my voice I cry to the Lord;
    with my voice I make supplication to the
      Lord.

2 I pour out my complaint before him;
    I tell my trouble before him.

3 When my spirit is faint,
    you know my way.
  In the path where I walk
    they have hidden a trap for me.

4 Look on my right hand and see—
    there is no one who takes notice of me;

*How it hurts, O Lord. The pain
runs through me, sapping me of
energy.*

*Life looks so bleak. Be with me.
Hold me. Comfort me. Let me not
fall victim to thinking pitifully that
no one understands.*

no refuge remains to me;
   no one cares for me.
5 I cry to you, O Lord;
   I say, "You are my refuge,
   my portion in the land of the living."
6 Give heed to my cry,
   for I am brought very low.
Save me from my persecutors,
   for they are too strong for me.
7 Bring me out of prison,
   so that I may give thanks to your name.
The righteous will surround me,
   for you will deal bountifully with me.

*You understand, Lord, loving me,
letting my anguish serve me and
others.*

*You see these attacks and, with a
heart of mercy, help them redound
to my good.*

Oppressive Thought: No one understands
  my pain.

Edifying Thought: God supports me.

Oppressive Image: Attack in the dark

Edifying Image: Release from confinement

My weakened faith, O Lord and God, adds to my pain in times of sorrow. When I turn to you, however, my soul is restored to steadfast confidence. Relying on your compassion and comfort, my spirit is refreshed. I know once more that by your ever-present power, you can make every trial work to my good. Let my love for you sustain me as I journey toward greater joy.

PSALM 143

Wanting Consolation

1 Hear my prayer, O Lord;
   give ear to my supplications in your
    faithfulness;
   answer me in your righteousness.
2 Do not enter into judgment with your
    servant,
   for no one living is righteous before you.
3 For the enemy has pursued me,
   crushing my life to the ground,
   making me sit in darkness like those long

*Burdened with sorrow, I feel
depressed, even lifeless, O Lord.
My mind and heart are lost in
darkness as, near despair, I fail to
see beyond the confinement of my
own misery and sins. Yet I dare to
approach you, my God, dare to
ask for your help in my time of
great need.*

dead.

4 Therefore my spirit faints within me;
　　my heart within me is appalled.
5 I remember the days of old,
　　I think about all your deeds,
　　I meditate on the works of your hands.
6 I stretch out my hands to you;
　　my soul thirsts for you like a parched land.
7 Answer me quickly, O Lord;
　　my spirit fails.
Do not hide your face from me,
　　or I shall be like those who go down to the
　　　Pit.
8 Let me hear of your steadfast love in the
　　　morning,
　　for in you I put my trust.
Teach me the way I should go,
　　for to you I lift up my soul.
9 Save me, O Lord, from my enemies;
　　I have fled to you for refuge.
10 Teach me to do your will,
　　for you are my God.
Let your good spirit lead me
　　on a level path.
11 For your name's sake, O Lord, preserve my life.
　　In your righteousness bring me out of
　　　trouble.
12 In your steadfast love cut off my enemies,
　　and destroy all my adversaries,
　　for I am your servant.

You have shown me in the past the wisdom of your ways. You have answered my prayers, at times disregarding my expectations, but, to my delight, exceeding them. I long to experience you again as my greatest consolation, as the Lord of my life. My mind tells me you are there. My heart longs to be rescued from the depths of doubt and to feel speedily your wondrous, kindly love.

Let me learn anew what I have learned before: that in doing your holy will I find my safest haven and greatest comfort.

Oppressive Thought: There is no way out of
　　this misery.

Edifying Thought: God's power to rescue
　　has been proven in my life.

Oppressive Image: Darkness

Edifying Image: The face of God

M*y misery, O God, is at times so great that I feel permanently imprisoned in gloom and pain. I long for release, for my soul's redemption. When I reach out to receive your loving touch, I sense anew that you are my Savior. You provide the freedom and light that salve my spirit, awaken my trust, and steady me on my new way. You reveal to me your Word of life.*

PSALM 144

Priorities

<table>
<tr>
<td>

1   Blessed be the Lord, my rock,
      who trains my hands for war, and my
            fingers for battle;
2   my rock and my fortress,
      my stronghold and my deliverer,
   my shield, in whom I take refuge,
      who subdues the peoples under me.
3   O Lord, what are human beings that you
            regard them,
      or mortals that you think of them?
4   They are like a breath;
      their days are like a passing shadow.
5   Bow your heavens, O Lord, and come down;
      touch the mountains so that they smoke.
6   Make the lightning flash and scatter them;
      send out your arrows and rout them.
7   Stretch out your hand from on high;
      set me free and rescue me from the mighty
            waters,
      from the hand of aliens,
8   whose mouths speak lies,
      and whose right hands are false.
9   I will sing a new song to you, O God;
      upon a ten-stringed harp I will play to you,
10 the one who gives victory to kings,
      who rescues his servant David.
11 Rescue me from the cruel sword,
      and deliver me from the hand of aliens
   whose mouths speak lies,
      and whose right hands are false.
12 May our sons in their youth
      be like plants full grown,
   our daughters like corner pillars,
      cut for the building of a palace.
13 May our barns be filled,
      with produce of every kind;
   may our sheep increase by thousands,

</td>
<td>

One of my greatest challenges,
Lord, is to maintain proportion in
my life. How often I err in manip-
ulating my schedule, in assigning
time and energy to various tasks
and activities, in providing appro-
priate leadership, in taking suffi-
cient time to rest. I need you, O
God, as a counterweight, as one
who keeps my life balanced and
sane. In your sublime subtlety, you
have made us—fragile as we are—to
be creative and bold.

Let your wisdom and majesty
show in me as courage to set prior-
ities: to delete the needless, to
resist the seductive, to rout the
iniquitous.

Give me a new tune by which to
dance. Let my work and play move
to music that dispels the somber-
ness of toil and tedium.

If I see progeny, success, or prosper-
ity, let them come not as burdens,
as the recompense of stretching
myself too far, but as blessings
from you, as the truly enjoyable
fruits of labors inspired by you, the
God of my life.

</td>
</tr>
</table>

by tens of thousands in our fields,
14   and may our cattle be heavy with young.
      May there be no breach in the walls, no exile,
          and no cry of distress in our streets.
15   Happy are the people to whom such blessings
          fall
      happy are the people whose God is the
          Lord.

Oppressive Thought: I must accomplish all
    of this.

Edifying Thought: God helps me to set
    priorities.

Oppressive Image: Building a mountain

Edifying Image: A new melody

Let my soul be soothed, O Lord my God, by sweet harmony. Let my life be ordered by your will. As I toil and struggle, let your grace move my work. As I hasten to succeed, let your love transfigure my effort. I long to hold you in my heart, to become both lively and peaceful. Help me, Lord, to pursue my spiritual and earthly goals with a calm bestirred by your steadying energy.

PSALM 145

Loving God

1   I will extol you, my God and King,
          and bless your name forever and ever.
2   Every day I will bless you,
          and praise your name forever and ever.
3   Great is the Lord, and greatly to be praised;
          his greatness is unsearchable.
4   One generation shall laud your works to
              another,
          and shall declare your mighty acts.
5   On the glorious splendor of your majesty,
          and on your wondrous works, I will
              meditate.
6   The might of your awesome deeds shall be
              proclaimed,
          and I will declare your greatness.

Your splendorous majesty, O God, rouses in me a sense of awe. My heart thrills to praise and love you. You so exceed my grasp, so elude the powers of my mind, that I reel in your presence, blush before you as you reveal yourself to my faint faith. You let me see that your love is boundless, your dedication ceaseless. My disposition to accept you into my life is partly due to my religious heritage, to my upbringing in the faith I hold so dear. In my enthusiasm for you and your great works, I want to do

7   They shall celebrate the fame of your
       abundant goodness,
       and shall sing aloud of your
       righteousness.

8   The Lord is gracious and merciful,
       slow to anger and abounding in steadfast
       love.

9   The Lord is good to all,
       and his compassion is over all that he has
       made.

10 All your works shall give thanks to you, O
       Lord,
       and all your faithful shall bless you.

11 They shall speak of the glory of your
       kingdom,
       and tell of your power,

12 to make known to all people your mighty
       deeds,
       and the glorious splendor of your
       kingdom.

13 Your kingdom is an everlasting kingdom,
       and your dominion endures throughout all
       generations.
   The Lord is faithful in all his words,
       and gracious in all his deeds.

14 The Lord upholds all who are falling,
       and raises up all who are bowed down.

15 The eyes of all look to you,
       and you give them their food in due season.

16 You open your hand,
       satisfying the desire of every living thing.

17 The Lord is just in all his ways,
       and kind in all his doings.

18 The Lord is near to all who call on him,
       to all who call on him in truth.

19 He fulfills the desire of all who fear him;
       he also hears their cry, and saves them.

20 The Lord watches over all who love him,
       but all the wicked he will destroy.

21 My mouth will speak the praise of the Lord,
       and all flesh will bless his holy name
       forever and ever.

my part to further such belief, both among my peers and among those whose faith will follow ours. The joys of my heart will thus be repeated. Your love and mercy will continue to be proclaimed.

Eyes will be opened anew to you and your wondrous ways. You have designed for all of us—for your children of every era—a place of permanent security and comfort.

Only our resistance to your grace, only our rebelliousness and love-lessness in face of your nurture and discipline will bar us from the multitude of saints who forever sing your glory. Your very presence is the surest food by which our every need is satisfied, now and in the age to come.

We sing with love your praises.

Oppressive Thought: God evades me.

Edifying Thought: God is more than my faith can assimilate.

Oppressive Image: A cold night

Edifying Image: A glorious fire

Spanning generations, nurtured from age to age, our love for you, O God, never equals your love for us. Yet with thankful hearts we are gladdened by your faithfulness. May our love for you be enduring. May we, who have been formed in our faith, be partners with you in fostering love of you in future generations. May we acclaim you as our God forever.

PSALM 146

Happiness

1 Praise the Lord!
  Praise the Lord, O my soul!
2 I will praise the Lord as long as I live;
    I will sing praises to my God all my life
      long.
3 Do not put your trust in princes,
    in mortals, in whom there is no help.
4 When their breath departs, they return to
      the earth;
    on that very day their plans perish.
5 Happy are those whose help is the God of
      Jacob,
    whose hope is in the Lord their God,
6 who made heaven and earth,
    the sea, and all that is in them;
  who keeps faith forever;
7   who executes justice for the oppressed;
    who gives food to the hungry.
  The Lord sets the prisoners free;
8   the Lord opens the eyes of the blind.
  The Lord lifts up those who are bowed
      down;
    the Lord loves the righteous.
9 The Lord watches over the strangers;

The key to my enduring happiness, to unquenchable contentment and peace, is joy in God. When my heart is merry, when—despite the trials of life—I am recurrently glad, I drink deeply of goodness. Knowing and loving the greatest good, namely God, I need wait for no others to bring me pleasure and contentment, not even those I might have once regarded as absolutely essential to my welfare. When I am in love with God, such persons' love, dedication, protection, generosity, guidance, or support become more cherished as expressions of overflowing divine care. I thus realize how goodness in God's kingdom has many forms.

he upholds the orphan and the widow,
but the way of the wicked he brings to
ruin.
10   The Lord will reign forever,
your God, O Zion, for all generations.
Praise the Lord!

*But they are decipherable only in
the context of a love that is everlasting and complete.*

Oppressive Thought: Above all, I need this
particular person's attention.

Edifying Thought: Above all, I need God.

Oppressive Image: Inordinate hunger

Edifying Image: Satisfied hunger

*No love of mine, O Lord my God, is as great as you. No gaze or word, no smile or touch, no
fond embrace endears as does your warming grace. Your love is the garden in which every other
love—constant, fast, and true—gladdens the heart and sweetens the soul. You are my happiness,
Lord, and I desire you all the more.*

PSALM 147

Togetherness

1   Praise the Lord!
How good it is to sing praises to our God;
for he is gracious, and a song of praise is
fitting.
2   The Lord builds up Jerusalem;
he gathers the outcasts of Israel.
3   He heals the brokenhearted,
and binds up their wounds.
4   He determines the number of the stars;
he gives to all of them their names.
5   Great is our Lord, and abundant in power;
his understanding is beyond measure.
6   The Lord lifts up the downtrodden;
he casts the wicked to the ground.
7   Sing to the Lord with thanksgiving
make melody to our God on the lyre.
8   He covers the heavens with clouds,

*The Lord is wondrous in many
ways. Our hearts swell with joy as
we sing the praises of the Lord, our
God. By divine kindness and
power, we have been gathered
together. We have become a community. Where necessary, God
instigated reconciliation and healing and supported them by grace.
Like stars that guide mariners on
the vast, forbidding sea, signs
came to us as heavenly blessings
by which we could summon
strength, surmount confusion, overcome obstacles, and resist evil.
Like a balm to our souls, our song
thus flows as a melody that heals*

prepares rain for the earth,
    makes grass grow on the hills.

9   He gives to the animals their food,
        and to the young ravens when they cry.

10 His delight is not in the strength of the horse,
        nor his pleasure in the speed of a runner;

11 but the Lord takes pleasure in those who
            fear him,
        in those who hope in his steadfast love.

12 Praise the Lord, O Jerusalem!
        Praise your God, O Zion!

13 For he strengthens the bars of your gates;
        he blesses your children within you.

14 He grants peace within your borders;
        he fills you with the finest of wheat.

15 He sends out his command to the earth;
        his word runs swiftly.

16 He gives snow like wool;
        he scatters frost like ashes.

17 He hurls down hail like crumbs—
        who can stand before his cold?

18 He sends out his word, and melts them;
        he makes his wind blow, and the waters
            flow.

19 He declares his word to Jacob,
        his statutes and ordinances to Israel.

20 He has not dealt thus with any other nation;
        they do not know his ordinances.
    Praise the Lord!

and inspires. Disposed to hymn making, we see a world transformed by God, a world clothed with forms and colors that delight, comfort, and energize.

Our hope centered on heaven pilots our life on earth. As a community protected and fortified by our Lord, we experience discomforts as tolerable phases in the divine scheme.

The patterns by which God reigns have become, for us, contours of a privileged revelation.

Oppressive Thought: We are totally on our
    own.

Edifying Thought: God has wonderfully
    brought us together.

Oppressive Image: Freezing rain

Edifying Image: Hearts warmed by song

How kind you are, O God, helping us to help each other. Mutual reliance is sweetened by mutual dedication. Goals achieved and joys attained are enriched by the gladsome spirit of conviviality. Our hearts incline to one another, Lord, because your creative love is the heart of our lives. Let our love always glorify your name.

PSALM 148

Creation's Glory

1 Praise the Lord!
Praise the Lord from the heavens;
   praise him in the heights!
2 Praise him, all his angels;
   praise him, all his host!
3 Praise him, sun and moon;
   praise him, all you shining stars!
4 Praise him, you highest heavens,
   and you waters above the heavens!
5 Let them praise the name of the Lord,
   for he commanded and they were
     created.
6 He established them forever and ever;
   he fixed their bounds, which cannot be
     passed.
7 Praise the Lord from the earth,
   you sea monsters and all deeps,
8 fire and hail, snow and frost,
   stormy wind fulfilling his command!
9 Mountains and all hills,
   fruit trees and all cedars!
10 Wild animals and all cattle,
   creeping things and flying birds!
11 Kings of the earth and all peoples,
   princes and all rulers of the earth!
12 Young men and women alike,
   old and young together!
13 Let them praise the name of the Lord,
   for his name alone is exalted;
   his glory is above earth and heaven.
14 He has raised up a horn for his people,
   praise for all his faithful,
   for the people of Israel who are close to
     him.
Praise the Lord!

To marvel at the extent and grandeur of God's magnificent designs is to savor extraordinary bliss, to anticipate celestial glory. But these present wonders of God's creation disclose as well a new creation. They awaken profound, assuring hope for an age akin to heaven on earth. Angelic personalities provoke attention to the divine splendor. Celestial bodies, set in bold relief by the blue of day and dark of night, glorify God's luminosity.

Creatures of the sea pronounce divine impenetrability. Meteorological elements celebrate the godly wisdom's unpredictability. The manifold facets of nature—landscapes and their animal populations—celebrate God's diversity, the grandiose expanse multiplicity, and variation. Persons of all generations and cultures attest that the Lord's marvelous munificence is complemented by careful attention to individuality. Truly, whoever knows God knows the godly desire to glorify all creation.

Oppressive Thought: All creation will collapse into nothingness.

Edifying Thought: All creation will be transformed by God's glory.

Oppressive Image: Bleak waters

Edifying Image: Angels everywhere

The vastness of your creation, Lord, is the constant herald of your endless grace. In ways uncountable you shower us with attention, kindness, and benevolence. You have fashioned a universe that assures us of your love while conveying your glory. May we never tire of exploring your work. May we glimpse each day another feature of your designs for our heavenly home.

PSALM 149

Success

1 Praise the Lord!
   Sing to the Lord a new song,
      his praise in the assembly of the
         faithful.
2 Let Israel be glad in its Maker;
      let the children of Zion rejoice in their
         King.
3 Let them praise his name with dancing,
      making melody to him with
         tambourine and lyre.
4 For the Lord takes pleasure in his
      people;
      he adorns the humble with victory.
5 Let the faithful exult in glory;
      let them sing for joy on their couches.
6 Let the high praises of God be in their
      throats
      and two-edged swords in their hands,
7 to execute vengeance on the nations
      and punishment on the peoples,
8 to bind their kings with fetters
      and their nobles with chains of iron,
9 to execute on them the judgment
      decreed.

I sing joyfully of those cherished achievements that mark our life together. God stands firmly at the center of our community, the family in which I, learning to meet ever new challenges, have grown in faith. Relying on the Lord's loving support, we can hope for further—and greater—success. My heart dances as I contemplate the care God lavishes on us, beyond our deserts, certainly beyond what I alone have earned.

There still are obstacles, lingering faults, and evils to overcome. Yet God's commitment to our cause is unflinching.

This is glory for all his faithful ones. Praise the Lord!

So the melody of my soul stirs me to praise.

Oppressive Thought: The obstacles are too great.

Edifying Thought: God is firmly in our midst.

Oppressive Image: Attackers unleashed

Edifying Image: A song of success

We claim success as a family, O Lord; we rejoice in achievements of this community in which we live. You have formed it and guided it. You have sustained and strengthened it. By your grace we thrive. May all that we share become a hymn of praise. May you, O Lord, be blessed unceasingly.

PSALM 150

Alleluia!

1 Praise the Lord!
Praise God in his sanctuary;
   praise him in his mighty firmament!
2 Praise him for his mighty deeds;
   praise him according to his
    surpassing greatness!
3 Praise him with trumpet sound;
   praise him with lute and harp!
4 Praise him with tambourine and dance;
   praise him with strings and pipe!
5 Praise him with clanging cymbals;
   praise him with loud clashing
    cymbals!
6 Let everything that breathes praise the
   Lord!
Praise the Lord!

The final utterance, the definitive Word, the ultimate truth, proclaims divine grandeur. All of us, with all creation, know our greatest glory in glorifying God. Let then the praise of God overflow, let it surpass mere creaturely limits in holy features of religion, in marvels of nature, in miraculous moments, in the orchestral wonder of myriad ages and cultures.

Let life itself sing of God, the Lord of life!

Oppressive Thought: Life ends without meaning or purpose.

Edifying Thought: All creation proclaims the glory of our God.

Oppressive Image: Crushing silence

Edifying Image: A resounding symphony

*H*ow grand, O God, is the Alleluia that rises from the work of your hands, from creation itself, and all its peoples. Echoing your providential love, the universe and its nations reach their height in a chorus of worshipful melody. Our God is all holy. May our song of praise resound forever!

Spirituality in the Psalms: A Panorama

The numbers refer to the psalms.

GOD AS OUR FOCUS

Centering our minds and hearts on God will inevitably bring enrichment (1). When confronted by evil, we can be provoked to rightful anger, but we must be careful to leave punishment ultimately to God (2). The Lord knows we are threatened in many ways and protects us according to our needs (3). We can find respite in our confidence that God is working for good (4). The Lord listens to our complaints so that we can express the anger and seek divine protection (5). Our fears of being abandoned by God give way to grief but should in good time lead to trust in steadfast divine love (6). Then our hurts are healed by firm hope in God's justice (7). For we need not see ourselves as mere victims of circumstances but can rejoice that we, made in God's image and guided by divine designs, are governors of our destinies (8). Such power should be accepted with thanksgiving and humility lest our weaker sides entice us toward false victories (9).

A HEALTHY OUTLOOK

Many seem to profit from injustice, but the Lord's justice will ultimately prevail (10). With God at our side, we can face evil with courage (11). Even persistent slander is purged by the power of God's utterances (12). Desolation leads to consolation (13). Bleakness yields to joyful expectation (14). For when we remain steadfast in divine ways, the benefits of God's presence endure (15). By this holy presence we gain great confidence and receive priceless counsel (16). By sincerity of heart we plead effectively for God's loving protection (17). And the powers by which we do good and repulse evil become, though pale reflections of God's majestic qualities, sufficient to warrant the powerful divine assistance by which we rise to victory (18). We must however be always ready to heed divine directives, to conform to God's laws revealed in nature's brilliance (19).

SORTING THINGS OUT

If we or others need help, we can approach the Lord, firm in our faith that prayers of petition are always heard (20). As revealed through God's Anointed One, the power of God works in us (21). Even in times of direst privation or desolation, we need only adhere to our traditional beliefs; they will sustain us until we praise and thank God anew (22). For the Lord loves us, tending to our every real need (23). What is essential is to open ourselves fully, to receive the divine glory into our lives (24). Our past failings need not remain obstacles to such enrichment, for our constant guide in the process is none other than the Lord (25). If there are wrongs for which we, despite appearances, are not personally responsible, we will be vindicated (26). For God is our most reliable protector and comforter (27). In face of such wrongs, God works to strengthen us (28). Stirring revelations of divine power are designed to bring us peace (29). Our human overconfidence is converted into the holy confidence of faith (30).

CONVERSION

We can find new courage in even the worst of afflictions (31). By confessing our sins, we can rest happily in God's kind forgiveness (32). We overrate ourselves and underrate our God when we do not trust the One who has created the universe (33). But we are transformed by growing confidence in God's providence (34). The Lord oversees our circumstances and reverses all threats to our blessedness and salvation (35). When, by our hypocrisy, we are enemies to ourselves, God's love for us remains a steadfast light of truth (36). We must disassociate ourselves from evil-doers and join the ranks of the meek, who will inherit an abundance of divine blessings (37). Indeed, because of our faults, we will at times be sorely afflicted, feel utterly crushed, realizing that we must admit our guilt and pray for mercy (38). Such prayer brings relief even when we are suffering the just deserts of our indiscretions and sins (39).

RENEWAL

Delivered from sin and other destructive forces, we become spiritually renewed; we find happiness in God above all else and are grateful for whatever we receive according to the divine will (40). Attending to needs of others, we become instruments of divine blessing ourselves and gain a refreshing, healthy sense of pride (41). Such a sense, while rooted in God, provides a sound foundation for greater hope in future times of sorrow and dejection (42). It also provides unwavering assurance of serenity when we feel wrongfully oppressed (43). In such distressing strife we are energized by divine resources, not our own (44). We thus can honor, sometimes even in ourselves, heroic virtues that emanate as sacred endowments (45). Through such faith we remain unshakable in our reliance on God, in our stalwart conviction that the Lord is almighty (46). We are inspired to shout for joy that God is so awesome (47).

HEIGHTENED SENSITIVITY

Our firmness of faith allows us to experience more profoundly the presence of God in sacred sanctuaries, in areas—both spacial and personal—where God dwells in special ways (48). The paths of goodness on which we walk provide assurance that we have a permanent home with the Lord, even beyond death (49). We are transported in spirit beyond the commonplace and understand that our customary expressions of religion must always be characterized by sincerity (50). It becomes clearer than ever to us that throughout our lives we give way to sin and must stir our hearts anew to repentance (51).

REGRESSION

At times humiliation must teach us of our recurrent faults (52). Our faith can become so distorted that, like the godless, we misconstrue the Lord's claims on us (53). Yet our kind and providential God protects us from all evil (54). Even when we feel betrayed by those close to us, God is at our sides supporting us (55). Even when we feel trampled, oppressed by cruelty, we can trust in God to deliver us (56). As ever, God's merciful protection provides security (57). Our desperate pleas for justice are heard, and the Lord rights us as well as the oppressors (58). Attacks on us are persistent, seeming to augment as we progress spiritually; here is our chance to augment our awareness of God's supportive and transforming presence (59). By such faith, our prayers for restoration are realistic and empowering (60). They seek the divine protection we identify as ours (61).

GREATER LIFE

God responds mightily to our expectations, and we again rest secure; no influence or resource of our own approaches the grandeur of divine power (62). Our greatest contentment is in the Lord, our source of true life (63). We need not fear any enemies, whatever their origins (64). Our eyes are opened anew to divine generosity, which overflows as boundless care for us and all creation (65). We want the whole earth to sing for joy before the Lord, to proclaim divine transforming power (66). With prayerful hearts we can look forward to even greater blessings (67). Our hearts swell as God, like a parent or spouse, complements our lives, bringing out the best in us, dispelling every reason for despair, helping us experience more fully all of life's treasures (68). Even when dishonored in many ways, we can do the otherwise impossible: watch our anger turn to praise, bear every burden with serenity (69). God's greatness thus outshines our puny contempt of wrongdoing (70). And we experience with new awareness what has come home to us before, that in the Lord we are utterly protected (71).

VIRTUE AS STRENGTH

Blessed abundantly by the Lord, we emulate those whose love for others radiates concern for justice and peace (72). For in our closeness to God we see the folly of abuse and exploitation (73). Even when wounded by defilement and related horrors, we trust in God's justice (74). We find our own equilibrium as the Lord balances the scales of justice (75). Divine might always triumphs over evil (76). Even when we feel utterly alone, we trust in God's powerful presence (77). God has charge over every generation, dealing appropriately with evil, showing mercy to the rebellious who repent, offering new partnership (78). Even when we feel devastated, the Lord strengthens us (79). Even when we are broken by sin, the Lord restores our wholeness (80). Obedience to God is a joy; faithfulness to divine ways is our greatest strength (81). God demands cooperation in distributing justice (82). Reliance on the

Lord's judgment fortifies us best to struggle against ungodly forces aimed at our destruction (83).

INTIMACY WITH GOD

To be intimate with God is to know the heights of joy and security (84). Our lives are imbued with sanctifying fidelity and love, with holiness exhibiting fairness and tranquility (85). Our helplessness becomes energy by which we glory in the Lord's power and love (86). For the Lord has sought us out, come to us according to our respective heritages (87). We may fall into depression, we may feel abandoned in darkness and even death (88). In recalling divine promises of love and fidelity, however, our confidence in God's wondrous power is renewed (89). Touched by God's constant and creative energy, we can, for all our weaknesses and for all life's trials, expect rejuvenation (90). Enjoying the divine presence, we feel invulnerable, protected by angelic powers (91). Singing the Lord's praises, we know an uncommon strength (92). Acknowledging God's majesty, we rest secure in knowing that the divine presence fills all creation (93). In confessing our sins and decrying evil, we declare that our just God stays close at hand, if only to discipline or punish (94). The Lord, who fills every mountain and ocean, fills our hearts to overflowing, to proclaiming godly majesty through our song of praise (95).

PROCLAIMING REDEMPTION

As we turn to others, our proclamation tells of salvation offered to all; with renewed fervor we herald that God reigns over us and for us (96). We declare that our Lord is just and forceful, that submission to divine loving discipline is enriching (97). God's majesty fills the whole earth; divine rule over all nations is a blessing (98). Godly authority is universal, firm, and holy (99). We long for all peoples to acknowledge the Lord's goodness and love (100).

INTEGRITY AND DEDICATION

Convinced of God's justice, we aspire to integrity and kindness (101). Should we waver, should our trust in divine goodness weaken, we recall the extent of God's benevolence (102). In our respect for divine commands, we recognize that the Lord's justice is marvelously complemented by godly mercy (103). We see the providential hand of God in the wonders of creation, in the orderly arrangement of our world, in the productivity of the environment that nurtures us (104). We give thanks that the Lord has formed us as a people, molded us in a tradition, and nurtured us in faith (105). Though confident in the divine grace that sustains our dedication to good deeds, we confess that numerous times, like too many of our ancestors, we have fallen short and sinned (106). We give thanks for God's loving assistance, for the divine favor that answers our prayers, exceeds our expectations, and helps us find our way to new integrity (107). By God's steadfast devotion to us, our steadfastness and dedication contribute once again to our spiritual renewal (108). If others attack our integrity and wish us ill, if we feel impoverished or worthless, we can count on the Lord to set things in right perspective (109). For our God has sent a Messiah, the anointed King whose judgment secures us against all evil, the priest whose sacrifice guarantees forever the efficacy of our dedication (110). Divine majesty is thus revealed as the eternal blessing of redemption, as the everlasting foundation of our integrity before God (111).

OBEYING GOD'S LAWS

When we delight in divine laws, when we respect godly authority, our obedience is manifested in virtues such as fairness, kindness and generosity, dispositions that bring ongoing rewards (112). The glory of the Lord shines everywhere, providing sustenance and instilling joy (113). God acts in our lives, and we are rejuvenated (114). So refreshed, our faith proclaims that without heavenly grace, our earthly deeds come to nothing (115). Knowing godly beneficence, we surrender our lives entirely to God and rest content that all our prayers are heard (116). There is no limit to God's faithfulness (117). With the Lord firmly at our side, we overcome weakness, are fortified beyond description, and attain righteousness befitting our unending faith (118). Our diligence in keeping the divine commands thus brings great spiritual enrichment: our lives are pure and happy; we gain insight and honor; we are strengthened and feel deeply loved by God; we sense the freedom that comes with commitment; we are comforted in our sorrows; we learn from our mistakes; our wills are strengthened by our acquired consistency; we become models of virtue; we learn patience; we have zest for life; we grow in wisdom and peace; we are protected from evil; and we know that God is near (119).

SELF-APPRECIATION

God can help us to see ourselves objectively, to be spared the oppression of falsehood (120). The Lord's assistance and protection are eminently trustworthy (121). Heeding God's call, we find serenity and draw toward one another in peace (122). By divine mercy we will not be deterred by any contempt (123). We are always safe in God's hands (124). Entrusting ourselves to godly care, we enjoy our truest worth (125). We rejoice in every blessing (126). We know that without the Lord, our accomplishments have no enduring value (127). Attention to godly things is the counterpart of our personal and familial happiness (128). So we are righteously indignant when we are maligned, when God's procedures are distorted (129). Should we be discouraged by our own contributions to our misery, we turn with hope to the Lord (130). This is our greatest security (131). For God has chosen to dwell in our midst and, because of the Messiah, has assured us extraordinary dignity from generation to generation (132).

COMMUNAL WORSHIP

We enjoy a sweet and permanent fellowship (133). Drawn together by divine grace, we lift our hands in praise of God (134). As a community we acknowledge the Lord's singular majesty and power; we recognize the wondrous providence by which divine graciousness is constantly and universally revealed (135). In this revelation we behold steadfast divine love that endures eternally (136).

SELF-SURRENDER

In times of intense grief, we can cling only to our dearest memories (137). God delivers us from our sorrow and gives us new strength; and our lament becomes thanksgiving (138). We realize once more that God, in ways inscrutable, permeates our lives, taking full charge even in areas that appear to us as dark and forbidding (139). We beg the Lord to deliver us from every onslaught and to let us rightfully hold our heads high (140). We pray for divine support as we resist temptations, as we discipline ourselves, wanting all thoughts, words, and behaviors to verify our solid relationship with God (141). We seek the Lord's comforting presence (142). Like servants we surrender to God's will, remembering that divine consolation revives us (143). In choosing God above all, in setting our priorities in a spiritually sound way, we prepare ourselves for blessings of every kind (144).

GLORIFYING GOD

Belonging to God, we lift our voices daily in praise of divine generosity, compassion, and steadfast love; from one generation to the next we sing God's awesome glory and expect to sing it with our own love forever (145). We proclaim the Lord as our truest benefactor and champion, as the ultimate source of our greatest happiness (146). By the Lord's wondrous designs, strains of love fill our world; and we, resonating with heaven's themes, are drawn together into a people, a new human family (147). All elements of the universe, all species, all races and cultures give praise to heaven, reflecting the glory by which the Lord has made them presagers of an everlasting order (148). The melody of our hearts is a faithful people's song of victory, a joyful declaration that by divine favor we will attain our most cherished goals (149). In the end, our lives become a symphony of praise, an orchestration of glory rendered to God above all (150).

RECAPITULATION: SPIRITUAL ENRICHMENT

As we increasingly focus our lives on God and trust in divine benevolence, we help our various dispositions—our many moods, thoughts, fantasies, and behaviors—become spiritually enriching and thus achieve their proper ends (1-9). Though many obstacles deter us, God is just and helps pain, sorrow and misfortune work to our good if we sincerely try to conform to godly ways (10-19). Prayer and our steady commitment of faith open us to the protective power and presence of God, who lovingly gives us comfort and strength (20-30). Confession of sins, amendment of lifestyle, and attunement to divine mercy are parts of our conversion, our ongoing change of heart (31-39). Thus renewed and thus more confident in God and ourselves, we become more loving and more enthusiastic about our faith (40-47). We become more keenly aware that God is with us everlastingly and that we have responsibilities in this relationship (48-51). Though we continue to fail, though we continue to be tested by new afflictions, we also continue to learn of the Lord's mercy and providence (52-61). With new life we look beyond our anger and fear; we appreciate the love, care, and protection the Lord lavishes upon us (62-71). As our trust in God's justice grows, we become stronger in virtue, more resistant to evil, and courageously dedicated to justice and peace (72-83). In closeness to God, we transcend weaknesses and sorrows, are energized by love, and moved to joyful songs of praise (84-95) We want all peoples to know of the Lord's universal authority, majesty, and love (96-100). In our response to divine commands, the Lord supports us in our progress and is merciful to us in our failures; our obedience becomes the rejuvenating soil of numerous virtues and countless blessings (100-119). With the Lord close to us, with hope in our Messiah contributing to our serenity, we become resistant to disparagement and learn to appreciate our true dignity (120-132). With like-minded persons of faith, we are drawn into a fellowship of worship (133-136). We acknowledge that life's inevitable sorrows become occasions of thanksgiving when, surrendering our whole lives to God, we prepare ourselves for finer blessings (136-144). Our voices resonate with hearts of joy as we sing of God's majesty and recognize the glory of our everlasting Lord, who brings all creation to its proper end (145-150).

Index of the Psalms

Numbers refer to selected psalms where the items are mentioned or inferred. **Bold** *numbers refer to psalms where the items constitute titles or major themes.*

Absence of God 10, 13, 22, 38, 71
Affliction (See also *Suffering*)
    22, 24, **38,** 94, 116
Alleluia! (See also *Praise*) **47, 150**
Angels 34, 35, 91, 103, 148
Anger **2, 5,** 101, 137
    of God (See also *Wrath of God*)
    78, 79, 85, 103, 106
Anointed One (see *Messiah, The*)
Authority **112**
    Divine (See also *Forcefulness of
    God*) **99,** 119

Betrayal **55**
Birds 8, 50, 84, 104, 148
Bitterness 14, 17, 64, 73, 106
Blessings 21, 67, **111,** 115, **134**
Brokenhearted, The, 34, 147

Centering **1**
Clarity (See also *Self-Knowledge*)
    19
Comfort 23, 71, 86, **123, 142**
Commitment to God 10, 22, 31,
    125
Companionship (see also
    Togetherness) **133**
Confession **32,** 38, **106**
Confidence **4, 16,** 27, **34, 89**
Consolation 94, **143**
Contentment (See also *Gladness,
    Happiness,* and *Joy*) **63**

Courage **11,** 27, **31, 118**
Creation's Glory (See also *Majesty
    of God*) 8, 19, 72, 104, **148**
Crying (See also *Tears*) 6, 22, 28,
    34, 86, 88, 102, 107, 119, 120,
    126, 130, 137, 142

Dancing 30, 87, 149, 150
Darkness 18, 88, 105, 139
Death 6, 13, 22, 49, 88, 116
Deer 18, 42
Defilement **74,** 79
Deliverance 3, 9, 18, 22, 34, 35, 40,
    53, 59, 69
Desolation **13, 77,** 40, 68, **88**
Detachment **40**
Discipline 6, 38, 94, 141
Discouragement **130**
Dishonor **69**
Distress **4,** 25, 32, 59, 107, 116
Dwelling Place of God, The, 43, **48,**
    76, **84,** 91, 132

Empowerment **8, 21,** 68, 106
Endurance **22**
Envy 68, 73
Eternal Life 37, 44, 45, **49,** 52, 61,
    89, 106, 111, 112, 145, 146
Evil (See also *Wickedness*) 7, 28,
    34, 35, 37, 59, 109, 140
Expectation (See also *Hope* and
    Optimism) **132**